To Victor,

with admiration

and best wishes.

Jordi

# IESE Business Collection

The Palgrave Macmillan IESE Business Collection is designed to provide authoritative insights and comprehensive advice on specific management topics. The books are based on rigorous research produced by IESE Business School professors, covering new concepts within traditional management areas (Strategy, Leadership, Managerial Economics, etc.) as well as emerging areas of enquiry. The collection seeks to broaden the knowledge of the business field through the ongoing release of titles, with a humanistic focus in mind.

More information about this series at
http://www.palgrave.com/gp/series/14856

Jordi Canals · Franz Heukamp
Editors

# The Future of Management in an AI World

## Redefining Purpose and Strategy in the Fourth Industrial Revolution

*Editors*
Jordi Canals
IESE Business School
University of Navarra
Barcelona, Spain

Franz Heukamp
IESE Business School
University of Navarra
Barcelona, Spain

IESE Business Collection
ISBN 978-3-030-20679-6        ISBN 978-3-030-20680-2    (eBook)
https://doi.org/10.1007/978-3-030-20680-2

Cover illustration: © vska/Alamy Stock Vector

This Palgrave Macmillan imprint is published by the registered company Springer Nature Switzerland AG
The registered company address is: Gewerbestrasse 11, 6330 Cham, Switzerland

# Preface

The current technology revolution is reshaping industries, disrupting existing business models, making traditional companies obsolete, and generating social change and anxiety. In particular, the emerging new world of big data that empowers Artificial Intelligence (AI) is redefining some basic principles on decision-making in organizations, and has the potential to make organizations simpler and leaner, and change the general manager's tasks.

The recent AI explosion and its applications to the business world have been propelled by a growing computer power, the collection of more abundant data and the development of sophisticated algorithms that help make complex decisions of predictive nature. This new AI world encompasses more autonomous, intelligent machines that run algorithms nourished with huge amounts of data, including a new generation of chatbots that engage in human interaction. AI, more specifically, Machine Learning (ML), has become the most important general-purpose technology of our time and with clear implications for the business world.

Senior executives are acting accordingly. In a recent 2018 survey among Fortune 1000 C-level executive decision-makers, an overwhelming 97.2% of executives reported that their companies were investing in launching big data and AI initiatives. Among those executives, a consensus was emerging that AI and big data projects were becoming closely intertwined. 76.5% of executives indicated that the growth and greater availability of data was empowering AI and cognitive initiatives (https://sloanreview.mit.edu/article/how-big-data-is-empowering-ai-and-machine-learning-at-scale/).

The rapid AI development is not only introducing new degrees of automation in many business' processes. It is also transforming industries—like retail, fashion, or financial services—by using more abundant data and deploying better prediction capabilities, developing new marketing and sales strategies to approach the final customer, and design more efficient business models. This means that many companies will become laggards and their assets and capabilities will become obsolete. This new competitive landscape will involve a huge reallocation of assets over the next few years.

At the same time, these technology-led changes generate colossal implications for society in terms of the future of human work, job destruction, new educational needs and the retraining of people. AI is unfolding new, complex societal challenges that involve companies and how companies interact with society. Among other dimensions, there are concerns on the impact of AI on jobs and communities; how companies will organize the education and training of employees in this fast-moving technology context; how technology-based companies—not only the big ones—will interact with society in areas such as privacy; how companies use data by respecting truth and generating trust; how platform-based, business ecosystems create situations and outcomes that require specific anti-trust policies; and, finally, whether tech companies using AI will be able to disclose, share, and control the evolution of ML and cognitive insights that their algorithms may generate. The growing impact of AI on companies and society clearly requires some new business leadership competencies.

In this book, we want to address the impact of AI on management and how companies will be managed in the future. Some AI new tools are improving managers' capabilities to make predictions, a very important dimension in different business functions, such as manufacturing, purchasing, sales, marketing, or logistics. This bigger and better prediction capability is opening up interesting possibilities for companies, encouraging firm creation, redefining business models, challenging companies and management, and making traditional corporate strategies outdated.

The world of technology start-ups today offers some new perspectives on the future of management. AI will not only destroy many traditional jobs, but change some general managers' tasks. As a result, management and the role of general managers, as we have observed and studied them for many decades, will evolve. In this new AI-based world, companies need to rethink their purpose, strategy, organizational design, people development, and decision-making processes. Moreover, they need to consider how to nurture and develop the business leaders of the future and the capabilities and skills that they will need.

AI is opening up some major challenges in the corporate world. The first is related to the quality of decision-making and the potential to combine vast arrays of data with better algorithms and growing computing power that may eventually help make better decisions. Will those algorithms be better than managers in making business decisions? The quality of those decisions will depend on the quality of data, the quality of algorithms used to make decisions, the internal biases that algorithms may contain or develop, and the quality of the learning that algorithms develop as they make more decisions. In this context, we argue that the impact of human judgment will become more relevant than ever.

The second challenge is related to the job of the CEO and general managers in AI-based organizations. It seems that previous knowledge and experience may be less relevant in the future, because big data and AI will provide in-depth knowledge about specific business insights, and consumers' and employees' behavior. But it seems that some leadership attributes will become more important than in the past. Among others, how to provide a sense of purpose that keeps the organization together and focused on the long-term; how to motivate and engage professionals and offer them meaning in their professional work; how to develop and retain high-performance professionals; how to think about strategy and long-term perspective in such a rapidly moving landscape; how to generate trust inside and outside of the organization; how to foster accountability in front of the different stakeholders; and how to make sure that companies respect human dignity and ethical values. The recent Facebook trust crisis around its users' data is a clear example of the new complex challenges in this rapidly changing business context driven by big data and algorithms.

As a result of the different functions that CEOs need to perform in an AI-based world, the capabilities, qualities, and tasks expected from them are changing fast. This is the third key challenge for companies and general managers. Organizational forms will evolve and the development of future leaders also need to be redesigned. The knowledge, capabilities, inter-personal skills, and attitudes that companies and society will expect from general managers in a few years' time will be slightly different. There is a clear need to provide hypothesis, frameworks and policy recommendations on how general management and organizations need to change in this new AI world.

The fourth challenge is how organizational design, team coordination, execution and management systems will need to evolve in this world dominated by data. Will strategic decisions, control and compensations systems still require human judgment? How to offset the potential bias or discrimination coming from AI algorithms that recommend specific decisions on people hiring and promotions, or assessing business performance? How will boards of directors assume responsibilities for the oversight of the company in a world where more decisions, including control and oversight, will be made by machines?

This book explores how management and business leadership need to change as a result of the accelerated penetration of AI in the business world, beyond analytics and big data. By design, this book is focused on changes in management and business leadership brought about by the technology revolution. It is inter-disciplinary and includes authors who are experts on decision-making theory, AI, organization theory, corporate strategy, and governance. This book has an international scope, with authors bringing their expertise from different cultures, professional backgrounds, and geographies, including Europe, Asia, and the Americas. It is also focused on the specific implication of AI on management and leadership, and how organizations will be managed in this new context. Finally, it is holistic, because it deals not only on how to use AI tools more effectively, or how to analyze big data better, but how business leaders will make decisions in this new context and how they need to engage their people to pursue the mission and goals of the firm.

## Book Structure

This volume is structured in four parts. Part I provides an overview of AI and its implications for management. Dario Gil and his colleagues describe in Chapter 1 the current growth in AI in a historical perspective and in the wider context of the Information Technology development. They discuss whether AI is similar to human intelligence and how it has developed and evolved. They also point out some potential contributions of AI to managerial decision-making.

Part II offers an overview of the impact of AI on companies and general management. Julian Birkinshaw reflects on the value of companies in the new AI world in Chapter 2. In particular, he discusses how AI changes the nature of the firm in two specific dimensions: the notion of strategy and the notion of management. He observes that AI is pushing firms towards a more constrained set of choices, which can help improve efficiency. Nevertheless, this trend will make more difficult to enable employees to do their best work and coming up with sources of sustainable competitive advantages.

Jordi Canals reflects on the basic functions of general managers in the new business world shaped by AI in Chapter 3. There is no doubt that the capabilities to make predictions are improving a lot with AI tools. But general management is not only about using better data and better algorithms to make decisions. Decisions also require wisdom, expertise, and prudence. And competitive companies also need some leadership attributes and dimensions that senior managers provide: purpose, governance, strategy, people engagement and development, sustainable performance and leadership with ethical values. In this context, AI will augment the general managers' capabilities, but will not replace them.

Part III covers some relevant issues on how people and leadership development will evolve in the AI world and how managerial competencies will be developed.

Jeffrey Pfeffer looks at people motivation and engagement in our highly intensive technology work context in Chapter 4. Based on many studies from different industries and disciplines, Pfeffer makes a clear statement: the work context for many employees is neither healthy nor very engaging. For some of them, it may even be unhealthy, creating serious health risks. By using a diversity of sources of data, he observes that the new digital economy, with automation, optimization, and pressure to seek growth, may contribute to a decline in people's health and engagement. He suggests some solutions that companies need to consider to offset this trend.

Peter Cappelli, Prasanna Tambe, and Valery Yakubovich address the transformation of HR with AI in Chapter 5. They present some major concerns with AI tools applied to HR: the quality of relevant data on what makes a good employee, the quality of algorithms used, how people perceive fairness in AI-decisions that affect them and how those tools have an effect on the level of employee engagement. The trade-off between efficiency and fairness that AI brings about is very clear in this area. The authors suggest some proposals to improve the quality of HR decisions.

Bernard Yeung discusses the new professional competencies and personal attributes of the workforce in the new AI context in Chapter 6. He presents the main drivers of change around the fourth industrial revolution and draws some implication for the education of future leaders. He touches upon knowledge and basic learning in a variety of disciplines, from science and technology to humanistic studies. He discusses the need for professional capabilities such as critical thinking and communication, and the ability to interact with other people in a variety of contexts. He also emphasizes the importance of life-long learning, as a system in our educational systems, but also as a personal attitude that each citizen should pursue.

Franz Heukamp discusses the impact of AI on the leadership development of the future in Chapter 7. AI-driven technologies are changing organizations and business practices in terms of business models, types of jobs and the ways in which people work. It is argued that AI will improve the capacity to make more accurate predictions. AI will help and enhance some decision-making capabilities, but will increase the value of some competencies. Using a simple framework—*knowing, doing, being*—he explores the traits that senior managers need to develop in order to successfully lead their organizations going forward.

Part IV raises some implications of AI on several critical, cross-functional managerial challenges. Dominique M. Hanssens presents the development of analytics in the Marketing area and develops a framework to think about sales and growth in Chapter 8. Dominique M. Hanssens distills what is new in AI, different from traditional analytics. Based upon his experience in understanding driving factors of sales, growth, and profitability in a variety of industries, he suggests that the AI potential in sales and marketing is huge. Nevertheless, there is still the need for creative, entrepreneurial, customer-focused managers who think how to create brands and better consumer experiences.

Thomas W. Malone introduces his concept of "superminds" in Chapter 9 and how the notion of supermind can be applied to corporate strategy and strategic planning processes. He pinpoints the need to develop organizational forms in which people can work with computers and get the most out of using technology. He highlights that growing computing power and hyperconnectivity will enhance human capabilities for strategy and strategic planning and, at the same time, will allow many more individuals to participate in the strategy process. Technology will allow to take into account an additional diversity of perspectives, and offer potentially better strategic options and decisions. By working with more powerful computers, people's capabilities will be augmented.

Joan E. Ricart looks at the CEO's job from the perspective of business models in Chapter 10. CEOs need to design and manage business models. AI tools are making business models more dependent on software and data, opening up new possibilities to use and combine different assets that companies have. Ricart argues that the potential for innovation that AI brings about is really big. He also cautions that companies will respond effectively to those challenges as far as they use them with creativity and discipline.

Javier Zamora discusses the connections between AI and business model innovation within a digital density framework in Chapter 11. The introduction of AI into an organization should not be considered as a new technology in isolation: it is applied in combination with other new technologies such as social media, mobile, cloud computing, big data and internet of things, among others. Together they constitute manifestations of a business environment with an exponentially increasing digital density. He defines digital density as the percentage of connected data that is available per unit of activity, being a unit of activity an industry, an organization or a business unit. Digital density is an indicator of how many of the processes that are conducted in a given unit of activity are based on data that can be accessed remotely (i.e., connected data. This chapter outlines the holistic guidelines that general management should follow to achieve a good AI governance within a digital density framework.

Barcelona, Spain                                                   Jordi Canals
March 2019                                                     Franz Heukamp

# Acknowledgements

The first version of most of this book's chapters were presented in the Conference on *The Future of General Management in an Artificial Intelligence-Based World*, organized at IESE Business School on April 19–20, 2018. The purpose of this Conference was to discuss the impact of AI on management, companies and management education. The Conference program was designed with an interdisciplinary perspective, provided by the diversity of speakers, including some experts on leadership, management, strategy, AI and big data, and their different geographical backgrounds. They had the opportunity to discuss those issues with other scholars, business school deans, and CEOs as well.

We want to thank the presenters and discussants of the April 2018 Conference for their most valuable contributions and their courage to tackle those issues from an interdisciplinary perspective: Africa Ariño (IESE), Ibukun Awosika (First National Bank of Nigeria), Julian Birkinshaw (LBS), Peter Cappelli (Wharton), Bruno Casiman (IESE), Marta Elvira (IESE), Fabrizio Ferraro (IESE), Ricardo Forcano (BBVA), John Gapper (FT), Dario Gil (IBM Watson), Dominique Hanssens (UCLA), Hansueli Maerki (ABB, Mettler Toledo), Ilian Mihov (INSEAD), Tomo Noda (Japan IGBS), Jeff Pfeffer (Stanford), Marc Puig (Puig), Anneloes Raes (IESE), Nico Rose (Bertelsmann), Sandra Sieber (IESE), Bernie Yeung (National University of Singapore), Bruno di Leo (IBM), Julian Villanueva (IESE), Eric Weber (IESE), Paco Ybarra (Citi), and George Yeo (Kerry Logistics). Tom Malone (MIT) could not attend this Conference and presented his paper in the IESE Symposium on Ethics, Business and Society on July 3, 2018.

The IESE Alumni and Institutional Development team took care of all the organizational details with great professionalism and service. We thank Marisa Bombardó, Wim den Tuinden, Sylvia Johansson, Luis Jover, Javier Muñoz, Eulalia Puig, Carmen Roch, and Patrik Wallen, and the whole Alumni Division team, for a magnificent organization.

We are also very grateful for the outstanding support that Mònica Mestres, Míriam Freixa, and Teresa Planell offered us. They helped us organize the Conference and edit the book, while keeping up with their ordinary and demanding work.

It is a great privilege for us to work again with Palgrave Macmillan and Liz Barlow and her team. Liz has also been very supportive of our projects, offered us terrific ideas, coming back to us very quickly and managing things in a very effective way. We are also grateful to Lucy Kidwell for her great support and professional guidance in the editing process. Finally, we thank Naveen Dass and Keerthana Muruganandham for their excellent help in the production of the book.

We have been very fortunate benefiting from the great work, useful suggestions and practical support of many outstanding individuals in preparing this book. Thank you all!

March 2019                                                         Jordi Canals
                                                                 Franz Heukamp

# Contents

**Part I    An Introduction to AI and Management**

1    **AI for Management: An Overview**                                    3
     *Dario Gil, Stacy Hobson, Aleksandra Mojsilović, Ruchir Puri
     and John R. Smith*


**Part II    The Changing Nature of Companies
             and General Management**

2    **What Is the Value of Firms in an AI World?**                       23
     *Julian Birkinshaw*

3    **The Evolving Role of General Managers in the Age of AI**           37
     *Jordi Canals*


**Part III    Leadership Development and Talent Management
              in an AI Age**

4    **The Role of the General Manager in the New Economy:
     Can We Save People from Technology Dysfunctions?**                   67
     *Jeffrey Pfeffer*

5      **Can Data Science Change Human Resources?**                   93
       *Peter Cappelli, Prasanna Tambe and Valery Yakubovich*

6      **University, Education, Technology, and the Future of Work**   117
       *Bernard Yeung*

7      **AI and the Leadership Development of the Future**             137
       *Franz Heukamp*

**Part IV    Some Key Managerial, Interdisciplinary Challenges**

8      **AI, Marketing Science and Sustainable Profit Growth**        151
       *Dominique M. Hanssens*

9      **How Can Human-Computer "Superminds"
       Develop Business Strategies?**                                 165
       *Thomas W. Malone*

10     **The CEO as a Business Model Innovator in an AI World**       185
       *Joan E. Ricart*

11     **Managing AI Within a Digital Density Framework**             205
       *Javier Zamora*

**Index**                                                             237

# Notes on Contributors

**Julian Birkinshaw** is Professor of Strategy and Entrepreneurship, Deputy Dean of Executive Education and Digital Learning, and Academic Director of the Institute of Innovation and Entrepreneurship at the London Business School. He is a Fellow of the British Academy, a Fellow of the Advanced Institute of Management Research (UK), and a Fellow of the Academy of International Business. Julian's main area of expertise is in the strategy and organization of large multinational corporations. He is the author of four-teen books, including *Mind Tools for Managers* (2018), *Becoming a Better Boss* (2013) and *Reinventing Management* (2010).

**Jordi Canals** is the IESE Foundation Professor of Corporate Governance, IESE Business School. He was the Dean of IESE Business School (2001–2016). He is the President of the IESE Center for Corporate Governance. His areas of expertise are corporate strategy and corporate governance. He is the author or co-author of sixteen books, including *Shaping Entrepreneurial Mindsets (ed.)* (2015), *Building Respected Companies* (2010) and *Managing Corporate Growth* (2001).

**Peter Cappelli** is the George W. Taylor Professor of Management, Wharton School, University of Pennsylvania. Director of its Center for Human Resources Research Center and a Research Associate at the National Bureau of Economic Research. He serves on the Global Agenda Council on Employment for the World Economic Forum. His recent research examines changes in employment relations in the U.S. and their implications. His publications include, among others *The New Deal at Work: Managing the Market-Driven Workforce*; *Talent Management: Managing Talent in an*

*Age of Uncertainty*; and *The India Way: How India's Top Business Leaders are Revolutionizing Management (With Colleagues)*; and *Why Good People Can't Get Jobs.*

**Dario Gil** is the Director of IBM Research, one of the world's largest and most influential corporate research labs. Prior to his current position, Dario was the Vice President of AI and Quantum Computing, areas in which he continues to have broad responsibilities across IBM.

**Dominique M. Hanssens** is the Distinguished Research Professor of Marketing at the UCLA Anderson School of Management. His research focuses on strategic marketing, in particular the assessment of short-term and long-term effects of marketing on business performance. From 2005 to 2007 he served as the Executive Director of the Marketing Science Institute in Cambridge, Massachusetts. Five of his articles won Best Paper Awards: in *Marketing Science* (1995, 2001, 2002), *Journal of Marketing Research* (1999, 2007) and *Journal of Marketing* (2010). In 2007 he was the recipient of the Churchill Lifetime Achievement Award of the American Marketing Association; in 2010 he was elected a Fellow of the INFORMS Society for Marketing Science; and in 2015 he received the INFORMS Society for Marketing Science Buck Weaver Award.

**Franz Heukamp** is the Dean and A. Valero Professor of Management, IESE Business School. He was the IESE Associate Dean for MBA Programs between 2012 and 2016. His main area of research is behavioral decision-making, with a special interest in Neuroeconomics. He is a member of The Institute for Operations Research and Management Sciences, and The Neuroeconomics Society.

**Stacy Hobson** is an IBM Research Scientist and currently leads efforts on AI research strategy with a particular focus on AI Challenges.

**Thomas W. Malone** is the Patrick J. McGovern Professor of Management at MIT Sloan School of Management and the founding director of the MIT Center for Collective Intelligence. Previously, he was the founder and director of the MIT Center for Coordination Science and one of the two founding codirectors of the MIT Initiative on Inventing the Organizations of the twenty first century. In 2004, Thomas summarized two decades of his research in his critically acclaimed book, *The Future of Work* (2004). His newest book, *Superminds*, appeared in May 2018. Thomas has also published four books and over 100 articles, research papers, and book chapters.

**Aleksandra (Saška) Mojsilović** is a Scientist, Head of the AI Foundations Department at IBM Research, Co-Director of IBM Science for Social Good, and an IBM Fellow.

**Jeffrey Pfeffer** is the Thomas D. Dee Professor of Organizational Behavior, Stanford University, Graduate School of Business. He has published extensively in the fields of organization theory and human resource management. He is the author or co-author of 15 books including: *Dying for a Paycheck*; *Leadership B.S.: Fixing Workplaces and Careers One Truth at a Time*; *The Human Equation: Building Profits by Putting People First*; *Power: Why Some People Have It—and Others Don't*; *The Knowing-Doing Gap: How Smart Companies Turn Knowledge Into Action*.

**Ruchir Puri** is the Chief Scientist of IBM Research and an IBM Fellow. He previously led IBM Watson as its CTO and Chief Architect from 2016–2019.

**Joan E. Ricart** is the Carl Shroeder Professor of Strategic Management at IESE Business School. He is a Fellow of the Strategic Management Society and a Fellow of the European Academy of Management, of which he was the founding President. He is the Academic Director of the IESE Cities in Motion Initiative and the UN Center of Excellence of PPP for Cities. Joan Enric is the author of several books and papers on strategy and business models published in leading journals such as *Econometrics*, *Journal of International Business Studies*, *Quarterly Journal of Economics* or *Strategic Management Journal*.

**John R. Smith** is an IBM Fellow and currently leads research and development on vision, speech, language, knowledge, and interaction.

**Prasanna (Sonny) Tambe** is an Associate Professor of Operations, Information and Decisions at the Wharton School at the University of Pennsylvania. His research focuses on the economics of technology and labor, the understanding the labor market for AI skills, and how workers choose to specialize in technologies. Prasanna received his Ph.D. in Managerial Science and Applied Economics from the Wharton School of the University of Pennsylvania.

**Valery Yakubovich** is an Associate Professor at ESSEC Business School in France. His research has been published in *American Sociological Review*, *Human Relations*, *Organization Science*, *Harvard Business Review*, and other journals and edited volumes. His current projects explore data-driven organizational and management innovations.

**Bernard Yeung** is the Dean and Stephen Riady Distinguished Professor, National University of Singapore, and President, Asia Bureau of Economics and Finance Research. His research work has featured in more than 110 research publications covering topics in finance, strategy, international trade or institutional economics. He has also won several scholarly awards and honours for academic excellence, including the Irwin Outstanding Educator Award (2013) from the Business Policy and Strategy (BPS) Division of the Academy of Management.

**Javier Zamora** is a Senior Lecturer of Information Systems at IESE Business School. He holds a Ph.D. in Electrical Engineering from Columbia University and a M.Sc. in Telecommunications Engineering from Universitat Politècnica de Catalunya. His current areas of interest are focused on how high digital density is transforming organizations and industries.

# List of Figures

Fig. 6.1    Economic growth (*Note* This figure was originally published
            open access under a CC-BY Creative Commons Attribution
            4.0 license. *Source* Max Roser [2018])                                119

Fig. 8.1    Illustration of the marketing → sales and marketing →
            profit relationship (*Notes* In this illustration, sales revenue
            [in $ millions] is $150 with no marketing support.
            The response elasticity is 0.15 and the gross margin is 50%
            of revenue. Sales rev ["rev"] is shown in solid line, and profit
            [contribution to overhead] is shown in grey line)                      153

Fig. 8.2    The evolution of brand value vs. customer relations value
            in mergers and acquisitions (*Source* Binder and Hanssens 2015)       161

Fig. 9.1    The basic cognitive processes needed by any intelligent entity.
            Entities that act intelligently (such as people, computers,
            and groups) usually need to do five things: create possibilities
            for action, decide which actions to take, sense the external world,
            remember the past, and learn from experience
            (Reproduced from Malone 2018, *Superminds*)                           171

Fig. 9.2    A "contest web" for developing strategies at different levels
            of a company. In each contest, people compete to develop good
            strategies for that part of the company. Contests at higher levels
            combine strategies from lower levels (Reproduced from Malone
            2018, *Superminds*)                                                    174

Fig. 10.1   The CEO's areas of responsibility (Andreu and Ricart 2014)            187

Fig. 10.2   The key tasks of a CEO (Andreu and Ricart 2014)                       188

Fig. 11.1   Business model and organizational model dimensions of AI              206

Fig. 11.2    Framework for digital transformation (left-side) and
its application in AI (right-side)    209

Fig. 11.3    Digital density architecture    211

Fig. 11.4    Impact of AI on the business model and organizational
model dimensions    232

# List of Tables

Table 4.1  Demographic and budgetary challenges, by country          75
Table 5.1  HR functions and prediction tasks                          96
Table 7.1  Key leadership attributes in the era of AI                147

# Part I

## An Introduction to AI and Management

# 1

# AI for Management: An Overview

## Dario Gil, Stacy Hobson, Aleksandra Mojsilović, Ruchir Puri and John R. Smith

## 1.1 Introduction

*Artificial Intelligence* (AI) has made very rapid progress in recent years. From smart speakers and question answering chatbots, to factory robots and self-driving cars, to AI-generated music, artwork and perfumes, to game playing and debating systems—we have experienced the transition of AI from a largely theoretical discipline into a practical tool empowering a plethora of new applications. Some might say that "AI is the new IT (Information Technology)," and we are seeing the evidence across the industry: machine learning and other foundational AI subjects have record-breaking enrollment on university campuses, while AI-enabled tools are already assisting doctors to spot melanoma, recruiters to find qualified candidates, and banks to decide whom to extend a loan to. Algorithms are powering product recommendations, targeted advertising, essay grading, employee promotion and retention, risk scoring, image labelling, fraud detection, cybersecurity defenses, and a host of other applications.

The explosion and broad adoption of algorithmic decision-making has spurred a great amount of interest and triggered a variety of reactions (along with a substantial amount of "hype")—from excitement about how AI capabilities will augment human decision-making and improve business

D. Gil (✉) · S. Hobson · A. Mojsilović · R. Puri · J. R. Smith
IBM Research, Yorktown Heights, NY, USA
e-mail: dgil@us.ibm.com

© The Author(s) 2020
J. Canals and F. Heukamp (eds.), *The Future of Management in an AI World*,
IESE Business Collection, https://doi.org/10.1007/978-3-030-20680-2_1

performance, to questions about fairness and ethics, fears of job eliminations and economic disparity, even speculations about a threat to humanity. Even the term "AI" itself has evolved and has come to mean different things to different people; it includes machine learning, neural networks, and deep learning, but has also become an umbrella term for many other analytics- and data-related subjects (part of the "*AI is the new IT*" phenomena).

The goal of this chapter is to give a brief introduction of AI and describe its evolution from the current "*narrow*" state to a point where capabilities are more advanced and are "*broad*", through to a futuristic state of "*general AI*". We also explore considerations for organizations and management, including the role of AI in business operations tasks such as strategy planning, marketing, product design, and customer support. Finally, we detail requirements for organizations in defining a comprehensive AI strategy, supported by an understanding of the value of AI to the organization and a focus on needs, including data and skills, to appropriately execute the AI strategy.

## 1.1.1  Defining AI

"Viewed narrowly, there seem to be almost as many definitions of intelligence as there were experts asked to define it," observed Richard Gregory in his book *The Oxford Companion to the Mind* (Gregory 1998), while one study identifies over 70 definitions of intelligence (Legg and Marcus 2007). Broadly speaking, AI is a field of computer science that studies how machines can be made to act intelligently. AI has many functions, including, but not limited to:

- *Learning*, which includes approaches for learning patterns from data. Two main types of learning are unsupervised and supervised. In unsupervised learning, the computer learns directly from raw data, whereas with supervised learning, human input is provided to label or identify important aspects of the data to define the training. Deep learning is a specialized class of primarily supervised learning built on artificial neural networks;
- *Understanding*, which includes techniques for knowledge representation required for domain-specific tasks, such as medicine, accounting, and law;
- *Reasoning*, which comes in several varieties, such as deductive, inductive, temporal, probabilistic, and quantitative; and
- *Interacting*, with people or other machines to collaboratively perform tasks, or for interacting with the environment.

## 1.1.2  A Brief History of AI

AI has received significant attention recently, but it is not a new concept. The idea of creating a "thinking" machine precedes modern computing. For example, the study of formal reasoning dates back to ancient philosophers Aristotle and Euclid. Calculating machines were built in antiquity and were improved throughout history by many mathematicians. In the seventeenth century Leibniz, Hobbes and Descartes explored the possibility that all rational thought could be made as systematic as algebra or geometry. The concept of artificial neural network is not new either. In 1943, Warren S. McCulloch, a neuroscientist, and Walter Pitts, a logician, tried to understand how the brain could produce highly complex patterns by using many basic cells, *neurons*, that are connected together, and they outlined a highly simplified computational model of a neuron (McCulloch and Pitts 1943). This work has made an important contribution to the development of artificial neural networks, which are the underpinning of many AI systems today. Another important contribution was made by Donald Hebb who proposed that neural pathways strengthen over each successive use, especially those between neurons that tend to fire at the same time (Hebb 1949). This idea was essential to the concept of Hebbian learning, and in the context of artificial neural networks, the process of setting and learning the weights between different neurons in the neural network model.

In 1950, Alan Turing, published his seminal paper "Computing Machinery and Intelligence", where he laid out several criteria to assess whether a machine could be deemed intelligent. They have since become known as the "Turing test" (Turing 1950). The term "artificial intelligence" was coined in 1955 by John McCarthy, then a young assistant professor of mathematics at Dartmouth College, when he decided to organize a working group to clarify and develop ideas about thinking machines. The workshop was held at Dartmouth in the summer of 1956, and AI as an academic discipline took off. Three years later, in 1959, IBM scientist Arthur Samuel coined the term "machine learning" to refer to computer algorithms that learn from and make predictions on data by building a model from sample inputs, without following a set of static instructions. Machine learning techniques were core to Samuel's game-playing program for checkers. It was the first game-playing program to achieve sufficient skill to challenge a world champion. Game playing continued to be a way to challenge AI and measure its progress over the next few decades and we have seen application in checkers, chess, backgammon and Go.

The period from 1956 to 1974 was known as the "golden years of AI". Many prominent scientists believed that breakthroughs were imminent and government and industrial sponsors flooded the field with grants.

The field of AI has gone through phases of rapid progress and hype in the past, quickly followed by a cooling in investment and interest, often referred to as "AI winters." The first AI winter occurred in the 1970s as AI researchers underestimated the difficulty of problems they were trying to solve. Once the breakthroughs failed to materialize, government and other funding dried up. During an AI winter, AI research programs had to disguise their research under different names (e.g. "pattern recognition", "informatics", "knowledge-based system") in order to receive funding.

Starting in the mid-seventies, by focusing on methods for knowledge representation, researchers began to build practically usable systems. AI came back in a form of *expert systems*—programs that answer questions or solve problems in a specific narrow domain, using logical rules that encapsulate and implement the knowledge of a subject matter expert. As an example, in 1980, Digital Equipment Corporation (DEC) deployed R1 to assist in the ordering of DEC's VAX computer systems by automatically selecting components based on the customer's requirements. By 1986, R1 had about 2500 rules, had processed 80,000 orders, and achieved 95–98% accuracy; it was saving the company $40M per year by reducing the need to give customers free components when technicians made errors, speeding the assembly process, and increasing customer satisfaction (Crevier 1993).

The 1980s also saw the birth of Cyc, the first attempt to create a database that contains the general knowledge most individuals are expected to have, with the goal of enabling AI applications to perform human-like reasoning. The Cyc project continues to this day, under the umbrella of Cycorp. The ontology of Cyc terms grew to about 100,000 during the first decade of the project, and as of 2017 contains about 1,500,000 terms.

In 1989, chess playing programs HiTech and Deep Thought defeated chess masters. They were developed by Carnegie Mellon University, and paved the way for Deep Blue, a chess-playing computer system developed by IBM, the first computer to win both a chess game and a chess match against a reigning world champion.

### 1.1.3   The Rise of Machine Learning and Neural Networks

Artificial neural networks are inspired by the architecture of the human brain. They contain many interconnected processing units, *artificial neurons*, which are analogous to biological neurons in the brain. A neuron takes an input and processes it in a certain way. Typically, neurons are organized in layers. Different layers may perform different kinds of operations on their inputs, while the connections between the neurons contain weights, mimicking the concept of Hebbian learning.

For close to three decades, symbolic AI dominated both research and commercial applications of AI. Even though artificial neural networks and other machine learning algorithms were actively researched, their practical use was hindered by the lack of digitized data from which to learn from and insufficient computational power. It was only in the mid 1980s that a re-discovery of an already known concept pushed neural nets into the mainstream of AI. *Backpropagation*, a method for training neural nets devised by researchers in the 60s, was revisited by Rumelhart, Hinton, and Williams; they published a paper, which outlined a clear and concise formulation for the technique and it paved its way into the mainstream of machine learning research (Rumelhart et al. 1986). The ability to train practical neural networks, the intersection of computer science and statistics, coupled with rapidly increasing computational power, led to the shift in the dominating AI paradigm from symbolic AI and knowledge-driven approaches, to machine learning and data-driven approaches. Scientists started to build systems that were able to analyze and learn from large amounts of labeled data, and applied them to diverse application areas, such as data-mining, speech recognition, optical character recognition, image processing, and computer vision.

The first decades of the twenty-first century saw the explosion of digital data. The growth in processing speed and power, and the availability of specialized processing devices such as *graphical processing units* (GPUs) finally intersected with large-enough data sets that had been collected and labeled by humans. This allowed researchers to build larger neural networks, called *deep learning networks*, capable of performing complex, human-like tasks with great accuracy, and in many cases, achieving super-human performance. Today, deep learning is powering-up a variety of applications, including computer vision, speech recognition, machine translation, friend recommendations on social network analysis, playing board and video games, home assistants, conversational devices and chatbots, medical diagnostics, self-driving cars, and operating robots.

## 1.2 The Evolution of AI: From "Narrow", to "Broad", to "General"

In recent years, machines have met and surpassed human performance on many cognitive tasks, and some longstanding grand challenge problems in AI have been conquered. We've encountered machines that can solve problems, play games, recognize patterns, prove mathematical theorems, navigate environments, understand and manipulate human language, but are they truly intelligent? Can they reach or surpass human capabilities, and where are we in this evolution?

The community of AI practitioners agrees that the practical applications of AI today belong to so-called *"narrow"* or *"weak"* AI. Narrow AI refers to computer systems adept at performing specific tasks in a single application domain. For example, Apple's Siri virtual assistant is capable of interpreting voice commands, but the algorithms that power Siri cannot drive a car, predict weather patterns, or analyze medical records. It is the same with other systems; factory robots, personal digital assistants, and healthcare decision support systems are designed to perform one narrow task, such as assemble a product, provide a weather forecast or make a purchase order, or help a radiologist in interpreting an X-ray. When they learn after deployment, they do so in the context of that narrow task, and do not have the ability to learn other tasks on their own, or apply them to different domains.

In contrast, *"strong"* AI, also referred to as *artificial general intelligence* (AGI), is a hypothetical type of AI that can meet human-level intelligence and apply this problem-solving ability to any type of problem, just as the same human brain can easily learn how to drive a car, cook food, and write code. Strong AI involves a system with comprehensive knowledge and cognitive capabilities such that its performance is indistinguishable from that of a human. AGI has not yet been developed, and expert opinions differ as to the possibility that it ever might be, the timeline for when it might happen, and the path toward it.

Narrow AI and General AI are two ends of the spectrum in the evolution of AI, with many years, or decades of development in between. We refer to that evolution and the period in between as *broad AI*. Here we outline several key challenges for advancing the field.

## 1.2.1 Learning with Less Data

Most of the recent progress in AI has been made possible due to advances in supervised machine learning, and in particular deep learning. In supervised machine learning, the system learns from examples it is presented with, to identify patterns, and perform tasks, such as classify images, recognize speech, or translate text. Humans provide examples to the systems during their training in the form of labeled data. But one of the significant drawbacks to deep learning networks is that to achieve desired accuracy and performance, they require massive amount of data to learn from. For example, ImageNet a database designed for use in visual object recognition tasks, contains over 14 million URLs of images that have been hand-annotated to indicate what objects are pictured. One of the standard approaches to collecting such datasets is crowdsourcing, and many developers and technology vendors turn to it to harvest and create large sets of labeled data needed for training models. But for many problems, especially in enterprise applications and business decision-making, crowdsourcing is not a viable approach, because either the data does not exist, the problem domain is too complex to allow for easy annotation, or the data is proprietary and sensitive.

Deep learning systems work less well when there are limited amounts of training data available, when the test set differs greatly from the training set, or when the space of examples is broad and filled with novelty. As such, their performance can degrade severely with small changes in the operating environment. For example, the performance of an image recognition service plummets if it is applied to image data collected under different lighting conditions or viewpoints, while speech recognition systems often break when encountering new dialects or pronunciations.

Humans on the other hand, learn differently. A child can learn to recognize a new kind of object or animal using only a few examples and is then able to generalize what it has seen to other circumstances. As a result, there is a broad agreement among machine-learning researchers that new techniques that can work using less data, or without labels are needed to advance the field beyond narrow intelligence.

## 1.2.2  Interaction Between Learning and Reasoning

Since the inception of the field, AI researchers have made enormous progress in developing both learning and reasoning capabilities. However, the two fields have developed independently, and production-grade AI applications deploy them in silos (consider a rule-based customer management system vs. a deep-learning powered customer chatbot). One of the reasons that AI field is still quite far away from general AI is that we are not able to build systems which use these mechanisms interchangeably. The state-of-the-art learning systems learn exceptionally well from data they are presented with but are now well integrated with prior knowledge. As a result, they are not able to handle problems that have less to do with classification and more to do with commonsense reasoning. For example, easily-drawn inferences that people can readily answer without anything like direct training, such as "Who is taller, Prince William or his baby son Prince George?" and "If you stick a pin into a carrot, does it make a hole in the carrot or in the pin?" prove impossible to answer with deep learning (Marcus 2018). Such apparently simple problems require humans to integrate knowledge across vastly disparate sources—something outside of the current deep learning acumen—indicating a need for new types of approaches that leverage a combination of machine learning and machine reasoning, if we are to reach human-level cognitive flexibility.

### 1.2.3  Ethics and Trust of AI

Today, AI-powered systems are routinely being used to support human decision-making in a multitude of applications. Yet broad adoption of AI systems will not come from the benefits alone. Many of the expanding applications of AI may be of great consequence to people, communities, or organizations, and it is crucial that we be able to trust their output. Trusting a decision of an AI system requires more than knowing that it can accomplish a task with high accuracy; the users will want to know that a decision is reliable and fair, that it can be accounted for, and that it will cause no harm. They will need assurance that the decision cannot be tampered with and that the system itself is secure. As we advance AI capabilities, issues of reliability, fairness, explainability, and safety will be of paramount importance.

In order to responsibly scale the benefits of AI, we must ensure that the models we create do not blindly take on our biases and inconsistencies, and then scale them more broadly through automation. The research community has made progress in understanding how bias affects AI decision-making and is creating methodologies to detect and mitigate bias across the lifecycle of an AI application: training models; checking data, algorithms, and service for bias; and handling bias if it is detected. While there is much more to be done, we can begin to incorporate bias checking and mitigation principles when we design, test, evaluate, and deploy AI solutions.

Another issue that has been at the forefront of the discussion recently is the fear that machine learning systems are "black boxes," and that many state-of-the-art algorithms produce decisions that are difficult to explain. A significant body of new research work has proposed techniques to provide interpretable explanations of "black-box" models without compromising their accuracy. These include local and global interpretability techniques of models and their predictions, visualizing information flow in neural nets, and even teaching explanations. We must incorporate these techniques into

AI model development workflows to provide diverse explanations to developers, enterprise engineers, users, and domain experts.

It has also been shown that deep learning models can be easily fooled into making embarrassing and incorrect decisions by adding a small amount of noise, often imperceptible to a human. Exposing and fixing vulnerabilities in software systems is a major undertaking of the technical community, and the effort carries over into the AI space. Recently, there has been an explosion of research in this area: new attacks and defenses are continually identified; new adversarial training methods to strengthen against attack and new metrics to evaluate robustness are being developed. We are approaching a point where we can start integrating them into generic AI DevOps processes to protect and secure production-grade applications that rely on neural networks.

Human trust in technology is based on our understanding of how it works and our assessment of its safety and reliability. We drive cars trusting that the brakes will work when the pedal is pressed. We undergo laser eye surgery trusting the system to make the right decisions. In both cases, trust comes from confidence that the system will not make a mistake thanks to extensive training, exhaustive testing, experience, safety measures, standards, best practices and consumer education. Many of these principles of safety design apply to the design of AI systems; some will have to be adapted, and new ones will have to be defined. For example, we could design AI to require human intervention if it encounters completely new situations in complex environments. And, just as we use safety labels for pharmaceuticals and foods, or safety datasheets in computer hardware, we may begin to see similar approaches for communicating the capabilities and limitations of AI services or solutions. Finally, it is worth emphasizing that deciding on whom to trust to train our AI systems will be the most consequential decision we make in any AI project.

## 1.3  Applications of AI in Management

AI will have an increasingly important role in business operations, including strategic planning, mergers and acquisitions, marketing and product design. As AI becomes more advanced and ubiquitous across enterprises and industries, its application for strategic planning will become more prevalent (Orsini 1986; Shrivastava et al. 2018; Spangler 1991). Strategic planning is an organizational management activity that is used to set priorities, focus resources, strengthen operations, and assess and adjust directions as needed

(Babafemi 2015; Porter 1980). Human decision-making is imperfect and subject to cognitive biases and gaps in rationality that can lead to suboptimal decisions. AI can be used within a multi-agent system that augments the cognition of individuals or groups of people in decision-making. The systems enable a human-agent team to collectively perform cognitive tasks better than human or software agents alone, especially in the realm of high-stakes decision-making. An example of this is the IBM cognitive room that supports decision-making for mergers and acquisitions (IBM 2017; Kephart 2015). The AI system allows groups of decision makers to effectively interact with a large amount of information using speech, gesture and data visualization techniques to assist the process of evaluating options for mergers and acquisitions.

AI has been gaining significant traction in the product marketing domain. AI infused marketing methods seek to leverage AI toward improving marketing efficiencies and outcomes (IBM IBV 2018; Katsov 2017; Kushmaro 2018; Olenski 2018; Siau and Yang 2017; Sterne 2017; Wiggers 2018). For example, AI can measure customer sentiment and track buying habits for sales and marketing. Brands and advertisers use the information to make ecommerce more intuitive and for targeted promotions. AI can be used to create more personalized communications to prospects and customers (André et al. 2018). AI can be used to create improved customer interactions through chat bots or to better understand how to match content to target users. AI will also have an important role in creative product design. New technologies in Deep Learning such as Generative Adversarial Networks (GANs) provide the capability to not only analyze data but also to synthesize data. As a result, we can learn from known products and be able to extrapolate from the learnings to generate new original ideas. This AI capability is being utilized today for creating digital work like art images or content for marketing campaigns. Early results are also being realized for domains as diverse as fragrance design (Goodwin et al. 2017; Goodwin 2018). The trend toward applying AI for generative tasks will continue, which will be important for organizations to exploit as an automated capability or as a tool to assist human creativity. AI will also expand workforce management applications into recruiting and hiring, managing employee turnover, and ensuring employee growth and satisfaction. AI models will also be able to tap into data within the organization to guide employees in developing skills and pursuing opportunities to grow within the company.

Several key management functions, such as human resources, recruitment, and decision support systems, have already benefited from applications of AI technology. As an example, IBM's Watson solution has been deployed as a talent solution offering deeper human engagement, cognitive process and operations, intelligent exploration and discovery, working as an employee and management assistant. It offers key insights from a vast web of knowledge in the enterprise to assist management and employees alike. IBM Watson has also been applied to wide array of use cases where its AI technology has been critical in providing insights to its users. Woodside, Australia's largest energy company, has used IBM Watson to retain the knowledge of senior experts and make it possible for employees to easily locate, analyze, and learn from it. Over 80% of employees adopted Watson for their day-to-day work easing the burden on senior experts and management. Employees reported previously spending more than three-quarters of their time in researching problems and seeking help from experts and less than one-quarter of the time in actually fixing the problem. Watson has helped Woodside reverse that. Additionally, the IBM Watson Recruitment solution has been applied to help management evaluate applicants to predict the likelihood of success for any given role. Indivizo, a Hungarian start-up company, has been helping businesses quickly and cost-efficiently identify applicants with the best fit for a role. It has successfully deployed IBM Watson solutions to help management hone in on the right candidates with the skills that will set them up for success.

These are just a few examples of the use of AI technologies in addressing specific business needs. As more companies adopt AI technologies to drive business value, many additional examples will emerge and the business functions that benefit will continue to expand.

## 1.4 Data, AI, and Skills Strategy

As organizations begin to deploy AI technologies in their business processes, they are faced with a myriad of choices: which capabilities to invest in, whether to develop the capabilities in house or acquire them externally, which platform and tools to use, and how to source or develop AI talent and skills. The first step to getting this right is the requirement to develop a comprehensive Data and AI strategy.

Data is the nucleus that enables today's AI solutions. A significant part of the appeal of machine learning is due to its ability to train more accurate models based on data—as opposed to traditional methods of manual rule writing that explicitly defined how the application would behave. Data continues to grow at an exponential rate, doubling every two years, and is expected to reach 175 Zettabytes by 2025 (Reinsel et al. 2018).

The diversity of enterprise data is also growing. What was once limited to traditional structured data in the form of relational databases and data warehouses is now dominated by unstructured data in the form of text, audio, video, and sensor data. This growth in volume and variety will continue to be driven by the ongoing need of organizations to capture and use unstructured data across all aspect of their business including supply chains, customer data, social media interactions, and more. Organizations are realizing the value of this data and need to maintain a strong information agenda in capturing, storing and exploiting data of all kinds as part of their business.

This trend in growth in amount and importance of data sets the stage for the next major wave of impact of AI on business. AI can be used to train models from unstructured data that can make more accurate predictions, drive better decisions, and transform business processes. Organizations will be able to use these AI models to increase operational efficiency, make more informed decisions, and innovate faster to create new products and services. An effective AI strategy begins with data, but also requires investment in data science to connect the AI models to the objectives of the business.

The most significant advances in AI come from data-driven learning techniques in a supervised setting. *What this means is that the data is labeled.* For example, an automobile insurance company may assign labels to the data during claims processing based on the damage depicted in photos of the vehicles. For a telecommunications provider, this could entail labeling customers subject to churn based on reason for switching. Labeling data requires investment, but it also creates added value and supports the creation of high-performing AI predictive capabilities. The consequence in the cases above is that labeled data can be used to train artificial neural network models that can improve or even transform business processes. In the case of insurance claims, the AI can assist the claim process by automatically detecting and assessing damage. In the case of customer churn, the AI model can make early and more accurate predictions of provider switching.

Where it is not possible or effective to invest in creating labeled data, it may still be valuable to capture and use unlabeled data. For example, an enterprise such as a telecommunications provider may have a very large number of human-to-human chat logs. This raw data can be captured and stored. If the data is labeled it may help to train an AI dialog model using supervised learning that can automate some of these chat sessions. If the data is not labeled, it may still help create an AI system that can automatically search for and retrieve documents or prior chat sessions to assistant human agents.

An important part of the enterprise AI strategy is to recognize that AI is not a single technology or solution. To get started, business leaders will need to educate themselves on what's available across the spectrum of AI technologies, how specific solutions integrate into the day-to-day operations of the business to deliver value, and how they fit in the existing technology stack and workflows. *A critical step in building a successful AI strategy is to discover which business processes in each enterprise can be reimagined as supervised machine learning driven workflows.* This approach represents the next frontier of productivity to be layered on top of recent *robotic process automation* (RPA) advances.

Organizational leaders can choose to work with third party companies to acquire AI capabilities or subscribe to AI services, assemble internal teams with AI skills to develop capabilities directly, or devise a combination strategy with some capabilities being brought in from the outside while others are developed in-house. Each of the options requires people with strong AI expertise to support these efforts. Utilizing AI effectively inside the organization involves having a diverse set of skills, such as data engineers (who would be responsible for data handling, integration and preparation), data scientists, AI researchers and engineers (who would develop and maintain the underlying core AI functions), UI/HCI experts (to guide the design of the technology and put it in the context of business processes and workflows), and software engineers (who would implement, deploy, and maintain the resulting business applications). Currently, there is a significant shortage of people with the necessary expertise to build AI systems. Recent reports have estimated that the number of people with the expertise in developing AI may be as low as 22,000 while less conservative estimates report a number around 200,000–300,000 people globally (Kahn 2018). With speculation that there are millions of available AI and data science roles (Daly 2018) and the demand for AI skills continuing to rise sharply, many large companies are engaged in a war for AI talent.

This point highlights another critical component of an AI strategy for business in identifying how to attract and retain people with AI skills. Skills education and training must be matched with the actual skills that will be required to make advances in AI, create new solutions, and work in partnership with AI systems. A recent report (Lorica and Loukides 2018) cited a number of impediments for the adoption of AI in businesses including data challenges, company culture, hardware and other resources, but the AI skills gap was listed as the number one barrier.

To address the needs for AI skills, companies may try traditional routes of posting open jobs and direct hiring of new college graduates or experienced professionals with AI specialization. Since universities are ripe with college students and professors studying and conducting research in AI fields, this has become a key channel for expertise and expertise development. As we've seen in the emergence of a focus on expertise development, leading online learning platforms such as Coursera (www.coursera.org) and edX (www.edx.org) offer online courses in AI, machine learning and other topics taught by leading university professors. Some companies have taken a more extreme tact in hiring large numbers of faculty and students (Hernandez and King 2016) or acquiring entire departments from a single university to staff their AI teams (Ramsey and MacMillan 2015).

Another tactic is in the development of programs to retrain and reskill existing employees. Some of these internal "*AI Universities*" or "*AI Academy*" efforts have been emerging in large businesses with companies like IBM (IBM 2018; Lopez 2018) and Amazon (Tumg 2018) offering these services for other companies to leverage. The particular choice of method in acquiring or training AI talent within an organization is one of the key components underlying the business AI strategy.

The AI field is continuously moving at a fast pace. As a result, enterprises need to employ AI researchers with advanced skills in order to stay current with the state-of-art. At a minimum, these AI researchers need be able to read the latest scientific literature, access the latest AI open source tools, identify and curate the latest neural network designs, learning algorithms and models, and connect them to enterprise applications. In more advanced contexts, these AI researchers need to design new neural networks, create new learning algorithms and develop new methods for training AI models. AI researchers need advanced skills in AI fields like machine learning, natural language processing, computer vision, speech processing, and robotics.

AI researchers work with AI engineers, who are responsible for developing and operationalizing the AI systems. The AI engineers integrate the latest neural networks, learning algorithms and models into enterprise applications. The AI engineers need to address both build-time and run-time aspects of these applications. Build-time requirements include training of neural network models as well as ensuring trust, fairness, explainability and other aspects of robustness. These efforts are not limited to a one-time build, and in practice, training needs to be performed continuously. Run-time requirements need to be addressed to support the necessary data rates and data volumes for applying the AI models within the applications. AI engineers need skills in programming languages like Python/C++/R/Java as well as experience with distributed computing, machine learning algorithms, and advanced signal processing. AI engineers will work with data scientists who are responsible for training specific models.

Data scientists need to curate and wrangle data sets for training, validating and testing of the AI models. The data scientists need knowledge of probability and statistics, data modeling and visualization and experience with relevant deep learning frameworks and data management tools like Hadoop and Spark. The data scientists need to work with domain experts to translate the requirements from applications to specific tasks for machine learning to train the required AI models. As application requirements change, data distributions change or drift, or as errors in deployed models are detected and fed-back, data scientists need to continuously retrain or refine the deployed AI models for applications.

## 1.5    Conclusion

We have seen significant advances in AI in the past few years and have reached a point where AI is beginning to move from a "narrow" state—being focused on a single task in a single domain—to the cusp of a "broad" era of AI where the technologies can be applied to tasks across multiple domains or problem sets. AI offers great promise in helping organizations with critical business operation tasks such as strategy planning, product design, marketing, and customer support. As business leaders aim to develop and deploy more AI within their organizations, a critical first step in this process is to determine the plan for the specific use of AI to meet their business objectives and the development of a comprehensive AI strategy. Critical components of the AI strategy include the plan for acquiring the necessary AI capabilities, whether through external sourcing or internal development, the method for assembling AI talent, and the availability and collection of the properly labeled data required to train the AI models. We encourage all leaders to be knowledgeable and intentional about these efforts to support successful deployment of AI within their business.

## References

André, Quentin, Ziv Carmon, Klaus Wertenbroch, Alia Crum, Douglas Frank, William Goldstein, Joel Huber, Leaf van Boven, Bernd Weber, and Haiyang Yang. 2018. Consumer Choice and Autonomy in the Age of Artificial Intelligence and Big Data. *Customer Needs and Solutions* 5 (1): 28–37.

Babafemi, Ilori. 2015. Corporate Strategy, Planning and Performance Evaluation: A Survey of Literature. *Journal of Management Policies and Practices* 3 (1): 43–49.

Crevier, Daniel. 1993. *AI: The Tumultuous Search for Artificial Intelligence*. New York, NY: Basic Books.

Daly, Ciaran. 2018. How You Can Bridge the AI Skill Gap in 2018. *AI Business*, January 11. https://aibusiness.com/bridging-ai-skills-gap-2018-long-read/.

Gregory, Richard. 1998. *The Oxford Companion to the Mind*. Oxford, UK: Oxford University Press.

Goodwin, Richard. 2018. Using AI to Create New Fragrances. *IBM*, October 23. https://www.ibm.com/blogs/research/2018/10/ai-fragrances/.

Goodwin, Richard, Joana Maria, Payel Das, Raya Horesh, Richard Segal, Jing Fu, and Christian Harris. 2017. AI for Fragrance Design. In *Proceedings of the Workshop on Machine Learning for Creativity and Design*, NIPS, December.

Hebb, Donald. 1949. *The Organization of Behaviour: A Neuropsychological Theory*. Oxford: Wiley.

Hernandez, Daniela, and Rachel King. 2016. Universities AI Talent Poached by Tech Giants. *The Wall Street Journal*. Dow Jones & Company, Inc., November 24. https://www.wsj.com/articles/universities-ai-talent-poached-by-tech-giants-1479999601.

IBM. 2017. Research Cognitive Environments, March. https://researcher.watson.ibm.com/researcher/view_group.php?id=5417.

IBM. 2018. AI Skills Academy. https://www.ibm.com/services/process/talent/ai-academy.

IBM IBV (Institute of Business Value). 2018. Redefining Markets: Insights from the Global C-Suite Study—The CMO Perspective. https://www-01.ibm.com/common/ssi/cgi-bin/ssialias?htmlfid=GBE03728USEN&.

Kahn, Jeremy. 2018. Sky High Salaries Are the Weapons in the AI Talent War. *Bloomberg Businessweek*. Bloomberg L.P., February 13. https://www.bloomberg.com/news/articles/2018-02-13/in-the-war-for-ai-talent-sky-high-salaries-are-the-weapons.

Katsov, Ilya. 2017. Introduction to Algorithmic Marketing: Artificial Intelligence for Marketing Operations. Retrieved from https://algorithmic-marketing.online.

Kephart, Jeff. 2015. IBM Research Symbiotic Cognitive Systems—Mergers and Acquisitions Prototype. https://slideplayer.com/slide/8434657/.

Kushmaro, Philip. 2018. How AI Is Reshaping Marketing. *CIO Magazine*, September 4.

Legg, Shane, and Marcus Hutter. 2007. A Collection of Definitions of Intelligence, June 25. https://arxiv.org/pdf/0706.3639.pdf.

Lopez, Maribel. 2018. It's Time to Reinvent Your Human Resources Strategy and IBM Watson Wants to Be Your Guide. *Forbes*. Forbes Media LLC, December 2. https://www.forbes.com/sites/maribellopez/2018/12/02/its-time-to-reinvent-your-human-resources-strategy-and-ibm-wants-watson-to-be-your-guide/#-3c33034a7053.

Lorica, Ben, and Mike Loukides. 2018. *How Companies Are Putting AI to Work Through Deep Learning*. Newton, MA: O'Reilly Media Inc., April. https://www.oreilly.com/library/view/how-companies-are/9781492040798/.

Marcus, Gary. 2018. Deep Learning: A Critical Appraisal, January 2. https://arxiv.org/abs/1801.00631.

McCulloch, Warren, and Walter Pitts. 1943. A Logical Calculus of the Ideas Immanent in Nervous Activity. *The Bulletin of Mathematical Biophysics* 5 (4): 115–133.

Olenski, Steve. 2018. How Artificial Intelligence Is Raising the Bar on the Science of Marketing. *Forbes*, May 16.

Orsini, Jean-Francois. 1986. Artificial Intelligence: A Way Through the Strategic Planning Crisis? *Long Range Planning* 19 (4): 71–77.

Porter, Michael. 1980. *Competitive Strategy: Techniques for Analyzing Industries and Competitors*. New York: Free Press. ISBN 0-684-84148-7.

Ramsey, Mike, and Douglas MacMillan. 2015. Carnegie Mellon Reels After Uber Lures Away Researchers. *The Wall Street Journal*. Dow Jones & Company, Inc., May 31. https://www.wsj.com/articles/is-uber-a-friend-or-foe-of-carnegie-mellon-in-robotics-1433084582.

Reinsel, David, John Gantz, and John Rydning. 2018. The Digitization of the World—From Edge to Core. *IDC*, November. Retrieved from https://www.seagate.com/files/www-content/our-story/trends/files/idc-seagate-dataage-white-paper.pdf.

Rumelhart, David, Geoffrey Hinton, and Ronald Williams. 1986. Learning Internal Representations by Error Propagation. In *Parallel Distributed Processing: Explorations in the Microstructure of Cognition*, vol. 1, ed. D.E. Rumelhart and J.L. McClelland. Cambridge, MA: Bradford Books.

Shrivastava, Puja, Laxman Sahoo, and Manjusha Pandey. 2018. Architecture for the Strategy-Planning Techniques Using Big Data Analytics. In *Smart Computing and Informatics: Smart Innovation, Systems and Technologies*, vol. 77, ed. S. Satapathy, V. Bhateja, and S. Das. Singapore: Springer.

Siau, Keng, and Yen Yang. 2017. Impact of Artificial Intelligence, Robotics and Machine Learning on Sales and Marketing. In *Proceedings of the Midwest United States Association for Information Systems Conference*, January.

Spangler, William. 1991. The Role of Artificial Intelligence in Understanding the Strategic Decision-Making Process. *IEEE Transactions Knowledge and Data Engineering* 3 (2): 149–159.

Sterne, Jim. 2017. *Artificial Intelligence for Marketing: Practical Applications*. Hoboken, NJ: Wiley.

Tumg, Liam. 2018. Amazon's Free Training: Internal Machine Learning Courses Are Now Open to Al. *ZDNet*. CBS Interactive, November 27. https://www.zdnet.com/article/amazons-free-training-internal-machine-learning-courses-are-now-open-to-all/.

Turing, Alan. 1950. Computing Machinery and Intelligence. *Mind* 49: 433–460.

Wiggers, Kyle. 2018. IBM's New Watson AI Marketing Suite Personalizes Ads for Individual Customers. *Venture Beat*, October 2.

# Part II

## The Changing Nature of Companies and General Management

# 2

# What Is the Value of Firms in an AI World?

Julian Birkinshaw

## 2.1 Introduction

Artificial Intelligence (AI) refers simply to the simulation of human intelligence by machines, especially computer systems. Over the last five years or so, advances in AI have occurred so rapidly that businesses are putting large investments into these technologies, and are starting to get to grips with the consequences of having computers undertake activities and jobs that were previously thought of as uniquely human (e.g. McAfee and Brynjolfsson 2017; Tegmark 2017). It is now widely accepted that computers can recognise and respond to human voices, recognise faces, diagnose cancerous cells, drive cars, and analyse legal documents, albeit with some form of human oversight (Agrawal et al. 2018; Polson and Scott 2018); and it is widely expected that further breakthroughs are on their way.

Many studies have looked at how AI is changing the workplace, in terms of how individuals' tasks and jobs might look in the future (e.g. Frey and Osborne 2017; Susskind and Susskind 2015). These studies focus on individuals, and on the skills and capabilities that will still be needed in the years ahead. My purpose in this paper is to consider the higher level of analysis, i.e. the firm itself, and to discuss what the distinctive attributes of firms might be in a world of hyper-efficient and hyper-intelligent machines.

J. Birkinshaw (✉)
London Business School, London, UK
e-mail: jbirkinshaw@london.edu

© The Author(s) 2020
J. Canals and F. Heukamp (eds.), *The Future of Management in an AI World*,
IESE Business Collection, https://doi.org/10.1007/978-3-030-20680-2_2

To structure the discussion, I will focus on two aspects of firms that will be very familiar to any reader: (1) Strategy—the choices executives makes about where and how the firm competes, an external perspective; and (2) Management—the choices executives make about how work gets done, an internal perspective.

To anticipate the main arguments of the paper, I will argue that AI is pushing firms towards a more constrained set of choices (in where and how they compete, and how they get work done) than their executives would readily choose. These constrained choices are not entirely bad, because they enable incremental improvements in efficiency, but if the goal of strategy is to create competitive advantage, and if the goal of management is to enable employees to do their best work, there are problems ahead. I therefore finish the paper with some ideas about the distinctive ways firms can create value, and therefore overcome the constraints of AI.

## 2.2    Background on the Digital Revolution and Artificial Intelligence

While the business world is in a perpetual state of flux, many observers believe that the changes underway at the current time are highly distinctive. Brynjolfsson and McAfee (2014) talk about the *Second Machine Age* which involves the automation of cognitive tasks that make humans and software-driven machines substitutes (whereas the First Machine Age, the industrial revolution, helped to make labour and machines complementary). Schwab (2017) uses the term *Fourth Industrial Revolution* to signify the new ways in which technology is becoming embedded within societies and the human body (the first three industrial revolutions were represented by steam engines, electrification, and microprocessors respectively). Others have used such terms as the *Information Age*, the *New Media Age*, the *Agile Age*, and the *Digital Age* (Castells 1996; Denning 2018). The common theme across these perspectives is that the exponential growth in the processing and transmission of information beginning in the late 1960s led to a major shift in the types of products and services sold to consumers, the internal workings of firms, and a dramatic shift in the basis of firm competitiveness.

The mechanisms by which technology has shaped firm activities and human behaviour are complex. For example, some studies have documented the shift from technology *supporting* work to technology *automating* work through to technology *complementing* human effort (Carr 2008; Davenport

1993), while others have emphasised the dialectic between technological innovations and social innovations that mitigate the limitations of those innovations (Bordrozic and Adler 2018).

My focus here is on one particular area of technological development, namely the rise of AI, defined as *the simulation of human intelligence processes by machines, especially computer systems.* Of course developments in AI have been underway since the beginning of the computer age. Over the years there has been considerable effort spent applying AI technology to the business world, and debating on its likely consequences (e.g. McAfee and Brynjolfsson 2017; Tegmark 2017).

Most discussions about the potential of AI in the 1990s and early 2000s were highly speculative, in large part because AI was developing very slowly—it had entered the "AI winter," a period when the promised advances failed to materialise. But over the last decade things have moved on rapidly. Winter has given way to spring, and to a suite of new technologies, such as deep learning and reinforcement learning, that are finally allowing AI to fulfil its business potential (Agrawal et al. 2018).

In the next two sections of the paper, I will consider how AI is shaping first the strategic choices executives are making for their firms and, second, the way executives are managing their activities internally.

## 2.3    The Impact of AI on Firm Strategy

Strategy can be defined as the choices executives makes about where and how the firm competes (Porter 1996; Rumelt 2011). Strategy is externally focused, meaning that these choices emphasise the firm's position in a marketplace—its value proposition to customers, and what differentiates it from competitors. Strategy also has an internal component, defined in terms of the firm's capabilities or the activities it undertakes, that enable it to deliver on its chosen position in the marketplace.

Over the last decade the term "business model" has come into popular usage (Zott et al. 2011). A firm's business model is its formula for making money, based again on a set of choices about where and how it competes. A business model is more generic than a strategy. Ryan Air and Easy Jet might have the same "no frills" business model, but their specific choices about which markets to compete in are different.

So what will the impact of AI be on firm strategies and business models? Consider first some of the broader trends that have occurred as a result of the digital revolution.

- Technology has increased the operational effectiveness of firms. Since the 1970s, firms have been investing large sums of money on Information Technology, and automating manual and repetitive tasks. AI advances are now leading to the automation of professional tasks, from auditing to legal work to medical diagnosis (Davenport and Ronanki 2018). Technology is also reducing transaction costs within and between firms (Williamson 1975). Firms frequently transact with one another without any human intervention, and greater transparency is, of course, making it easier for disputes and problems to be resolved.
- Firms are becoming less vertically integrated and more horizontally specialised. This is a very long-cycle trend. Think back to the post-war industrial era, when many firms controlled their entire value chain (Ford Motor Co had its own rubber plantations for its tires, IBM developed its own processors). Gradually, it became clear that this level of vertical integration was inefficient and lacked flexibility, and firms increasingly focused on a narrower set of activities where their "core competences" were (Quinn 1992; Prahalad and Hamel 1990 ). Moving into the 1990s and 2000s, this trend towards greater horizontal specialisation continued, and the norm among digital era firms is to aim for narrow expertise in one business area, but on a global scale. Google and Facebook exemplify this trend, as do "unicorn" firms like Uber, WeWork, and Palantir.
- One of the most visible changes over the last decade is the emergence of "platform" businesses. A platform is simply a technological interface that mediates transactions between two or more sides. Fast-growing firms such as Uber, LinkedIn, WeWork and Facebook are pure platform businesses. Others, including Microsoft, Apple and Amazon are platform-based businesses operating with a mix of physical and digital offerings. A related feature of the digital economy is the increasingly important role of business ecosystems in shaping consumer and firm behaviour. An ecosystem is a community of interacting firms and individuals who co-evolve and tend to align themselves with the direction set by one or more central companies (McIntyre and Srinivasan 2017).

New technologies are also having an effect on the behavioural dimensions of strategy, in terms of how executives analyse their strategic options and make decisions. While AI is improving the quality of many decisions, it also creates risks and blind spots if it is overused. These include:

- Analysis paralysis. AI excels at pulling together and interpreting large bodies of data. It is good at identifying anomalies, finding patterns, and making predictions (Agrawal et al. 2018). Because it's so easy to use, some executives are seduced into using it as a substitute for their own critical judgment, or they fall into the trap of over-analysing a situation, and not actually making a decision.

- Loss of contextual understanding. AI is still "narrow" in scope, meaning that on a specific assignment or task it can be every bit as smart as a human, but without any ability to tackle slightly different tasks. The increasing use of AI in the business world is therefore helping executives to optimise their answers to well-defined questions, while potentially reducing their ability to see the bigger picture. Many investment decisions, for example, are based on Net Present Value analyses, which means that if a potentially important factor cannot be quantified, it doesn't get included.

- Lack of differentiation. The race to develop new AI technologies is fierce, which means that advances are quickly copied. Of course, some of the firms developing AI technologies generate a temporary advantage, but their business model is typically to embed that technology in as many of their client firms as possible (e.g. IBM's Watson business unit). This leads to a predictable "arms race" where competitors invest in very similar technologies, to avoid falling behind, but they end up even less differentiated than before. The fund management industry, for example, increasingly uses "robo advisors" to make investment choices for their clients, but competitors all have similar algorithms for making their trading decisions, they will inevitably end up with very similar investment returns.

Taken together, these points suggest a rather bleak view of strategy-making in an AI world. By embracing these new technologies, executives are likely to end up making more constrained decisions than they might have in the past. They will emphasise evidence-based, rigorous decision-making, but in a way that leads them to converge on similar choices to those of their competitors. This approach might be less risky ("safety in numbers") but it is completely at odds with the core notion of strategy as a way of making difficult choices to differentiate a business from its competitors.

So what is the advice to executives in today's AI-obsessed world? It is important, as always, to treat new technologies with caution and to understand their limits as well as their potential benefits. So investing in AI to some degree is a good thing, as a way of enhancing basic operational effectiveness. But AI is no substitute for creative thinking or intuitive leaps forward. As I have written elsewhere, the imperatives for firms that are seeking to capitalise on the opportunities in today's fast-changing world involve acting on opportunities more quickly, and being prepared to follow an intuitive or experience-based point of view, rather than relying heavily on empirical support (Birkinshaw and Ridderstråle 2017). The latter part of this paper will explore some of the ways to make these types of creative or intuitive leaps.

## 2.4  The Impact of AI on Management

The second half of the paper shifts the focus inside the firm, in terms of how work gets done. Again, the rise of AI is just the latest part of a secular shift towards greater automation and greater use of technology within firms. For example, studies in the 1980s were already predicting the demise of the middle manager because the computer revolution was enabling the sharing of information down and across organisations more efficiently than before.

I focus here on the practice of management: getting work done through others. Again, there are many ways to define the activities of management, so I will use framework I developed before (Birkinshaw 2010) to structure the discussion.

Management involves making choices in four linked areas: how work is coordinated, how decisions are made, how objectives are set, how employees are motivated (Birkinshaw 2010). I will consider how AI and related technologies are changing each one.

- *Coordinating activities.* Coordination in the business world occurs through a combination of two mechanisms. One is the use of standardised rules and procedures (typically through hierarchical governance) to ensure conformity of behaviour and to generate consistent outputs, the other is a process of mutual adjustment between parties, involving give-and-take on both sides (typically in a market-based setting; Birkinshaw 2010).

  As observed earlier, AI and other related technologies are helping to dramatically reduce the costs of coordination within and between firms. To use a trite example, when you say to Alexa "order more dog food," a chain of activities is initiated that leads to the delivery of a fresh supply of Kibble twenty four hours later, with little or no human intervention. This work is coordinated by a single firm, Amazon, but it often involves third parties (makers of dog food, delivery companies) whose systems interact seamlessly with Amazon's.

A simple transaction cost logic (Williamson 1975) would suggest that these lower transaction costs make firms less important, and would increase the prevalence of market-based transactions. There is some truth to this, but of course transaction costs are also being lowered *within* firms, which makes it possible for a giant firm like Amazon to still operate efficiently. So as the costs of transacting within *and* between firms are reduced, the role of humans in these relationships becomes much smaller. People still oversee these types of relationships, to ensure that everything is done legally and fairly, but even here there are signs that technology might one day take over. For example, the Ethereum ecosystem, built on blockchain technology, is experimenting with so-called *smart contracts* which are processed automatically once a transaction has occurred (Christidis and Devetsikiotis 2016).

- *Making decisions.* There has always been a tension between algorithmic and heuristic decision-making. Algorithmic decisions are based on logic and empirical evidence, heuristic decisions are based on the subjective judgment of experienced individuals. Most decisions, of course, involved some combination between the two, but as discussed earlier the dramatic advances in AI are making algorithmic judgments more and more accurate. There are countless examples now of computers making more accurate judgments than experts, in such areas as wine prices, cancer diagnosis and route selection (McAfee and Brynjolfsson 2017).

- *Defining objectives.* There are two schools of thought on how to define objectives. One is based on the principle of linear alignment. A specific firm might define an intended outcome, say five years into the future, and then define the specific plans and targets for all the various parts of the firm over the coming years, to ensure that outcome is achieved. The alternative school of thought is that a firm (or individual for that matter) has multiple objectives that cannot all be optimised at the same time. Many firms, for example, speak about their "triple bottom line" of financial, social and environment goals, and it is widely accepted that there are short-term trade-offs between these different goals.

How does AI affect objective setting in firms? AI research has always struggled with goals and objectives. Tegmark (2017: 249) wrote: "If I had to summarise in a single word what the thorniest AI controversies are about, it would be goals." Nonetheless, as a first approximation, it is valid to observe that "Narrow AI," which is the state-of-the-art today, works best when it is directed towards tackling a singular goal. Indeed, the success of machine learning techniques, such as reinforcement learning, is based in large part on algorithms that "reward" choices that get closer to a pre-specified goal.

- *Motivating employees.* Finally, there are two schools of thought about how to motivate employees. Using the language of MacGregor (1966), Theory X assumes that motivation is extrinsic, and people therefore work hard because they are being offered material rewards; Theory Y assumes that motivation is intrinsic, i.e. it comes from within.

  There is merit to both these theories, and of course human motivation is complex and highly variable from individual to individual. But to keep things simple, and relevant to the current paper, the salient point is that AI technologies make it possible today to monitor and evaluate how well individuals are performing specific tasks. Many factories, call centres, and delivery companies track the activities of their workers in real time, and they analyse this data to help them increase the efficiency of the work being done. This is the modern-day equivalent of FW Taylor's Scientific Management (1914), and of course it helps to reinforce a Theory X worldview of human motivation.

Putting these four points together, we once again end up with a rather bleak prognosis of the impact of AI on today's workplace. I have previously referred to this as the "Brave New Workplace" in homage to Aldous Huxley—a world of hyper-efficient coordination, algorithmic decision-making, narrow linear objectives, and a neo-Taylorist approach to human motivation.

Fortunately, just as with the discussion of strategy, there is an alternative future open to enlightened executives who are seeking to make a difference in the organisations they run. This alternative view is best opened up by asking the question, "what are firms for?" The transaction cost view, discussed earlier, sees firms narrowly as a nexus of contracts, as a way of minimising transaction costs (Jensen and Meckling 1976; Williamson 1975). But there are several alternative views in the organisation theory literature. For example, Moran and Ghoshal (1999) argued that one of the key reasons we have firms is because they do things markets cannot, specifically they are able to take resources away from their short-run efficient optimal use, and put them into activities that have the potential for the creation of greater value in the long run. Kogut and Zander (1996) argued firms have a social identity that individuals relate to, which increases their discretionary effort towards the firm's goals.

These theoretical arguments suggest some important ideas about the potentially distinctive qualities of firms in an AI world. Without claiming to be exhaustive, I propose there are four such qualities. The first two are more about coordination and decision-making, the latter two are more about objective setting and motivating employees.

## 2.4.1 Firms Create Value by Managing Tensions Between Competing Priorities

In today's parlance, firms have to exploit their established sources of advantage (to make profits today) while also exploring for new sources of advantage (to ensure their long-term viability) (March 1991). However, getting the right balance between these two sets of activities is tricky because each one is to a large degree self-reinforcing. Hence the notion of organisational ambidexterity—the capacity to balance exploitation and exploration (Tushman and O'Reilly 1996).

AI is evidently helping many firms to exploit their existing sources of advantage—whether through process automation, improved problem-solving or quality assurance. AI can also be useful in exploring new sources of advantage: in the famous case of AlphaGo, the winning "strategy" was one that no human player had ever come up with; and computers are increasingly writing new musical scores and painting Picasso-like landscapes.

But AI is not helpful in managing the tension between these activities, i.e. knowing when to do more of one or the other. Such choices require careful judgment—weighing up qualitative and quantitative factors, being sensitive to context, or bringing emotional or intuitive factors into play. These are the capabilities that lie at the heart of organisational ambidexterity and I don't believe AI can help us with them at the current time. IBM's recently announced Project Debater is a case in point: it showed just how far AI has come in terms of constructing and articulating a point of view, but equally how much better humans are at balancing different points of view (Slonim 2018)

## 2.4.2 Firms Create Value by Favouring a Long-Term Perspective

As a variant of the first point, firms don't just manage trade-offs between exploitation and exploration on a day to day basis, they also manage trade-offs *over time*. As noted earlier, firms deliberately take resources away from their short-term best use, in order to give themselves the chance to create even more value over the long term (Moran and Ghoshal 1999). This "one step back, two steps forward" logic manifests itself in many ways—risky R&D projects, pursuing sustainability goals, paying above-market wages to improve loyalty, and so on. We actually take it for granted that firms will do many of these things, but again they involve judgments that AI is ill-equipped to help us with. AI can devise seemingly cunning strategies that look prescient (remember AlphaGo) but only when the rules of the game are pre-determined and stable.

An example: the "Innovator's Dilemma" is that by the time it's clear an invasive technology is going to disrupt an incumbent firm's business model, it is too late to respond effectively (Christensen 2013). The incumbent therefore needs to invest in the invasive technology *before* it is definitively needed. Successful firms, in other words, need to be prepared to commit to new technologies in periods of ambiguity, and to have a "willingness to be misunderstood," in Jeff Bezos' terms. This isn't an easy concept for AI to get used to.

### 2.4.3   Firms Create Value Through Purpose

There is a second dimension to long-term thinking, and that is its impact on individual and team motivation. We typically use the term purpose here, to describe what Tata et al. (2013) call a "moral or spiritual call to action" that leads people to put in discretionary effort—to work long hours, and to bring their passion and creativity to the workplace.

This notion that a firm has a social quality—a purpose or identity—that goes beyond its economic *raison d'etre* is well established in the literature, from March and Simon (1958) through to Kogut and Zander (1996). But it still arouses suspicion among those who think of the firm as a nexus of contracts, and who believe that people are motivated largely through extrinsic rewards.

My view is that you just need to look at charities, open-source software movements, and many other not-for-profit organisations to realise that many people work harder when money is not involved. And it is the capacity of a leader to articulate a sense of purpose, in a way that creates emotional resonance with followers, that is uniquely human.

Successful firms, in other words, institutionalise a sense of identity and purpose that attracts employees and customers. For example, even though blockchain technology is—by definition—about building a system that cannot be hacked, or misused by a few opportunists, its limited uptake at the current time suggests people still prefer to put their faith in other people.

### 2.4.4   Firms Create Value by Nurturing "Unreasonable" Behaviour

There are many famous cases of mavericks who succeeded by challenging the rules, such as Steve Jobs, Elon Musk, and Richard Branson. With apologies to George Bernard Shaw, I think of these people as unreasonable—they seek to adapt the world to their view, rather than learn to fit in. And if we want to see firms move beyond what is already known and proven—to create new market opportunities—more of these types of people would be useful.

Unreasonableness is antithetical to the world of AI. Computers work either through sophisticated algorithms or by inference from prior data, and in both cases the capacity to make an entirely out-of-the-box leap doesn't exist. As noted earlier, in the world of investment management, robo advisors are not just making trades, they are also providing investment advice to investors, and at a fraction of the cost of human financial advisors. But as the Financial Times (Johnson 2017) said last year, "when it comes to investing, human stupidity beats AI." In other words, if you want to beat the market, you need to be a contrarian—you need to make investments that go against the perceived wisdom at the time, and you need to accept the risk that your judgment or your timing might be wrong. These qualities are—at the moment—distinctively human.

So one of the distinctive qualities of *firms* is that they nurture this type of unreasonable behaviour. Of course, many firms do their best to drive out variance, by using tight control systems and punishing failure. My argument is that as AI becomes more influential, though the automation of basic activities and simple contracts, it becomes even more important for firms to push in the other direction—to nurture unorthodox thinking, encourage experimentation, and tolerate failure.

## 2.5   Conclusions

The purpose of this paper was to offer a critical evaluation of the impact of AI on the nature of the firm, and specifically on the types of strategies and management styles adopted by firms. Even though many observers think of AI as a potentially liberating force, my analysis suggests it is more likely to serve as a constraint on the actions of executives and the activities of firms. Many firms, in fact, are adopting AI and related technologies in a manner that makes them more streamlined and efficient, but actually less distinctive and less attractive as places to work.

Despite this somewhat gloomy prognosis, the paper finishes with a more upbeat message by identifying some of the things executives can do to reaffirm the distinctiveness of their firms, to help them avoid the constraints discussed above. Of course, these paths towards individuality involve greater courage and risk than following the herd, but they also offer greater long-term potential.

# References

Agrawal, Ajay, Joshua Gans, and Avi Goldfarb. 2018. *Prediction Machines: The Simple Economics of Artificial Intelligence*. Brighton, MA: Harvard Business Press.

Birkinshaw, Julian. 2010. *Reinventing Management: Smarter Choices for Getting Work Done*. Hoboken, NJ: Wiley.

Birkinshaw, Julian, and Jonas Ridderstråle. 2017. *Fast/Forward: Make Your Company Fit for the Future*. Stanford: Stanford University Press.

Bodrozic, Zlatko, and Paul Adler. 2018. The Evolution of Management Models: A Neo-Schumpeterian Theory. *Adminitsrative Science Quarterly* 63 (1): 85–129.

Brynjolfsson, Erik, and Andrew McAfee. 2014. *The Second Machine Age: Work, Progress, and Prosperity in a Time of Brilliant Technologies*. New York: W. W. Norton.

Carr, Nicholas G. 2008. *The Big Switch: Rewiring the World, from Edison to Google*. New York: W. W. Norton.

Castells, Manuel. 1996. *The Rise of the Network Society. The Information Age: Economy, Society, and Culture Volume I*. Information Age Series. London: Blackwell.

Christensen, Clayton. 2013. *The Innovator's Dilemma: When New Technologies Cause Great Firms to Fail*. Boston: Harvard Business Review Press.

Christidis, Konstantinos, and Michael Devetsikiotis. 2016. Blockchains and Smart Contracts for the Internet of Things. *IEEE Access* 4: 2292–2303.

Davenport, Thomas H. 1993. *Process Innovation: Reengineering Work Through Information Technology*. Boston: Harvard Business Press.

Davenport, Thomas H., and Rajeev Ronanki. 2018. Artificial Intelligence for the Real World. *Harvard Business Review* 96 (1): 108–116.

Denning, Stephen. 2018. *The Age of Agile: How Smart Companies Are Transforming the Way Work Gets Done*. New York: AMACOM.

Frey, Carl Benedikt, and Michael A. Osborne. 2017. The Future of Employment: How Susceptible Are Jobs to Computerisation? *Technological Forecasting and Social Change* 114: 254–280.

Jensen, Michael C., and William H. Meckling. 1976. Theory of the Firm: Managerial Behavior, Agency Costs and Ownership Structure. *Journal of Financial Economics* 3 (4): 305–360.

Johnson, M. 2017. When It Comes to Investing, Human Stupidity Beats AI. *Financial Times*, April 11.

Kogut, Bruce, and Udo Zander. 1996. What Firms Do? Coordination, Identity, and Learning. *Organization Science* 7 (5): 502–518.

March, James G. 1991. Exploration and Exploitation in Organizational Learning. *Organization Science* 2 (1): 71–87.

March, James G., and Herbert Alexander Simon. 1958. *Organizations*. New York: Wiley.

McAfee, Andrew, and Erik Brynjolfsson. 2017. *Machine, Platform, Crowd: Harnessing Our Digital Future*. New York: W. W. Norton.

McGregor, Douglas. 1966. *The Human Side of Enterprise*. Classics of Organization Theory. New Delhi: McGraw-Hill.

McIntyre, David P., and Arati Srinivasan. 2017. Networks, Platforms, and Strategy: Emerging Views and Next Steps. *Strategic Management Journal* 38 (1): 141–160.

Moran, Peter, and Sumantra Ghoshal. 1999. Markets, Firms, and the Process of Economic Development. *Academy of Management Review* 24 (3): 390–412.

Polson, Nick, James Scott, and Nick Polson. 2018. *AIQ: How People and Machines Are Smarter Together*. New York: St. Martin's Press.

Porter, Michael E. 1996. What Is Strategy? *Harvard Business Review*. 74 (6): 61–78.

Prahalad, C. K., and Gary Hamel. 1990. The Core Competence of the Corporation. *Harvard Business Review* 68 (3, May–June): 79–91.

Quinn, James Brian. 1992. *Intelligent Enterprise: A Knowledge and Service Based Paradigm for Industry*. New York: Simon and Schuster.

Rumelt, Richard. 2011. *Good Strategy/Bad Strategy: The Difference and Why It Matters*. London: Profile Books.

Schwab, Klaus. 2017. *The Fourth Industrial Revolution*. New York: Crown Business.

Slonim, Noam. 2018. Project Debater. In *Computational Models of Argument: Proceedings of COMMA 2018* 305: 4.

Susskind, Richard E., and Daniel Susskind. 2015. *The Future of the Professions: How Technology Will Transform the Work of Human Experts*. New York: Oxford University Press.

Tata, R., S.L. Hart, A. Sharma, and C. Sarkar. 2013. Why Making Money Is Not Enough. *MIT Sloan Management Review* 54 (4): 95–96.

Taylor, Frederick Winslow. 1914. *The Principles of Scientific Management*. New York: Harper.

Tegmark, Max. 2017. *Life 3.0: Being Human in the Age of Artificial Intelligence*. New York: Alfred A. Knopf.

Tushman, Michael L., and Charles A. O'Reilly III. 1996. Ambidextrous Organizations: Managing Evolutionary and Revolutionary Change. *California Management Review* 38 (4): 8–29.

Williamson, Oliver. 1975. *Markets and Hierarchies*. New York: Macmillan.

Zott, Christoph, Raphael Amit, and Lorenzo Massa. 2011. The Business Model: Recent Developments and Future Research. *Journal of Management* 37 (4): 1019–1042.

# 3

# The Evolving Role of General Managers in the Age of AI

Jordi Canals

## 3.1    Introduction

For many years, the role of semi-autonomous machines or robots undertaking tasks in the workplace or making some decisions was limited to the shop floor. They were programmed to execute some physical actions. Today, those machines have been introduced slowly but effectively in many manufacturing plants and warehouses, handling operations and logistics with high reliability, effectiveness, speed and physical safety. Many of them are not robots as the popular literature tends to characterize them. They are simply machines programmed to perform certain tasks. With increasingly sophisticated software, data and learning, these machines undertake now many office functions and services, such as answering questions in call centers, offering customer service, deciding how to invest some money in financial products, or doing facial and voice recognition in security functions.

Some companies' experiences show the advance in recent years of artificial intelligence (AI) which is increasingly being applied across industries. Inditex, the world's leading fast-fashion retailer, is allocating most of its IT investment in using big data and AI tools to improve their sophisticated online shops, with new attributes, such as customers' facial recognition, or recommendations of specific clothes according to personal lifestyles and

J. Canals (✉)
IESE Business School, University of Navarra, Barcelona, Spain
e-mail: jcanals@iese.edu

© The Author(s) 2020                                                                                      **37**
J. Canals and F. Heukamp (eds.), *The Future of Management in an AI World*,
IESE Business Collection, https://doi.org/10.1007/978-3-030-20680-2_3

preferences. Inditex' s retail business in traditional stores is slowing down in some geographies, but online sales—where the application of AI tools is deep—are growing.

BlackRock, the world's largest asset manager, with a top reputation for the quality of its management and investment decisions, set up its Lab for AI in Palo Alto, California, in 2018. It is investing in applying AI to improve the performance of their investment managers, automate back office functions, cut costs and enhance their client service, by analyzing vast amounts of data. AI has become a key tool for sophisticated asset managers.

MD Anderson and Mass General Hospital—two of the leading medical centers in the United States, among others—are spending significant resources in applying AI tools to diagnose and treat more effectively some specific diseases with a higher success rate. These tools are developed based on the evidence of thousands of patients who followed different medical therapies and treatments, with a diversity of outcomes.

Many companies are using Siri, Apple's virtual assistant, or Amazon's Alexa for basic customer service purposes. The potential for applying autonomous, smart machines to highly sophisticated office jobs is growing quickly, thanks to the combination of bigger computer power and available data. The former CEO of a large European bank declared recently that half of its workforce—close to 100,000 people—could be replaced by robots and virtual assistants in a short period of time. This may be a bit exaggerated, but the substitution of people by machines is a trend that is spreading outside of the physical work—the traditional domain of robotics—to qualified office work, including some managerial decisions.

Growth in AI applications in the business world has been propelled by a combination of factors: a growing computer power, the development of sophisticated algorithms that help make complex decisions of predictive nature, and more abundant data, that train and improve those algorithms. AI tools that use big data and sophisticated algorithms are replacing some types of human work, traditional robots—those that simply do some physical functions more effectively—and computers with special software—those that run accounting o sales reports with speed and accuracy, like spreadsheets. New AI capabilities include not only search capabilities, but also artificial vision, language processing and face recognition. This new world of AI encompasses more autonomous, intelligent machines—including a new generation of chatbots—that run algorithms nourished with huge amounts of data. AI, more specifically Machine Learning (ML), has become the most important general purpose technology of our time (McAffee and Brynjolfsson 2017).

The AI new wave is improving managers' capabilities to make predictions: this is a very important ability in all key business functions, such as manufacturing, purchasing, sales, marketing, finance or logistics (Agrawal et al. 2018). These changes are not only introducing new degrees of automation in many companies. They are challenging organizations and management, and transforming industries—like retail, fashion or financial services—by introducing new strategies to approach the final customer and developing more efficient business models. If AI tools are truly effective, many companies may become laggards and their assets and capabilities will become obsolete. This will involve a huge reallocation of assets. As a result, these changes have colossal implications for society in terms of the future of human work, job destruction, new educational needs and the retraining of people.

The implications of widespread AI use for management are big. Senior managers need to learn about them and consider some experiences around the functionality, possibilities, deployment and impact of AI. As these AI tools do more sophisticated, intelligent work, and come up with some recommendations or solutions to problems, they are helping frame some managerial decisions better and make better predictions. In some business areas like logistics, marketing or trading, they are already doing a good job, improving productivity and efficiency, but also replacing traditional jobs and layers of intermediate managers.

With its success in these managerial functions, AI is starting to question the future role of CEOs and senior managers. This is the specific focus of this chapter. We will refer both to CEOs and senior managers as general managers, without making explicit the distinctions among them every time. The CEO is the top manager of a company, holding the final and overall responsibility in its major decisions, activities and performance, and sharing it with the board of directors. Senior general managers are managers with the overall responsibility for a business unit or a corporate division (CFO, CTO, CHRO or CMO, among others). They share the overall responsibility for the whole company as members of the top management team.

The structure of this chapter is the following. Section 3.2 presents an overview of the potential implications of AI for managerial decision-making in different management functions. It also outlines how management can test and monitor the implementation of AI tools in managerial decision-making, with some specific goals and timing: the decisions around the why, what, how, where and when of AI are clear functions and responsibilities of senior managers in any company.

Section 3.3 discusses how key senior management functions will evolve in the age of AI. By discussing the experience of two international companies that are making extensive use of big data and AI tools, I identify the areas where those tools are making some progress and the areas and functions where good general managers are needed to keep developing their companies.

With the background of those cases, I discuss in Sect. 3.4 the CEOs tasks and responsibilities that are required in an AI world. In particular, I describe how competent CEOs think about the firm's purpose, consider what makes a company unique and makes some specific decisions to reinforce this uniqueness, develop the next generation of leaders or ponder the broader social impact of the firm. This and other functions and requirements makes the job of a CEO truly human. Section 3.5 offers some final reflections on the future of general management.

## 3.2    The AI Potential in Management Functions

Over the past years, increasing industrial automation and highly capable robots have been introduced in many manufacturing companies around the world, with a positive impact on productivity. AI recent developments clearly have a high potential to help companies and senior executives make better decisions based on data. With the availability of more powerful computing power, AI algorithms can carry out many tasks—including data analysis—quicker and more accurately, in ways that individuals do not have the capacity to do.

A new round of process automation is the first area of AI deployment and impact (Davenport and Ronanki 2018). It can be seen as the next step in the design and use of Information Technology (IT). It is a natural expansion of traditional IT capabilities, which means that many companies already have people and skills to understand and use them. It includes applications such as software that reads documents—for instance, financial information or bills used for audit purposes—or software that screens and manages data from call centers or servers.

The second AI area of influence is related with cognition (McAffee and Brynjolfsson 2017; Davenport and Ronanki 2018). In this case, AI tools use algorithms that map sets of data, identify patterns of behavior from data and suggest how to interpret and use data, and make some decisions. It includes functions such as digital advertising placement in a personalized way, predictions about future consumer behavior and implications from data on traffic in shopping malls or online stores. These tools are a bit more sophisticated than traditional analytics or predictive models. They use not only statistical correlations, but also deep learning techniques (see Gil et al., Chapter 1 in this book). These techniques try to mimic how the human brain works with data and makes some decisions. Voice recognition—like the one provided by Siri or Alexa—and image recognition—like the one offered by Facebook and other apps that recognize a face and encourages to tag them with their names—belong to this category. Intelligent machines—like chatbots—can also engage with humans using the information they have and provide customer service or offer answers to some frequently asked questions.

AI that aims at cognition is making progress, although it is more expensive that traditional analytics and needs strong human monitoring to make sure that cognitive insights offer reasonable answers. AI that aims at cognitive insight is also opening up the dangerous world of fake news and deepfakes, the AI powered imitation of speech and images that can create alternative realities. They make somebody appear to be doing things or saying things that person never did or say. The growing problem of fake news and deepfakes is increasing with the use of AI tools and create a huge challenge of trust in online media and other companies using and selling private data.

In this paper, I will specifically refer to the impact of AI developments on senior management and managerial decision-making. Recent AI developments in automation and cognitive insights are covering data clustering and estimation. As Agrawal et al. (2018) point out, the current wave of AI may not bring a lot of general intelligence, but a greater capacity for prediction. Prediction itself is not the whole business decision. A decision involves data, judgment and a final action. But it is true that algorithms that can make business predictions are getting better because the data that nourishes them is more abundant and richer than ever, and the computing power to analyze and classify that data is also bigger.

Algorithms that make use of large sets of data may help identify hidden patterns in consumers' behavior or prices and demand elasticity. In other key business functions—like global supply chain or finance—they help understand better some complex problems in today's business world and provide stronger data-based evidence to make decisions.

It is true that there might be some hype around the potential of AI. Its development has also awakened some sharp criticisms, some of them coming from people from the AI field, such as Pearl (2018), one the leading scholars in developing Bayesian networks and bringing a probabilistic approach to AI. AI does not have all the answers, but offers some tools to collect and analyze vast amounts of data on consumer behavior or purchasing decisions, establish some patterns of behavior of some variables and eventually make decisions or suggest some recommendations. In some particular business functions, AI is making some inroads by helping improve the quality of decision-making.

*Manufacturing and operations.* AI tools can help manufacturing companies plan and make better decisions on purchasing based on historical prices, demand, quality, reliability, inventory levels and service (Sanders 2016). They help allocate manufacturing capacity in different factories around the world more effectively, and run manufacturing networks smoothly. Car manufacturers are making better use of robots and other intelligent machines in their operations. SEAT, a Volkswagen subsidiary, employs close to 10,000 people, and has already 4000 robots in its manufacturing plant and warehouses, many of them in performing complex tasks, with a positive impact on human health—replacing people in heavy physical activities—and productivity.

New sets of data reveal patterns of obsolescence of physical assets and suggest in advance policies to improve their maintenance or, eventually, their replacement. Sensors and satellites can track better the delivery of merchandising, improving the quality of the distribution system of any company. These traditional business functions do not disappear, but the use of algorithms with vast amounts of data change the need for human optimization and human supervision.

*Marketing and sales.* Companies like Inditex, Ermenegildo Zegna or Wal Mart are using AI tools to deliver better customer experience. Amazon is improving its capacity to make useful recommendations to online buyers by using more accurately data on their behavior. Google and Facebook have become the largest advertising platforms due to their capacity to personalize ads to specific consumers by using big data and AI.

Fast-moving consumer goods companies, like Henkel, Nestlé, P&G or Unilever, launch dozens of new products or varieties of products every year. With AI tools, they can now understand better why so many new product launches fail, and the factors that help successful product development in a wider variety of markets, segments and types of customers' profiles.

*Finance and investment decisions.* Financial officers can go through investment decisions with much better estimates of their Internal Rate of Return or Net Present Value simply because of the richer and more diverse data to be used in analyzing a complex decision. They can also make better estimates of the firm's future profitability and financial structure, by using better data and fine tuning it, depending on different scenarios. Fund managers are using AI tools to make better decisions on portfolio management based upon richer information about historical prices, yields, companies' performance, interest rates and the economic cycle.

Banks, insurance firms and other financial institutions are using risk assessment models that take into account a wider and richer variety of data on their clients, including company's historical performance, its industry and the overall state of the economy.

*Human resources.* Once considered one of the less sophisticated business function in many companies in terms of technology, it has become a hot area in terms of applications of AI tools. HR departments used to have some challenges, that AI tools may help solve. We highlight just two of them. The first is the screening of CVs and the hiring process, in particular, when companies have hundreds or thousands of applicants to choose from. AI tools are helping screen the candidates, match their profiles with the companies expected skills and capabilities. They help detect basic and hidden attitudes in interviews. AI tools have many challenges—in particular, avoiding data biases that may distort the decisions by preferring candidates with some qualities, as we will discuss later. The second is to help identify and select internal talent. Some companies are very good at this; others are not. AI tools are helping track all the company's talent pipeline, organize it according to certain variables, and suggest, for instance, horizontal moves within an organization when an opening is happening in any division within the company.

*Strategy and M&A.* AI tools are helping investment banks and consulting firms develop better scenarios for corporate strategies, contemplating different outcomes depending upon some key external or internal factors. They can also develop quicker better combinations of companies through M&A, not only by crunching quicker the numbers with different scenarios, but also including other data related to customer acquisition, synergies that can be achieved or product portfolio enhancement.

The cases that have been briefly described above highlight that AI tools are introducing new decision-making capabilities in any organization based on algorithms and the more effective use of more abundant data. They are helping shape decisions with more abundant data, higher speed, better accuracy, and draw more diverse scenarios. The possibilities of AI in managerial decision-making are becoming not only bigger, but also encompassing a wider scope of activities and business functions in organizations, from purchasing and manufacturing, to marketing, sales, logistics and distribution, and affecting corporate functions such as HR or finance as well.

*Management, data and the adoption of AI tools.* A key management issue is how CEOs and senior managers should consider the adoption of AI tools to improve their decision-making. In the adoption of AI tools, senior managers should know and understand them, including its potential and its limitations and risks. The introduction of robots in manufacturing and logistics is easy to understand and plan. The introduction of chatbots in customer service is easy to understand, but more expensive to develop and its risk of failure may easily lead to some crisis. The introduction of the deep learning technique is even more complex, because most algorithms do not provide a clue on why they make the decision that they make.

The experience of some companies that use AI tools—including large high-tech companies—share some common features. The first is that their scope is very specific on some tasks and goals (like improving marketing effectiveness in online sales). Second, they search and select data for that specific purpose that they aim at (for instance, what customers buy and when). Third, the predictive power of algorithms is based upon causality factors, not only correlations. Fourth, there is a monitoring of AI tools by human experts. In most of those cases, we observe that the replacement of human work by machines is more related with the increasing automation of certain processes, rather than the replacement of experts. Fifth, leading firms select one or a few pilot programs out of those projects, learn from them, see the outcomes in terms of customer satisfaction or operational effectiveness, and fine tune the human needs for data analysis and data filtering. It is also important to establish some key milestones. Finally, AI requires the education of people: firms need to have an explicit educational strategy for their employees to use AI in an effective way.

In the deployment of AI tools, there are some caveats that companies need to take into account, in order to prevent them from major organizational mistakes. The most relevant is on the use of data and the capability of algorithms. The combination of big data, algorithms and computer power may not be enough to make sure that decisions improve simply because there is more data available. To start with, quality data is essential. The use of biased data will lead to major disasters in decision-making, including its impact on corporate reputation and customers' trust.

It is not only the effect of the quality of data on decision-making itself that is relevant, but the quality of data has a strong influence on how algorithms develop their own learning to make recommendations or decisions. Algorithms are good in making decisions depending upon the quality and amount of data that feed them to train them. Data is used to train algorithms with the aim of including new potential solutions to different problems that algorithms are supposed to solve. It is often said that AI may eliminate human bias in decision-making. This may happen only if algorithms make decisions with unbiased data. Biases in the data used to make predictions and data used in training algorithms can have a devastating impact. A clear example of this situation is the potential for discrimination that there is in an algorithm that selects CVs that has been trained with data on successful individuals that only come from certain groups of people. The problem here is not only about data selected and used, but data not used by omission: the failure to include some data to be used by algorithms is another type of bias. Data is not neutral.

The debate on privacy and data is also very relevant. AI is based on using vast amounts of data. The way companies—both high-tech and other companies—manage data of third parties has and will have an impact on corporate reputation and trust, and the long-term survival of those firms. The 2018 Facebook data crisis over Cambridge Analytica highlights the new challenges that AI raises for companies and senior managers. The reputation of many companies and the whole AI field is at stake if governance and some critical ethical issues related with AI are not taken into account.

The quality of algorithms themselves and their transparency to AI users are also causes for concern. Algorithms need to offer a comprehensive and reasonable modeling of the real world, beyond what traditional big data and analytics do. They need to capture the different connections of causes and effects—not only correlations—in understanding certain phenomena. Most AI algorithms are good at recognizing patterns, but are not able to distinguish between causes and effects. They should be understood by decision-makers, who will be the final agents responsible for the decisions made. The way algorithms are modeled and how they are trained with quality data are key to a functional development of AI. This requires transparency on how algorithms are designed and described.

In a nutshell, AI tools should be explicit about data used and data not used—including omissions—and respect the truth about data. AI tools should also be explicit about how algorithms suggest decisions to be made. These are essential qualities in making AI functional, reliable and trustable.

Both the AI potential and its limits are compelling reasons why CEOs and senior managers have the responsibility to become familiar with these tools and gradually test their application in their companies in an effective way. The challenge to implement AI tools highlight the need for competent management in AI deployment as well. AI is a more complex form of IT and, as it already happens with IT, needs a very capable management to become an effective tool for positive change in any company.

## 3.3   AI and the Future of General Management

The AI potential to improve decision-making increases the value of good management. Management is not only about making decisions. Management, in particular, the work of CEOs, senior executives and other general managers, can offer an answer about why the company actually exists and why it does what it does. General management requires thinking about the future of the company and making that future happen. It involves setting goals—that are framed by the personal preferences of the different stakeholders—in an integrated way. It designs policies and executes actions in a consistent way. It aims at engaging and developing people. It needs to serve a wide variety of stakeholders. It tries to balance different requirements and constraints, in the short and the long term (Birkinshaw 2011).

In some professions, such as law, accounting and consulting, among others, the threat of technology disruption is large (Susskind and Susskind 2015). In management, the prospects are a bit different. Management is not only about some specialized knowledge and data. It is also about reason, freedom, empathy, engagement, entrepreneurial mindset, humility to learn and prudence in making good judgment, qualities that AI can complement, but is unlikely to replace. Moreover, the deeper impact of AI may come from management making use of algorithms and data, not from machines talking to machines (Malone 2018).

Management is indispensable in an AI world. It is a clear observation—even in technology-based start-ups—that the long-term success of most companies depends on developing good management teams that can engage people and harness technology innovation to serve customers.

Most successful companies have a CEO and a senior management team—general managers—who want to have a positive impact on the long-term performance of the firm (Wasserman et al. 2010). The CEO and senior managers think about the strategy of the firm; discuss and present its major strategic challenges and decisions to the board of directors; hire and develop the future leaders of the firm; engage and develop people; focus the organization on serving customers and creating economic value; and try to design and operate a functional organization.

Respected senior managers think about the future, undertake new business projects and help create the future with energy and passion. They are keen to develop new ideas with an entrepreneurial mindset. The adventure of creating a new business to serve customers better and help solve some human needs is a source of inspiration for many of them. There is a truly human factor in this process of creating new products, services or companies that can make a positive difference. It is impossible to create something new and relevant without the human passion for discovery, innovation, people growth and desire to have a differential impact. These areas are the natural domain of senior managers.

The role of management in the AI world can be better understood by highlighting the technology challenge in the context of wider problems that large companies face. I will briefly present and discuss two cases of successful international companies that are leaders in their industries and that are investing a lot in technology, big data, analytics and ML. They show the type of management and leadership challenges in today's world and the role of technology in them. They will help us understand the role of good management in tackling those challenges.

### 3.3.1 Unilever

In November 2010, under the leadership of CEO Paul Polman and the support of its board of directors, launched the Unilever Sustainable Living Plan (USLP), that aimed at making sustainable living commonplace (Canals [2018b] provides the background of this business situation). This Plan, unlike other Corporate Social Responsibility initiatives, took the responsibility of the whole value chain and included some ambitious targets to be achieved by 2020: source 100% of its agricultural raw materials sustainably, halve the greenhouse gas impact and water consumption, help more than 1bn people improve their health and hygiene, and double the proportion of the product portfolio meeting the highest nutritional standards. Polman also established that those goals should not only be achieved by some business units—for instance, boosted by outsourcing some activities—but across the whole value chain.

A unique quality of the USLP was the integration of those goals into the business and strategy of Unilever. USLP was at the center of a strategy that aimed at engaging consumers, driving growth, reducing costs, sustaining innovation and inspiring employees. These ideas fit well with the history and tradition of Unilever, a company that was already distinguished as a caring organization for its social impact. Nevertheless, in the years before Polman's arrival in 2009, Unilever's growth was flat and financial performance was behind other firms in its industry.

Paul Polman and his team were concerned about outlining a new strategic vision that could mobilize the company to pursue some long-term goals and develop a new growth strategy. These objectives should be reached within the backdrop of a global economy sunk in the deep hole of the 2008 global financial crisis and the accelerated digital transformation of companies. In particular, consumer goods companies faced the need to connect with the new generation of young consumers with different consumption habits and preferences, and most of them native digitals. Polman thought that the growth crisis at Unilever and the crisis in the global economy were opportunities to rethink the way companies pursue growth, following a different pathway from doing more of the same as many of the used to do. Polman decided that Unilever had to do different things in different ways.

The USLP had some core elements: it served to reinforce the values of Unilever; it gave the company a clear sense of purpose; it was well integrated into the new corporate strategy aimed at growth; and offered a good balance between delivering financial results and achieving some clear social goals.

Unilever was investing a huge amount of money in new technology tools, both to operate manufacturing, purchasing and logistics more efficiently, and to be more active in online media advertising and marketing. In its digital transformation, Unilever started to use the AI tools available in the market.

The transformation process of Unilever since 2009 had been impressive, becoming one of the leading firms in the world in integrating purpose and broad social impact with economic performance and operational effectiveness. It became one of the leaders in the fast-moving consumer goods industry in terms of economic performance between 2009 and 2017. Technology had been a key driver in this process. What is truly interesting about Unilever's transformation was that the huge investment in technology had not been the essential driver of transformation at Unilever. Technology had been an enabler of change, but not the engine of change.

It is assumed by all stakeholders that the driver of change at Unilever since 2009 was Paul Polman and his top management team. They were able to be explicit about a purpose and a strategic vision. They made the effort to mobilize thousands of managers and other employees around the world behind purpose and strategy, and turn those frameworks into specific action plans to be implemented. Polman and his team convinced the board of directors to support that plan, engaged with shareholders to explain the value of than plan, worked with suppliers to make that plan feasible and eventually they deliver results.

Unilever's transformation process had been remarkable and it became an excellent example of what a multi-stakeholder company is. This case highlights some of the key factors that can be identified as the outcome of good general management that AI tools will not replace: a sense of purpose and support of some values, a clear strategic vision, integration of sustainability and social goals in the strategic vision, specific goals to be achieved, engage and develop people, execute and deliver value, manage a complex organization and communicate well with all stakeholders. Unilever invested a lot in technology and new AI tools. These tools are very important, but without good general management, they would have been valueless.

## 3.3.2 Cellnex: A Successful Growth Story in Telecom Infrastructure Management

By the end of 2018, Cellnex, an international telecom infrastructure management firm based in Spain, had become one of the leaders in the industry in Europe, with accelerated growth and a strong reputation for technology and service capabilities. Cellnex went public in 2015. Under the original name of Abertis Telecom, it was the spin-off of Abertis and had evolved from a small business unit in the late 1990s that provided radio and TV signals to networks in Spain. Abertis was an industrial holding firm with a global leading position in highway management.

Cellnex's exponential growth in less than four years, to a total market value of close to €6bn by the end of 2018, in a very competitive and sophisticated telecoms industry, was a remarkable story. Canals (2018a) provides the background of its evolution.

The management of telecommunications infrastructure—mainly, communication towers—for the transmission of mobile phone signals (voice and data) had become vertically disintegrated in the US in the early 2000. Major telecom operators (ATT, Verizon, etc.) decided to sell their infrastructure business units in the late 1990s to specialized companies to generate cash for content development and other purposes. American Tower was the leading US telecom infrastructure management company in 2018, with a total market value close to $60bn. In the EU, most telecommunications operators were still vertically integrated, and owned and control their infrastructure. Nevertheless, the need to reduce debt after the 2008 financial crisis and to invest more in 5G and content was forcing EU telecom companies to rethink their level of vertical integration. The use of big data and some AI tools was becoming increasingly important for telecom operators and, in particular, for the management of their telecommunications infrastructure.

In this context, Abertis Telecom top managers started to consider in 2012 how to speed up the potential growth of this new industry in the wake of the highly probable divestment of infrastructure assets by telecom operators. In 2012, Abertis Telecom bought 4000 towers to Telefonica and Yoigo in Spain, and 300 towers in Italy owned by TowerCo in 2014. New opportunities arose in the horizon, being the most important the telecom infrastructure assets of Wind, the second largest mobile telecom operator in Italy in 2015.

The orientation of the new Cellnex in 2015 was a combination of corporate governance, strategic foresight and good leadership deployed by Francisco Reynés, CEO of Abertis and Chairman of the new Cellnex, and Tobias Martinez, CEO of Cellnex, and their colleagues in the top management of Cellnex.

The first step that they took was to provide a long-term strategic framework for the future growth of Cellnex, by the end of 2014. It was based upon the resources and technology capabilities that the company had at that time and the market opportunities that were unfolding. Reynés and Martínez put together a small team of senior executives from the former Abertis Telecom to develop some clear strategic guidelines and a financial model to help fund the future growth of the company.

With this plan and their personal commitment, they could convince the board of directors of Abertis to approve the spin-off of Cellnex and its eventual IPO in 2015. This was a very complex, emotional situation for Abertis' board members. The professionalism and commitment of the Cellnex leaders was powerful enough to convince board members about the decision to be made. The Abertis board of directors established as a condition for the operation that Abertis, the holding company, would not issue new debt to fund any of Cellnex' s acquisitions. Any new investment project should be funded by Cellnex itself, which was an additional challenge for the newly created company that had to go to capital markets without the financial backing of the parent company. This constraint helped improve the quality of the project and fostered the firm's entrepreneurial mindset.

Third, Cellnex top management had to deal simultaneously with the normal operations of the company, the IPO and the potential acquisition of Wind's telecom infrastructure. The CEO put together some small teams to manage the different projects trying to maximize communication and minimize interferences.

Fourth, the development of a comprehensive and credible equity story for Cellnex to convince potential investors and asset managers, still a challenge in the post-financial crisis European landscape. It included a vision, a mission, a corporate governance model based on the independence of the board of directors, a clear strategic plan, some key capabilities, and an experienced and entrepreneurial management team. In the strategic plan, technology, big data and analytics played a very important role, but also the sophisticated service to its demanding customers.

Cellnex went public in May 2015. Its growth through the end of 2018 was spectacular, with a solid organic growth and selected acquisitions of infrastructure assets in France, Italy, The Netherlands and Switzerland, among others. Cellnex became one of the leading European telecom infrastructure management firm by the end of 2018.

In the Cellnex growth process, the role of information technology and big data was very relevant. And the technology capabilities were essential to provide outstanding services to telecom operators that were outsourcing those services to Cellnex. Technology was a demanding requirement that Cellnex could offer; but it was a capability also available to other telecom operators and technology-based companies in the EU.

Cellnex's recent growth provides some useful references on the role of AI and technology in a highly competitive industry. What truly set Cellnex apart from its competitors was not the quality of technology capabilities or AI tools: it was the combination of a highly competent and motivated management team who developed a clear strategic orientation, their entrepreneurial mindset, a sense of innovation, their aspiration for a culture of customer orientation, and the support of its board of directors, including some clear guidelines for its corporate governance. The quality of leadership and management, and the culture of customer service, really made Cellnex a unique and successful company in its industry.

The Cellnex and Unilever transformation processes discussed above highlight some key managerial challenges and responsibilities, beyond the adoption of advanced technology and AI tools. Their senior managers did a job that went beyond the challenge of optimization, which is the function where AI has some superior qualities in many cases, due to its huge computing power. They offer us a reminder that optimization is only one of the challenges that managers face. There are many others relevant areas where the need for good general management is very clear.

## 3.4  Some Critical Functions and Responsibilities of General Managers in an AI World

No matter how transformational AI may be for companies, CEOs and senior executives are still left with some very basic responsibilities and challenges that only competent leaders can address. Good managers do so with a combination of knowledge and experience, rational judgment, emotional intelligence, ethical principles and wisdom to make decisions with a holistic perspective.

Cellnex and Unilever experiences, among others, highlight the value of general managers' job as presented by some management authors. In his classical piece, Mintzberg (1975) suggests that managers undertake some key jobs: interpersonal roles (including figurehead, leaders and liaison), informational roles (including monitoring, disseminator and spokesman) and decisional roles (entrepreneur, disturbance handler, resource allocator and negotiator).

Kotter (1982) approaches the general manager's job by distinguishing general managers' challenges related with responsibilities and challenges related with relationships. Some of them coincide with Mintzberg's categories.

Porter and Nohria (2018) explain some basic CEOs challenges and tasks by studying carefully the agenda of CEOs. They observe that CEOs are agenda driven work face-to-face, rely heavily on their direct reports, manage using broad integrating mechanisms and deal with many external constituencies.

In a nutshell, even with sophisticated AI tools, CEOs and senior executives will still need to address some basic management challenges. Based upon the Unilever and Cellnex experiences, I will highlight some of those critical functions and responsibilities that CEOs and general managers have.

### 3.4.1 Purpose

One of the first functions that a good CEO has is to offer a good answer to the question: "Why does my company exist?". In other words, a company needs to be explicit about its purpose. This is a key responsibility for the CEO and the top management. Shareholders returns are an indispensable condition for any company, but not a sufficient condition for a company to exist in the long term. Companies need to nurture and grow their reputation with small and big steps. Their purpose is one of them (Canals 2010). And the way this purpose is deployed and reflected in large and small decisions is a litmus test for any company. An engaging purpose is also one of the key anchors that a company has to attract and retain good professionals. It is also an important step in convincing potential shareholders and talented professionals about how serious is a company on the type of impact that it wants to have (Mayer 2018). Top asset management companies such as

Blackrock, Vanguard or State Street are also increasingly clear about it and are vocal about why they value this quality in the companies they invest in.

Purpose has always been a cherished topic among leadership scholars. Barnard (1938) highlighted the need for a common purpose in any organization, one that would go beyond the individual goals of the different stakeholders and that could help the company develop in the long term. Drucker (1954) emphasized that the purpose of any company is to make a client. He also highlighted the importance of the human side of management over optimization and wrote early about the wrong approach of maximizing shareholder returns, even when this notion was not yet very popular. Drucker also was a great supporter of the relevant role of business in society beyond creating economic value.

Selznick (1957), in his *Leadership in Administration*, discussed how companies can become institutions. In this process, business leaders need to perform some basic functions related with purpose: the definition of institutional mission, the institutional embodiment of purpose, the defense of institutional integrity and the ordering of internal conflict. More recently, Moss Kanter (2011), among others, highlighted the need for a clear purpose in organizational change and the process of institutionalizing a company. The firm's purpose is one the distinguishing features or relevant companies: it helps anchor the strategic vision, strategic plans, and action plans, and makes the company different in front of employees, customers and other stakeholders. It is also true that purpose gains legitimacy as far as the top management knows how to make decisions in coherence with it across the organization.

The definition of the firm's purpose and its translation and application into different areas is a key function of the CEO and the senior managers. It involves a combination of vision, values, determination, passion, consistency and creativity, all of them key attributes of good managers. We will need to keep asking the question about why a specific company exists, whatever the level of technical progress that AI tools may offer.

## 3.4.2 Governance

The second challenge is the design of a good governance model for the firm. Governance is not the specific job of the CEO alone. It is more accurate to say that the governance model of any company is a key function of its board of directors. The board has a special mission to design a good governance model, by taking into account the nature of shareholders, and the history and identity of the firm; it also has to protect the firm from the private interests of some shareholders or other stakeholders, and develop it for the long term (Carter and Lorsch 2004; Canals 2010). We assume here that the CEO is a board member and the unique link between the board and the top management team, and has a special responsibility in helping the board design the best corporate governance model that a company needs.

Most successful companies, including the largest tech-based firms that use AI—as Apple or Microsoft, among others, show—have strong boards. A good board of directors sets the reference for the governance of the firm, chooses the CEO and other senior executives, and discusses and approves the company's strategy, among other key functions. The firm's governance may need some special assistant of AI in gathering data or preparing some specific scenarios. But governance is essentially a human activity that requires integration of perspectives and good judgment, aimed at the development of the company for the long term, and the right balance of interests among the different stakeholders.

A good corporate governance model includes clear criteria for the election or replacement of the CEO; some rules on the structure and composition of the board of directors; a process to evaluate the strategic orientation of the company, including the approval of major strategic decisions; regular financial and non-financial monitoring; and the supervisory and compliance functions that any board has to fulfill. These are key strategic leadership functions that are not only essential for any good company, but also critical to make companies stable. In this process, boards of directors need to establish and consolidate relationships based on trust, professionalism and service. Companies that are not good at managing the different criteria that different shareholders may have about the firm, or conflicts between some shareholders and the board of directors, may be a serious threat to the firm's survival. On a positive note, good corporate governance mechanisms help boards of directors and top management teams make the right decisions and choices to develop the company for the future.

It is an interesting observation that the leading asset managers that have become the dominants shareholders of large, publicly traded firms throughout the world—companies like BlackRock, Vanguard or Fidelity, among others—have been recently highlighting that two of their top criteria for investing as shareholders in some companies are that those firms have a good corporate governance model and a clear definition of purpose that the company aims at. The fact that dominant shareholders are using those criteria highlights very clearly the importance of those issues for boards of directors and senior managers.

Corporate governance is the key activity of the board of directors in collaboration with the CEO and the top management. It is a key condition for the long-term development of any firm. Due to its very nature, governance will remain a truly human activity in organizations.

## 3.4.3 Strategy and Uniqueness

The third top management challenge is how the board, the CEO and the top management team take some key decisions that can make a company unique and different. A good strategy is about uniqueness, a quality that makes a company special in front of its customers (Porter 1996; Hanssens, 2019, Chapter 8 in this book). Those specific decisions help develop the unique value proposition that a company wants to offer its customers: either a superior perceived quality of the product or the overall buying experience; or a great operational effectiveness that helps the firm have a very competitive cost structure and allows it to offer lower prices. This value proposition is based upon some competitive advantages developed through specific decisions that a company has made over the years, including irreversible investments (Ghemawat 1991).

The combination of the specific value proposition, the positioning of the firm in the industry and the decisions to support this positioning define the specific business model that a firm chooses to have (Casadesus-Masanell and Ricart 2011; Zott et al. 2011). The decisions about the business model involve specific choices about where the company wants to compete and where it doesn't.

These strategic decisions should be based on data. AI tools may analyze large sets of data about the industry, customers patterns and positioning data faster and more accurately than in the past. Those tools may also develop richer scenarios and describe strategic options more accurately. AI tools may help model better some strategic decisions, although one should not forget that those decisions are surrounded by uncertainty and depend on the data used.

Wisdom and prudence in decision-making are indispensable both to verify that the process by which the quality of data is validated and the internal processes by which algorithms make recommendations or final decisions are reasonable and coherent. Without good judgement, decision-making is flawed. There is an individual and social need to monitor the outcomes of some machine decisions, in particular, when they have an impact on the well-being of individuals. The failures associated with AI tools due to fake data or incomplete algorithms are already abundant.

Prudence is a key quality in strategic decision-making. It develops the ability to make wise judgments on situations with a variety of constraints; it also helps choose the best pathways to govern oneself and others through the use of reason, while promoting the common good of the organization. AI can complement wisdom and prudence well when data are reliable and algorithms are well-designed. As recent experience with sophisticated IT systems shows, in situations where complex human behavior and human interaction are critical, we need good human judgment. We all want relationships based on trust and to deal with people who assume their own moral and legal responsibilities on their decisions at any time.

Competent CEOs and senior managers come up with good ideas about strategy out of entrepreneurial management; frame those decisions; try to balance the requirements that different shareholders and other investors in the company may have; offer some solutions to trade-offs between the short term and the long term; and consider how those decisions may have an impact on people, culture, values and the firm's reputation. It is clear that AI may help model decisions and design richer and different scenarios, but coming up with entrepreneurial attitudes and proposals and making and executing those strategic decisions are still a key attribute of CEOs and general managers.

A less known attribute of a good strategy and its uniqueness is how some strategic decisions shape the soul of the firm and reinforce the corporate culture and values that the firm has: the activities at which the firm is really special in the eyes of customers and employees. Pondering the different qualitative and quantitative implications of those strategic decisions on people and culture also requires a combination of wisdom, experience and human empathy that good managers display—and technology doesn't.

### 3.4.4 Developing People, Nurturing Teams

Successful companies in the long term are thriving groups of individuals who like to work together with a shared purpose. A critical task of management is to attract, retain, engage and develop people. In an age of more powerful technology, this challenge for management is more important than ever. AI tools may make our companies a bit less human than what most of us would like to see in the workplace.

The potential impact of technology on the engagement of employees with their firms is a key factor in the debate about the future of human work in the age of AI. Unfortunately, technology is not very good at motivating and engaging employees (see Cappelli and Travis 2018; Cappelli et al. 2019, Chapter 5 in this book), who feel that technology-driven innovation may put their jobs at stake, and fear that technology will require new skills and capabilities that they do not have and most of them do not know how to get them.

It is very unfortunate, but the growing role of technology and digitalization in many companies has mainly advanced in the direction of optimization and operational effectiveness, not in the direction of making companies more attractive for talent and offering a better context for professional and personal development (Pfeffer 2018). Technology has a potential for helping people, not only final customers, but also employees.

If technology makes people perceive that the level of personalization in the company diminishes with growing automation, people will feel less engaged. The challenge of integrating millennials in the current workplace is a signal of that problem. It is true that some AI tools for managing people may help make more personalized approaches to people development. But there is nothing more motivational for any person in any company that working with a good manager who not only allocates resources effectively, but also sets new challenges for people, helps people tackle them, promotes good human values, offers flexibility, encourages participation and allows people to learn and grow in this process.

Developing talent and helping talent work effectively in a team is a very relevant quality of the agile economy that technology is contributing to expand. The art and science of developing teams requires a combination of mission, sense of direction, quality and motivation of the team members, flexibility and empathy. These are great attributes of the best leaders. AI tools can offer some criteria on how to combine the members of a team according to their background, culture and expertise. In the end, it is the job of general managers to help develop people's skills and attitudes and make sure that a team is ready to tackle a challenge and turn a problem into an opportunity to learn and improve.

The impact of technology in job creation and destruction is also a very relevant issue in people's motivation and engagement. AI will likely involve job losses and higher unemployment in the short term. It is a fact that technology advancement looks more like a threat rather than an opportunity for people. This negative effects of technology generate personal anxiety and the potential for social unrest. It is important that companies—in particular, tech-based companies—and senior executives seriously consider what needs to be done to train and re-train people to succeed in this new world. Technology innovation that brings about this level of potential disruption requires that business leaders and senior executives think holistically about the impact that their technology decisions have on their companies, people and wider society. The reputational impact of mishandling of data used by tech companies is only the tip of the iceberg of the huge risks that are looming in the AI world.

In particular, large high-tech companies should think more holistically about the overall impact of the technology solutions that they are offering on employees, rather than emphasizing the disruptive effect of those technology solutions. Innovation is good and indispensable, but when an innovator introduces disruptions, in particular, in the workforce and its community, shareholder maximization should not be the only criterion. Technology innovation is creating social negative effects that need to be taken into account. Technology-based companies should use their capabilities to innovate to find also innovative solutions on how to use those tools so that employees feel more engaged, not more disengaged.

What is clear is that few technological innovations will succeed in the long term if their implementation comes with a high human cost. Social unrest will slow it down, and regulation and public policy will shape its future development, unless it aligns its goals with the wellbeing of society. AI transformational effects may be really big, not only in terms of efficiency, but also in the future of work and the nature of work itself. We need to make sure that it is being deployed in a way that actually helps and empowers people, and not in a way that threatens jobs or diminishes people's potential to contribute.

All in all, the role of general managers in attracting and developing people will increase with AI. There might be some useful AI tools that may help track people's performance a bit better. But managing people seems to be still a task and a mission that should be entrusted to competent and good general managers, not AI tools.

### 3.4.5  Sustainability and Sustainable Performance

The fifth challenge is how to make sure that the company is not only unique and special, but also that it creates economic value in a sustainable way. A good firm needs to make sure that the economic value creation process can be sustained over the years, by avoiding the threats of imitation and substitution that may diminish the value of its advantages, through continuous investment, product development and process improvement. Again, these considerations may lead to some sophisticated analysis with some simulation tools or software to help visualize the impact of those changes, but the wise judgement of good CEOs is indispensable.

There are other risks that threaten sustainability, that are not related to increasing product market competition or the emergence of new entrants. There are three areas that have an impact on sustainable performance that are especially important in today's business world. The first is related with the ownership structure and the type of shareholders that companies have. The increasing role of private equity firms, hedge funds and activist investors as large shareholders of companies has generated less stable ownership structures, the need for quicker financial returns and some boardroom fights that reflect the growing role—and noise—that some of those investors have on their companies. This is a different type of capitalism, away from a system with more dispersed shareholders who used to have longer-term horizons. Engaging constructively with those shareholders and investors is a key function of the CEO, the CFO and maybe other members of the top management team. The potential that they have today of rocking companies is enormous.

The second challenge regarding sustainability is the increasing influence of some geo-political factors on the strategy of international firms and their performance. Some issues that we thought were a relic of the past have come back to the board room. Protectionism, trade barriers, foreign direct investment barriers, trade retaliation, unstable international rules, lack of stable regulatory frameworks and other forms of political influence have become very relevant. These geo-political issues add to a new world of more unstable financial markets, higher international savings and liquidity, and more erratic currency volatility, in particular, in emerging markets. International companies cannot forget about those issues without putting their companies in jeopardy.

The third challenge related with sustainability is the firm's impact on the environment. The need to decarbonize the economy is clear. Even if the specific impact of carbon emissions is still the object of some debate, it is clear that they have a negative impact on global warming. This impact is even bigger in emerging markets that are also suppliers of raw materials for companies in more advanced economies. Wise general managers need to think about the role of their companies in society, also in terms of their impact on the environment. Legislation to cut emissions will become tougher around the world. More important, there is the moral responsibility that any leader has to leave behind a better legacy.

It is clear that good CEOs and general managers need to address and manage those risks and threats to the sustainability of any company. Technology may help, but general managers' competence, wisdom and personal values are indispensable in tackling those challenges and define the quality of the decisions that they make. They also shape the firm's overall reputation.

## 3.4.6  Broader Social Impact

Companies need to think not only in terms of how much economic value they create, and which purpose they have, but also about the wider impact that they may have on society. This approach involves more than managing different stakeholders as some notions of corporate social responsibility suggest. Companies need to be responsible citizens in the society where they live and operate. As a result, they need to integrate in a coherent way different objectives that sometimes may seem to be in contradiction: short-term and long-term performance, shareholders and others stakeholders, operational effectiveness and people engagement, or financial performance and impact on a local community, among others.

An attractive quality of good management is that it balances different criteria and objectives, and allows for innovation and creativity in finding solutions to new problems, for which there may not be historical data. AI may be very good at dealing with large sets of data. But many challenges are new, there is no data to help make a decision and there is a need to solve the problem.

Management is also about exploring the facts as they are, understanding different opportunities and options, establishing different criteria to evaluate the options, making a final decision and evaluate its impact. In defining the firm's broader social impact, a company should not choose to undertake many different social challenges, but should be known for using some specific capabilities to tackle some of those challenges and integrate them into their overall strategy. Unilever, with its Sustainable Living Plan, did actually so, and executed it very well. Unilever has had a broader social impact bigger than many other companies of its size and potential. In this way, it has helped not only tackle some issues around carbon emissions and sustainable sourcing of raw materials, but also integrate those dimensions in its wider strategy and become a reference for many other companies.

In this coherent integration of specific business goals and strategy, and broader social impact, the unique role that a CEO can play as a leader and orchestrator is more relevant than ever. Caring about people and the environment, and integrate those dimensions in the firm's strategy—as companies such as Unilever are trying do—are attributes of the best human leadership. More important, only good CEOs are able to do so. It is truly professional, truly human and truly unique.

### 3.4.7  The Moral Dimension of the CEO's Job: Leading with Ethical Values

A CEO takes up the responsibility of the whole company. The CEO is entrusted the care of people and clients, shareholders and other stakeholders. When there is a corporate failure or the company dives into a corporate crisis, all stakeholders look at the CEO. These relationships entail moral and legal duties that the CEO should assume. Through different leadership actions, the CEO has an impact on other people, and can grow professionally and personally through those actions.

Machines that learn with data are neither designed to make judgements about good and evil, nor can assume responsibilities. Experts can make progress in training machines by feeding data of what is good or bad in some specific cases, but machines cannot learn from specific data to make a general ethical judgment: this is a human capability. The more sophisticated AI tools do not have and will not have any responsibility about the negative impact that they may have on people and companies. The responsibility belongs to human beings, who freely make decisions and should accept their effects. CEOs and senior executives have the freedom to make a wise use of those tools and the related responsibility.

People may not always agree on the ethical dimensions of every single decision to be made. Nevertheless, there are some ethical values with universal appeal, such as the respect for the dignity of every person and individual freedom, the value of our own conscience, and the need to be fair and respect the truth, among others. These are values that most people consider important. They are part of the United Nations' Universal Declaration of Human Rights, stem from the dignity of each person and have been recognized as such in the fight for human rights. They are criteria coming from human reason and the search for the common good, should be the paradigm for any managerial action and should prevail over any form of AI.

Through different managerial actions, a CEO has an impact on other people and oneself: for this reason, the job of a CEO has an ethical nature. The use of AI tools only amplifies this quality. A CEO is supposed to define some strategic pathways, engage and lead people and manage resources in an effective way for all stakeholders. It is not only about respecting laws and established norms, and following some procedures. It is about considering that companies are made up of people; they are complex organizations that should allow different stakeholders to achieve their goals in a balanced and fair way, so that all parties can at least get some sufficient results. This outcome may not necessarily be the maximum that they can get, because there are other parties that are also necessary for the company to exist and operate.

In any thriving society, social interactions require trust. So do companies. Trust is developed by responsible persons who deal with one another in a professional and responsible way, and is supported by appropriate social institutions, like the legal system or a well-functioning government. Algorithms can help humans do part of the job in making decisions, but managerial decision-making still needs human wisdom and prudence.

CEOs deal with people, customers and other stakeholders. They manage resources and need to do it with efficiency. Their behavior has to search the common good, not just one's own good, and be fair to the different stakeholders. Leading by example is a clear condition of successful leadership. Example is a human and social language through which individuals learn from other individuals, and each generation of citizens learns from their predecessors. CEOs' behavior has a resonating echo in the ears of employees, customers and the rest of society. It can be a great force for good, as some business leaders are, by performing their social function with professional excellence and integrity.

This is one of the key features of CEOs and their jobs. It involves a moral dimension that AI and machines do not have. The moral character of managerial decision-making and the consideration of ethical values, such as the respect for the dignity of each person, the well-being of others and the common good of society, make the job of CEOs different from that of machines. They make the job of CEOs truly human. The moral nature of the job of a CEO is today more important than ever. Moreover, it is one of the few pathways through which companies' leadership can regain credibility and legitimacy in contemporary society.

## 3.5   Some Final Reflections

Based upon the discussion of some successful companies in transforming their business model, I have articulated the case for the role and responsibilities of CEOs and general managers in an AI world. Senior managers need to understand AI tools and their applications to companies. The general deployment of those tools needs excellent general managers who understand the business, can engage people to use those tools and monitor effectively their implementation.

More important, those companies highlight that CEOs and general managers are indispensable, even in a world dominated by big data and smart algorithms. There are key top management decisions and functions that CEOs need to take up and address. I have highlighted some key areas: purpose, governance, strategy, people development, sustainability, broader social impact and leadership based upon ethical values. There are many relevant business functions where AI and other technologies will make inroads and help make better decisions. But in those areas, good general managers are indispensable.

Those managerial functions make companies social institutions, not only efficient organizations that are engineered to do a job, as Barnard (1938) and Selznick (1957) highlighted. In particular, the institutionalization of an organization requires that top managers infuse it with values, beyond the technical dimensions of the functions to be performed (Selznick 1957). Companies can become social institutions if they adopt a broader logic than the dominant shareholder value maximization (Moss Kanter 2011). CEOs and senior managers can make a unique contribution to their companies by providing the sense of purpose and direction that we highlighted here. This is part of the process by which companies can become respected institutions in society (Canals 2010), an attribute that companies and society desperately need.

Senior executives are dealing with fascinating changes in the business world, with technology and data being used in much smarter ways. At the same time, we need to ask ourselves those fundamental leadership questions. AI neither knows how to frame them, nor provides an answer to them. Good CEOs and senior managers can do it. CEOs' challenge is how to use AI tools to make our companies not only more competitive, but also more human, and turn them into respected institutions in society.

# References

Agrawal, A., J. Gans, and A. Goldfarb. 2018. *Prediction Machines*. Boston: Harvard Business Review Press.

Barnard, C.I. (1938) 1968. *The Functions of the Executive,* 1968 ed. Cambridge, MA: Harvard University Press.

Birkinshaw, J. 2011. *Reinventing Management. Smarter Choices for Getting Work Done*. New York: Wiley.

Canals, J. 2018a. Cellnex: A Growth Project. IESE Case SM-1662.

Canals, J. 2018b. Unilever: The Role of the Board of Directors and the CEO in Corporate Governance and Strategy. IESE Case SM-1671.

Canals, J. 2010. *Building Respected Companies.* Cambridge: Cambridge University Press.

Cappelli, P., and A. Travis. 2018. HR Goes Agile. *Harvard Business Review* 96 (2): 46–53.

Carter, C., and J.W. Lorsch. 2004. *Back to the Drawing Board.* Boston: Harvard Business School Press.

Casadesus-Masanell, R., and J.E. Ricart. 2011. How to Design a Winning Business Model. *Harvard Business Review* 89 (1–2): 100–107.

Davenport, T.H., and R. Ronankin. 2018. A Real World Guide to Artificial Intelligence. *Harvard Business Review* 96 (1): 108–116.

Drucker, P. 1954. *The Practice of Management.* New York: Harper & Row.

Ghemawat, P. 1991. *Commitment.* New York: Free Press.

Kotter, J.J. 1982. *The General Managers.* New York: Free Press.

Malone, T. 2018. *Superminds.* New York: Little, Brown.

Mayer, C. 2018. *Prosperity.* Oxford: Oxford University Press.

McAffee, A., and E. Brynjolfsson. 2017. *Machine, Platform, Crowd.* New York: Norton.

Mintzberg, H. 1975. The Manager's Job: Folklore and Fact. *Harvard Business Review* 53 (4): 49–61.

Moss Kanter, R. 2011. The Institutional Logic of Great Global Firms. In *Towards a New Theory of the Firm: Humanizing the Firm and the Management Profession,* ed. J.E. Ricart and J.M. Rosanas, 84–108. Madrid: Fundación BBVA.

Pearl, J. 2018. *The Book of Why: The New Science of Cause and Effect.* New York: Basic Books.

Porter, M.E. 1996. What Is Strategy? *Harvard Business Review* 74 (6): 61–78.

Porter, M.E., and N. Nohria. 2018. How CEOs Manage Time. *Harvard Business Review* 96 (4): 42–51.

Pfeffer, J. 2018. *Dying for a Paycheck.* New York: Harper Business.

Sanders, N.R. 2016. How to Use Big Data to Drive Your Supply Chain. *California Management Review* 58 (3): 26–48.

Selznick, P. 1957. *Leadership in Administration: A Sociological Interpretation.* New York: Harper & Row.

Susskind, R., and R. Susskind. 2015. *The Future of Professions.* Oxford: Oxford University Press.

Wasserman, N., B. Anand, and N. Nohria. 2010. When Does Leadership Matter? In *Handbook of Leadership: Theory and Practice,* ed. N. Nohria and R. Khurana, 27–63. Boston: Harvard Business School Press.

Zott, C., R. Amit, and L. Massa. 2011. The Business Model: Recent Developments and Future Research. *Journal of Management* 37 (4): 1019–1042.

# Part III

## Leadership Development and Talent Management in an AI Age

# 4

# The Role of the General Manager in the New Economy: Can We Save People from Technology Dysfunctions?

## Jeffrey Pfeffer

## 4.1 Introduction

The originally proposed subtitle for this paper was, "Can We Save Organizations from Technology Dysfunctions?" I have changed that subtitle, substituting the word "people" for "organizations." Organizations, in the U.S. and in many other countries do not need any saving. Many indicators make this simple but important point.

For instance, the proportion of economic output (GDP) going to corporate profits currently stands at close to 10% in the U.S., compared to a long term average since 1950 of 6.6% (Tully 2017). The rising percentage of GDP going to company profits reflects a steady and worldwide shift of economic returns toward capital and away from labor since the early 1970s (Thompson 2013). An OECD report (ILO 2015: 3) noted that between 1990 and 2009, "the share of labour compensation in national income declined in 26 out of 30 advanced countries." Moreover, "in many emerging and developing countries, the decline in the labour income share is even more pronounced." Capital and labor's share of national income is important because, as Piketty (2014) noted, a higher share of economic output going to capital is associated with higher inequality in the distribution of income. Other data show that a declining labor share of national output "negatively affect the main macroeconomic aggregates, namely household

J. Pfeffer (✉)
Graduate School of Business, Stanford University, Stanford, CA, USA
e-mail: pfeff@stanford.edu

© The Author(s) 2020
J. Canals and F. Heukamp (eds.), *The Future of Management in an AI World*,
IESE Business Collection, https://doi.org/10.1007/978-3-030-20680-2_4

consumption private sector investments, net exports and government consumption" (ILO 2015: 2). This shift in the distribution of the fruits of economic activity provides one explanation for why wages have stagnated even as productivity and economic activity has grown (e.g., Mishel et al. 2015).

As another measure of business strength, economic concentration is increasing both worldwide (Schecter 2017) and in numerous industries. This increasing concentration derives in part because companies can use their market power to gain political power, and that political power then allows those companies to intervene in the public policy arena in ways that further increase their market power. One manifestation of this phenomenon is the absence of effective antitrust enforcement that has enabled substantial consolidation through mergers in many industries including airlines, health insurance, concerts and ticketing (LiveNation), newspapers, telecommunications including cell phone service, and entertainment.

There is growing evidence that this economic concentration affects not just corporate profits through expanding margins, or consumers through higher prices, poorer service, and less choice, but also impacts labor markets. Research suggests that growing economic concentration depresses wages. For instance, Benmelech et al. (2018) reported that local-level employer concentration had increased over time, resulting in increased monopsony power. Importantly, they observed a negative relationship between employer concentration and wages over the period 1977–2009.

Even as companies have prospered, workers face not only wage stagnation (e.g., Mishel et al. 2015) but also increased economic insecurity. Layoffs are now a regular occurrence almost regardless of macroeconomic conditions, and people more frequently confront precarious employment with the continued growth of the so-called gig economy. Companies have effectively declared a "war on jobs" as they grow contingent employment and increase their use of outsourcing and contract labor in an effort to hold down their labor costs. One study found that the proportion of US workers in alternative work arrangements had increased by 50% between 1995 and 2015 (Katz and Krueger 2016). That study also reported that 94% of the net job growth over the preceding decade had come in alternative work arrangements such as part-time, freelance, and contract work. The trend toward less secure, contingent employment is a worldwide phenomenon, as many countries emulate the labor deregulation of the U.S. and workers increasingly find themselves in temporary or irregular employment arrangements that negate the protections offered to full-time, regular workers.

In many ways, the challenges posed by artificial intelligence—and particularly the enormous threats to regular jobs and incomes and the increasing economic insecurity that people confront from the rapid automation of work—could come to reflect yet another manifestation of an organizational reality that places little to no emphasis on the well-being of individuals. Whether, and to what extent, AI eventuates in harm to individual economic, psychological, and physical well-being depends on the policies, and how the priorities, societies, and workplaces adapt.

In this chapter, I first *briefly* document the sorry state of employee well-being and the potential threat to labor posed by artificial intelligence—briefly because these facts are, or should be, already well-known. I then argue that, not surprisingly, people's physical and mental health are connected to their economic security and other dimensions of work environments on the one hand, and to their work performance—and health care costs—on the other. Therefore, in the face of ever-rising health costs that burden national budgets, it is actually in the interests of governments to promote workplace well-being, and frequently, because of the connection between well-being and productivity, in companies' interests as well. Moreover, jobs provide people with more than income. Work provides meaning and status and was also once a place where people enjoyed social contact and the social support and friendship that workmates provide.

If we want to understand the likely effects of artificial intelligence and continued automation in the workplace on people, we need to understand the decision logics that seem to guide organizational and public policy decisions. The sorry state of the contemporary workplace and its connection to both health and productivity raises the question of why and how things have gotten to the condition they have, as understanding decision criteria provides one way of forecasting the future. Part of the problem is a collective action issue, in which no individual company wants to undertake potentially costly actions that its competitors can avoid. Another part of the problem is the evolving conception of general management from a concern with balancing stakeholder interests to one of single-mindedly pursuing the interests of one group—shareholders—of prioritizing the interests of capital over all others and theories and values that legitimate this prioritization. A third determinant of decision logics is the taken-for-granted language used to describe economies and businesses, and the dominance of narrowly economic conceptualizations of decisions with a concomitant emphasis on costs, profits, and productivity. If societies are to solve, or even address, issues such as inequality in health and lifespans, declines in life expectancy, and ever-increasing health care costs, fundamental changes in management practices—and therefore fundamental reorientations in priorities and decision criteria—will be required. It is therefore important to understand the plethora of forces working against prioritizing the well-being of people.

What all of this means is that, for better or worse, general managers are and will continue to be front and center in addressing some fundamental social issues. This expanded role for general management requires both new measures and a different orientation to companies' responsibilities to the people who do its work. Although the challenges posed by AI and other manifestations of workplace automation are potentially addressable, I am far from sanguine about the willingness of companies and their leaders to do what needs to be done, for the political system to impose regulations that would ensure that they do, or for governments to make adequate investments in human sustainability.

## 4.2    The (Sorry) State of People's Well-Being

Even before we witness the full impact of artificial intelligence and the continuing automation of work, work arrangements are already problematic for people's income, job security, and workplace stress, and therefore for their physical health and psychological well-being. There are many, many indicators that demonstrate problems with the employment relationship and the conditions confronting most working people. Here are just a few.

Labor market arrangements and workplace practices affect people's health and thus contribute to the worldwide problem of soaring health care costs and rising inequalities in lifespans and other health indicators. We know that income inequality has adverse health effects (e.g., Wilkinson and Pickett 2006), and not just for people at the bottom of the distribution. In part because income is tied to health and because the conditions of work differ ever more widely depending on people's level of education (Goh et al. 2015b), inequalities in health both within and across countries are increasing. For instance, a recent study found that inequalities in life expectancy among counties in the U.S. are growing, with there being a 20-year difference in life expectancy between the counties with the highest and lowest life expectancy (Dwyer-Lindgren et al. 2017). For the last two years, average life expectancy in the U.S. actually *decreased*, in part because people at the top of the income distribution are enjoying longer life while for those at the bottom, life expectancy is going down (Belluz 2018). As I have argued in *Dying for a Paycheck* (Pfeffer 2018), substantial epidemiological evidence demonstrates a direct and important connection between work environments and people's physical and mental health and mortality.

According to the Conference Board, job satisfaction has rebounded since the depths of the recent recession. Nonetheless, it is still the case that in the U.S., barely 50% of people are satisfied with their jobs, and job satisfaction is low worldwide. Moreover, the report notes that job satisfaction is unlikely to return to levels seen in the past because of trends such as "the emphasis on maximizing shareholder value, declining unionization, outsourcing (both foreign and domestic) and market concentration" (Conference Board 2017). Meanwhile, Gallup reports that based on a worldwide survey, "85% of employees are not engaged or actively disengaged at work" with a cost to the global economy of $7 trillion in lost productivity (Harter 2018).

To take another indicator, the 2017 Edelman Trust Barometer showed "the largest-ever drop in trust," with CEO credibility falling 12 points to "an all-time low of 37 percent, plummeting in every country studied" (Edelman 2017).

As Crabtree (2017) noted, "the percentage of a country's population that is employed full time for an employer—which Gallup refers to as having a 'good job'—is one of the most fundamental statistics of productivity." Gallup has presented data showing a strong positive relationship between the proportion of people with good jobs and countries' per capita GDP. Gallup's survey of people in 155 countries found that just 32% of working-age adults have good jobs, a percentage that has not changed much if at all since Gallup began collecting and computing this statistic. "Great jobs" are jobs where people are engaged with their work. As Ray (2016) commented, "Great jobs are scarce. Across the world, the percentage of adults with great jobs rarely tops 10%" and fewer than 200 million people in the world have great jobs.

Gallup has also developed a well-being index, based on metrics that comprise five dimensions of well-being: purpose, social (having supportive relationships), financial (security and reduced stress), community (liking where you live and feeling safe), and physical (having good health). In 2017, "nearly half of U.S. states saw their well-being scores decline by a statistically significant margin…[a]nd for the first time in nine years of tracking changes in state well-being, no state saw statistically significant improvement" (Witters 2018).

Well-being issues are not just a US problem. A 2017 worldwide survey by the HR consulting firm Willis Towers Watson reported that around 30% of employees had suffered "severe stress, anxiety, or depression in the last two years" (Willis Towers Watson 2017). That same report noted that financial satisfaction had taken a turn for the worse, declining from 48 to 35%. In the U.S., 37% of respondents said they could not come up with $2000 in an emergency, while the comparable figure for the U.K. was even higher, at 41%. The same survey revealed that "employees' long-standing desire for greater security continues to intensify" and more than 20% of people still expected to be working at age 70 or later.

Similar results illustrating the dismal state of employees' sense of security, trust in their leaders, and satisfaction with their jobs and lives come from surveys conducted by other organizations around the world.

## 4.3    The Likely Impact of Artificial Intelligence

As noted by Datamation (2018), "artificial intelligence has exploded in the past few years with dozens of startup companies and major AI initiatives by big name firms" such as Google, Amazon, Microsoft, Facebook, IBM, Twitter, and Salesforce. However, artificial intelligence, absent the sort of public policy innovations and interventions that have been exceedingly, astonishingly rare, will only make workers' situations worse. Recall Gallup's definition of a good job—someone working *full-time* for an *employer.* The adoption of artificial intelligence and the spread of automation promises to either destroy or transform many jobs and to disrupt employment relationships that are already under considerable stress.

The World Economic Forum's report on the future of retail noted that automation threatened "over 40% of consumer goods jobs and at least 20% of retail jobs in the next ten years" (World Economic Forum 2017). In many countries, retail jobs are the largest occupational category. McKinsey's (2017) study of the effects of automation estimated that some 60% of occupations have at least 30% of their content that could be automated. McKinsey calculated that some 75 million to 375 million people globally would need to switch occupational categories. In the U.S., the report estimated that by 2030, between 39 million and 73 million jobs could be destroyed. Even accounting for new job creation, some 16–54 million workers would need to be retrained for entirely new occupations. Frey and Osborne (2013) estimated the probability of computerization for 702 detailed occupational categories. Based on their analysis, some 47% of total US employment is at risk, with low wage and less education occupations being most subject to computerization. *The Economist* (2016) reported that the comparable figure for Britain was 35 and 49% for Japan.

Brynjolfsson and Mitchell (2017: 1530), exploring the impact of machine learning, an aspect of artificial intelligence, on work, noted that "the implications for the economy and the workforce going forward are profound." That is because of the primacy of efficiency and economic mindsets in decision-making: "Each time an ML [machine learning] system crosses the threshold where it becomes more cost effective than humans on a task, profit-maximizing entrepreneurs and managers will increasingly seek to substitute machines for people" (Brynjolfsson and Mitchell 2017: 1531).

Business intelligence makes it increasingly possible to schedule people to work only when they are needed, to avoid paying for excess labor. Growing sophistication of artificial intelligence and machine learning will only improve the accuracy of such forecasts. According to a 2015 report from the Economic Policy Institute (Golden 2015), about 17% of the US workforce has unstable work schedules. People with unstable work schedules report more than twice the rate of work–family conflict as those with regular schedules. Nearly half of the people surveyed "by the International Social Survey Program said their 'employer decides' their work schedule," with just 15% saying that they were free to decide their schedule.

The available evidence suggests that automation promises job loss and growing economic insecurity for the people who retain their jobs, at least as far as the forecasts prove accurate.

## 4.3.1 Why Policies to Mitigate the Harmful Effects of AI Are Unlikely to Be Implemented

The counter argument to these dire warnings about the effects of automation and AI on labor is that proper policy interventions can mitigate or even completely remediate many of the anticipated deleterious impacts. In theory, this is probably true. Investments in education and job training can help people transition to new jobs and new occupations. Income maintenance policies, including unemployment insurance, guaranteed income, and other social welfare interventions can mitigate the harmful effects of income reduction or the loss of income arising from job displacement. The question is not if such policy interventions are, in principle, possible. The real issue is what are the prospects for such policies and programs actually being implemented?

With some exceptions, such as Germany, that has implemented shared working subsidies to avoid layoffs and has an active apprenticeship training effort, advanced industrialized countries have not historically done a great job with previous job dislocations coming either from recessions or from the transition from extractive industries and manufacturing to services. Now these countries face the task of helping with the transitions necessitated by AI, and for the most part, have less capacity to do so.

First of all, almost all industrialized countries have below replacement-level birthrates. Low birthrates have several effects. First, "any reduction in birth rates promotes population aging" (Coleman and Rowthorn 2011: 223) and a higher proportion of older people. Because health status is related to age (World Health Organization 2018), a higher proportion of older people entails higher health care costs and also greater pension and social insurance costs as older people participate in the labor force at lower rates. When birthrates are below replacement level, unless there is sufficient immigration, countries' populations shrink. Coleman and Rowthorn (2011: 226) noted that "because labor (equivalent to population) is one of the key inputs to production, it is axiomatic that population growth increases total GDP.... With given productivity, GDP declines *pro rata* with numbers of people." Of course, per capita GDP may increase and there are other advantages of smaller populations such as less environmental impact. However, "other things being equal, big countries have more political and military power than small ones" (Coleman and Rowthorn 2011: 227).

Second, most countries are running, and have run for years, budget deficits, leaving them little discretionary spending capability to invest in income maintenance, training, or both. Table 4.1 presents data, by country, on fertility, budget deficits, and share of GDP represented by public debt. Few countries, and none of the advanced industrialized countries, have a birth rate that is above replacement level. Virtually all of the countries are running budget deficits, and in many instances, accumulated public debt is a substantial fraction of GDP. These data make the point that even if governments had the will and policy-making skill to formulate interventions to help labor deal with AI-induced changes in employment, it is not clear that countries have the *capacity* to handle the coming shocks to the employment relationship.

If education and training are to be an antidote to the adverse effects on labor from artificial intelligence and automation, the global historical record on investment in human capital development is mixed at best. Margaret Thatcher, just two years into serving as prime minister, cut government funds for universities by 20% (Docherty 2013). That action began a process in which student tuition would rise substantially as universities in the U.K. were increasingly privatized and forced to seek funds from commercial activities such as business and executive education programs and admitting foreign students who would pay higher fees.

**Table 4.1** Demographic and budgetary challenges, by country[a]

| Country | Fertility (births/ woman) | Current budget (as % of GDP) | Total debt (as % of GDP) |
|---|---|---|---|
| Argentina | 2.26 | −6.1 | 53.7 |
| Australia | 1.77 | −1.7 | 47.1 |
| Austria | 1.47 | −1 | 81.7 |
| Belgium | 1.78 | −2.1 | 104.3 |
| Brazil | 1.75 | −1.1 | 78.4 |
| Bulgaria | 1.46 | −1.4 | 28.6 |
| Canada | 1.6 | −2 | 98.2 |
| Chile | 1.8 | −3.1 | 25.2 |
| China | 1.6 | −4 | 18.6 |
| Columbia | 2 | −3.3 | 53 |
| Croatia | 1.4 | −2.1 | 81.5 |
| Czech Republic | 1.45 | −0.1 | 35.1 |
| Denmark | 1.73 | −0.6 | 35.1 |
| Ecuador | 2.19 | −5.5 | 41 |
| Finland | 1.75 | −1.6 | 63.8 |
| France | 2.07 | −2.6 | 96.1 |
| Germany | 1.45 | 0.7 | 65.7 |
| Greece | 1.43 | −1.3 | 180 |
| India | 2.43 | −3.3 | 50.1 |
| Italy | 1.44 | −2.3 | 131.2 |
| Japan | 1.41 | −4.6 | 223.8 |
| Korea (South) | 1.26 | 0.9 | 43.3 |
| Netherlands | 1.78 | 0.6 | 59 |
| Pakistan | 2.62 | −4.5 | 159.4 |
| Poland | 1.35 | −2.2 | 46.2 |
| Portugal | 1.53 | −1.8 | 127.7 |
| Saudi Arabia | 2.09 | −8.3 | 30 |
| Spain | 1.5 | −3.3 | 96.7 |
| South Africa | 2.29 | −3.2 | 50.1 |
| Sweden | 1.88 | 0.9 | 39 |
| Switzerland | 1.56 | 0.2 | 32.9 |
| Turkey | 2.01 | −2 | 29.6 |
| United Kingdom | 1.88 | −3.6 | 90.4 |
| United States | 1.87 | −3.4 | 77.4 |

[a]Fertility rate comes from the Central Intelligence Agency World Factbook; Budget surplus or deficit comes from the Central Intelligence Agency Work Factbook, the ratio of total public debt to GDP comes from Wikipedia (https://en.wikipedia.org/wiki/List_of_countries_by_public_debt). All figures are for 2017

In the U.S., public disinvestment in higher education began more than three decades ago. In 2017, state spending on higher education remained well below what it had been prior to the onset of the recession a decade earlier. As state support for higher education has declined, student tuition has soared and become an increasingly larger share of public university budgets.

In 2008, tuition accounted for 35.8% of public higher education funding, but by 2013, tuition represented 47.8% of all higher education revenue in the U.S. (Bauman 2018). Mortenson (2012) noted that the 2011 "funding effort was down by 40.2 percent compared with fiscal 1980." He also made the connection between declining public support of education and soaring tuition: "inflation-adjusted tuition charges that were declining in the 1970s have surged since 1980. Inflation-adjusted tuition and fee charges increased by 247 percent at state flagship universities." Not surprisingly, soaring tuition is associated with ever-declining proportions of students from lower-income families, increasing numbers of foreign and out-of-state students who can and will pay more, rising student debt which in the aggregate now exceeds $1 trillion and burdens graduates with loan payments for years, and declining completion rates as more students have to work while they are in school.

While universities in Scandinavian countries remain free or nearly so, the trend toward public disinvestment in higher education is a common issue as higher education has to compete everywhere with other budget priorities including declining physical infrastructure, particularly in the U.S., and spending on health care and the elderly almost everywhere. Universities and colleges, an important locus for the retraining needed for people displaced by AI, confront funding challenges that leave them not particularly resource-ready for this growing responsibility.

The story about other forms of training is much the same. Individual companies are reluctant to invest in training, particularly more general skills, because when people leave, their investment in training that individual goes with them. Training has been among the first thing to get cut at most companies as soon as they face any economic stringency. Few countries mandate a certain level of investment in training. The U.S. is a particularly bad example. A Hamilton Project report (2014) noted that "since 1985 the amount budgeted for key U.S. Department of Labor training programs declined by 20 percent in real terms." That report found the U.S. was near the bottom in terms of labor market training expenditures as a percent of GDP. But even the leading countries spend only about one-half of one percent of their GDP on labor market training. While there is widespread recognition that reskilling workers for the new economy is essential, much of the needed investment relies on the voluntary, completely discretionary action of private employers, supplemented by government encouragement and some level of government spending. It is hard to see this approach ensuring a successful transition in the face of the rapid automation of work and the enormous amount of job dislocation that is already occurring and will occur in the future.

Simply put, there is more recognition of the need for investment in training and skills than there is action consistent with this recognition. Budgets are under strain virtually worldwide and face further problems emanating from aging and shrinking—populations. It is difficult to see either adequate investment in education or in creating a sufficient social safety net to buffer people from job displacement given demographic realities and past trends. Wishes, recommendations, and hope are not strategies that inspire much confidence that countries or companies are going to do what would be required to assure a reasonably smooth transition to a world increasingly dominated by AI-influenced work.

## 4.4 The Relationship Among Economic Insecurity, Well-Being, and Performance

Work environments and economic security matter, not just for people's financial well-being, although that is obviously important, but also for people's physical and mental health and mortality. For instance, Goh et al. (2015a) conducted meta-analyses on the effects of ten different workplace "exposures" including long working hours, economic insecurity, shift work, work–family conflict, an absence of job control, and not having social support in the workplace on self-reported physical health, self-reported mental health, having a physician-diagnosed illness, and mortality. They found that most of the exposures were as harmful to health outcomes as second-hand smoke, a known and regulated carcinogen. In a study estimating the combined effects of these stress-inducing aspects of work environments and also access to health care through health insurance on health and health care costs, Goh et al. (2016) found that work environments were responsible for approximately 120,000 excess deaths and about $190 billion in excess costs annually in the U.S. This would make workplaces the fifth leading cause of death in the U.S. and responsible for somewhere between five and eight percent of total health care costs.

Workplaces are a public health crisis with enormous effects on health care costs, mortality, and morbidity worldwide. The World Economic Forum (2010: 3) noted that chronic diseases "account for the lion's share of health-care costs" with an even greater impact on productivity. "Globally, the toll from chronic disease…is estimated at US $2 trillion in lost productivity each year." The Centers for Disease Control reported that "eighty-six percent of the nation's $2.7 trillion health care expenditures are for people with chronic and mental health conditions. *These costs can be reduced*" (emphasis added). One of the reasons the costs from chronic disease are widely thought to be controllable is that chronic disease comes from stress and the behaviors such as smoking, drug use, alcohol abuse, and overeating that stress helps cause, and presumably the sources of stress can and should be reduced. Numerous surveys by the American Psychological Association and the American Institute of Stress, among other organizations, consistently show that the workplace is among the top three causes of stress (Pfeffer 2018).

We already have a workplace-induced health crisis, even without additional implementation of AI and the automation of many jobs. Particularly relevant for discussions of the effects of automation and artificial intelligence on people is the large research literature examining the health effects of various forms of economic insecurity and instability. One form of economic insecurity arises through layoffs and job loss. Layoffs adversely affect people's financial well-being but also their sense of self as they wonder, "what did I do to deserve this?" The evidence shows that layoffs increase mortality, and by a substantial amount. One study in Sweden found that the overall mortality risk for men increased by 44% in the four years following a job loss (Eliason and Storrie 2010). The effect of job loss on mortality has been observed in studies not just in the United States but in countries such as New Zealand, Sweden, Finland, and Denmark that have more robust social safety nets (Pfeffer 2018). Mortality rises in part because of a substantial increase in the suicide rate following job loss but also from increases in heart attacks and other causes such as alcohol-related deaths.

Layoffs also contribute to poor health, not just mortality. A longitudinal study by sociologist Kate Strully (2009) found that job loss following an establishment closure increased the odds of reporting poor health by more than 50%, and for employees healthy at the beginning, losing a job from a plant closure increased the odds of having a new health condition by more than 80%. Even for respondents who were able to find a new job, the health effects of layoffs persisted. And research shows that layoffs adversely affect the health of people in units experiencing layoffs who manage to retain their jobs (Kivimaki et al. 2000). Layoffs also have ill-effects on the managers responsible for doing the layoffs (Grunberg et al. 2006).

Layoffs lead to an increased incidence of workplace violence. One study found that people laid off were six times as likely to report violent behavior than those not laid off (Catalano et al. 2002).

Losing one's job leads to unhealthy individual behaviors. For example, research shows that being unemployed increases the use of alcohol, cannabis, and other drugs. One study of Swedish men found that being unemployed for more than 20 weeks increased the incidence of heavy drinking by 400% (Janlert and Hammarstrom 1992).

The state of employee health affects productivity and job performance and also, not surprisingly, health care costs. Emeritus University of Michigan professor Dee Edington has documented that unhealthy employees incur higher worker compensation costs (Burton et al. 1999) and that less healthy employees are also less productive. One review of some 113 published studies found that there was convincing evidence for a relationship between employee health and productivity (Schultz and Edington 2007). Other studies find that people with poor physical health have higher turnover intentions (Grandy and Cropanzano 1999). A study in Europe found that job insecurity increased people's mental health complaints and also their intentions to quit their jobs (Chirumbolo and Hellgren 2003). Turnover is obviously costly. Virtually none of the people I interviewed for *Dying for a Paycheck* were still in the workplaces that had caused them stress and made them ill.

Thus, economic insecurity affects employee health and well-being. In turn, people's health affects their productivity and job performance, and of course, their health care costs. Economic insecurity and the job environment more generally are, as the data make clear, pressing public health issues that should be of concern to governments and employers facing ever-increasing health care costs. The coming job disruptions from AI that virtually every report forecasts are only going to make a bad situation even worse.

## 4.5 How—And Why—Companies Came to Disregard People's Well-Being

Organizational work environments matter for people's health and well-being and also for their engagement and job performance. Not a particularly novel or controversial idea. But then, why do outcomes such as health and mortality—and even health care costs—receive such short shrift in most managerial decision-making?

A few years ago at a conference I attended at UCLA, Lawrence Fink, the CEO of Blackrock and someone known for advocating that companies take a long-term view and invest in their futures, made what I consider to be a striking comment. He said that the U.S. had made progress in achieving greater competitiveness during the 2008 recession and its incipient recovery because, to take one example, employees in the US auto industry were now earning about as much as their counterparts in Mexico (because the severe recession resulted in wage give-backs and the implementation of two-tier wage structures in which new employees were paid at a lower rate). That statement, coming from one of the more presumably enlightened CEOs, illustrates the extent to which worker well-being is missing from business and social policy discussions, which instead focus on costs, mostly narrowly defined, and profits.

Low wages are not an unalloyed social good. There is extensive evidence showing the relationship between people's wages and their physical health (e.g., Leigh and DeVogli 2016). Moreover, we know that life span follows a social gradient, with higher income and education associated with better health and longer life spans (Marmot 2004). Reducing workers' wages to the level of Mexico has consequences not just for the people's standard of living but also for their physical and psychological health.

There are several reasons why people receive such little priority in company decision-making. One important reason is the prominence of shareholders—capital—over all other company constituencies. As Robert Reich, former U.S. Secretary of Labor, has written (2014), 60 years ago, "most CEOs assumed they were responsible for all of their stakeholders". 'The job of management,' proclaimed Frank Abrams, chairman of Standard Oil of New Jersey, in 1951, "is to maintain an equitable and working balance among the claims of the various directly interested groups…stockholders, employees, customers, and the public at large." Other large companies made similar statements at that time.

Over time, so-called stakeholder capitalism (e.g., Freeman et al. 2007) has been replaced by shareholder capitalism, in which the primacy of shareholder interests is presumed, even at the expense of other constituencies (Clarke 2005). This prioritization of stock price and profits occurs even in some of the most presumably humanistic companies. Howard Behar, a member of the board of directors and formerly the person who ran Starbucks' international operations, severed his ties with the company when during the severe recession of 2008 the company, under the leadership of Howard Schultz, laid off many employees in an effort to maintain its profits.

This change in the priority given to shareholders compared to other constituencies has been so extensively documented as to have become almost taken-for-granted. It is sometimes attributed to the rise of shareholder activism and a resulting increase in hostile corporate takeovers or threatened takeovers. These actions, which often result in incumbent management losing their jobs—a prospect that makes those managers much more attuned to the financial markets and stock price—are made possible by the financing instruments such as junk bonds and the debt accessed by private equity firms that facilitate these buyouts.

While these changing values and priorities probably began in the U.S., shareholder primacy is a doctrine that has spread throughout much of the world, as stock markets, debt financing, the operation of private equity, and hostile takeovers are increasingly all global in scope. The idea of maximizing shareholder value as the most important, if not the sole, objective of management is taught in most business schools throughout the world as received truth (e.g., Ghoshal 2005). However, as Bagley and Page (1999) among others, have noted, there is no *legal* mandate to ignore interests other than those of shareholders, and in fact, courts have frequently sided with managements on the increasingly rare occasions that they seek to make business decisions incorporating the interests of other constituencies.

The primacy of shareholder interests reflects not just changes in corporate governance and the debt and equity markets. Fundamentally the maximizing of shareholder value above all else, also indicates the privileging of economic considerations—money—over all others. Maybe even the privileging of money over human life. *The New York Times* reported the death of a New Jersey woman who had fallen behind on her electric bills (Rojas 2018). When Public Service Electric and Gas cut off her electricity during a July heat wave, that individual lost not only access to air conditioning but also to the power that ran her oxygen machine. Davis (2009) extensively documented the growing primacy of a market orientation to everything ranging from housing to childcare, while other research has shown the growing prominence of finance in society (e.g., Krippner 2005).

A second contributing factor to the rise of shareholder capitalism and the neglect of employee well-being may be the decline in the strength of labor organizations such as unions, entities that traditionally were able to argue for and obtain some priority for the interests of their members. In the U.S., the union membership rate declined from 20.1% in 1983 to 11.1% in 2015 (Dunn and Walker 2016), continuing an erosion of union power that began even earlier. In Western Europe, union influence is also declining (e.g., Gumbrell-McCormick and Hyman 2013). Although union decline in advanced industrialized countries is undoubtedly caused in part by the shift away from manufacturing and the increased internationalization of economic competition, changes in the willingness of managers to fight rather than accommodate unions is a significant factor. So, too, is the more hostile governmental attitudes and policies toward collective bargaining (e.g., Kochan et al. 1994).

Of course, there are counter-movements, such as conscious capitalism (Mackey and Sisodia 2013) and the World Business Council, among many others, that seek to provide more priority to constituencies other than shareholders and considerations other than stock price. Various academics, including Jordi Canals (2010), and executives have added their voices to arguments advocating for a different, more balanced view of the role of companies in society. But such efforts notwithstanding, I see little evidence of much impact. Companies such as 3G Capital earn plaudits, not opprobrium, when, following the Heinz-Kraft Foods merger, they laid off a substantial fraction of the workforce. Venture capitalists have told me for years that if a potential investee does not have a plan to offshore and outsource work, they will probably not invest—under the assumption that anyone without such a plan in place must be incompetent.

Furthermore, in spite of the proliferation of studies showing the profitability of high commitment work practices that "put people first" (e.g., Pfeffer 1998), including studies and books written by human resource consulting firms, few companies seem to act on these insights. Why they don't is a question yet to be definitely resolved. But certainly, a part of the answer comes from what is routinely measured and what is not. As we learned from the quality movement, measurement matters. Profits and costs are typically measured and reported on in detail. Human well-being is measured only occasionally, if at all—and therefore necessarily comes to play a lesser role in organizational decision-making.

Another part of the answer about why human health and well-being is so often neglected comes from the language and theoretical perspectives that have come to be inextricably entwined in business management. Ferraro et al. (2005) argued that social theories can become self-fulfilling because of their effects on the design of institutional arrangements and the use of language and assumptions that become widely used and accepted. Economics language and assumptions have come to dominate not only business but many considerations of public policy and even daily life. The conception of time as a resource and the consequent pressure to "invest" and "manage" time has reified the connection between time and money. As DeVoe and House (2012) demonstrated, thinking about time as money reduced people's pleasure from surfing the internet or listening to a pleasant song, because thinking about the monetary aspects of time made people impatient.

Moreover, companies confront an increasingly competitive environment in which cost avoidance and cost reduction reign supreme. Therefore, firms are naturally reluctant to do anything, such as taking care of their employees, that might put them at a competitive cost disadvantage—an example of a classic collective action problem. The only way to obviate such collective action issues is to mandate prosocial behavior so that any given company does not have to fear defections by its competitors. But in a worldwide push for labor market deregulation and ever-more prominent beliefs that markets solve everything, such mandates are hard to introduce and the ones already in place are increasingly under attack, either directly through outright repeal, or indirectly by starving the agencies charged with enforcing labor market rules for the resources necessary for them to do their jobs.

## 4.6 Raising the Importance of People's Well-Being in Organizational Decisions

If we are serious about human sustainability and well-being and if we want to put pressure on companies and governments to take action to improve sustainability, what needs to be done is clear. First, we need appropriate measures because as already argued, measurement matters. If companies and governments are serious about people's well-being, they need to measure it. And second, once those measures are compiled, they need to be publicized so that companies can compete to do better, while those organizations that sacrifice human well-being can be potentially shamed into changing their practices.

Fortunately, measurement is not that difficult to do. For instance, as I discuss in my book on the workplace and its effects on health (Pfeffer 2018), a *single item* measure of self-reported health, on a five-point scale, *prospectively* predicts people's subsequent mortality and their use of health care resources. The predictive value of a single-item measure of self-reported health holds in some studies even after numerous other demographic measures and indicators of health status are statistically controlled. And this single-item measure of self-reported health has been validated in samples of the young, the old, and different ethnic populations. Indeed, the OECD uses country-wide survey-obtained measures of self-reported health as one of their national health indicators. Since health status varies by education and income, analyses should control for those factors in comparing across organizational units.

A second measure of health is prescription drug use, obtained either from survey self-reports or, better yet, from actual prescription data. When workplaces are toxic and people are suffering and stressed, those individuals will seek medications to help them tolerate the workplace pressures. Many of the people I interviewed for *Dying for a Paycheck* explicitly talked about turning to antidepressants and other drugs to help them cope with the psychological pain their workplaces were producing. Michael Dahl (2011; Dahl et al. 2010) has used prescription data to examine the consequences of becoming an entrepreneur and the effects of organizational change. The use of antidepressants, sedatives, sleeping pills, and ADHD drugs that promote wakefulness and concentration are all possible indicators of unhealthy workplaces. Again, of course, one would want to norm for age, education, and income, and most informative would be changes over time, data that permit controlling for stable individual differences.

An extensive epidemiological literature demonstrates the negative consequences of excessive work hours for indicators of both physical and psychological well-being, including actual mortality (Pfeffer 2018). Studies of work hours and their health effects cover many countries, including Japan, and find consistent, albeit small, health effects. It is relatively straightforward to measure working hours, either through self-report or other data.

There are well-validated survey measures of virtually every cause of workplace stress: an absence of social support, a lack of job control, work-family conflict, workplace bullying and abuse, and gender- and race-based discrimination that people often experience as stressful (Pfeffer 2018). Stress itself can be measured by assaying cortisol from saliva (e.g., Pfeffer and Carney 2018).

With the growing emphasis on environmental sustainability and social responsibility, organizations have made great strides in developing indicators to assess how well companies are doing in stewarding physical resources. And companies themselves tout their accomplishments in their self-generated materials. It is completely feasible to accomplish similar assessments of work organizations' performance with respect to their work practices that affect human sustainability. Public policy would benefit enormously from knowing the mean levels and distribution of human sustainability performance. Regulation, if desired, requires valid and reliable indicators to be effective. The gathering—and publication—of measures capturing aspects of workplace human sustainability would do more than any other single thing to advance the cause of building workplaces that do not, either intentionally or inadvertently, sicken and kill the people who work for and in them.

Beyond measurement, if we want business leaders to prioritize human life and well-being, it is certainly useful for them to learn about these issues in business schools. As one recent business school graduate has noted (Benjamin 2018), business school classes say almost nothing about labor unions. Benjamin argues that business schools "are ideological institutions committed to a strict blend of social liberalism and economic conservatism," promoting innovation and free markets as the solution to almost all social problems. The guests invited to business schools seldom include representatives of labor (dare we say never) or political movements questioning fundamental tenets of capitalism and its values. Dame Carol Black told me that she and Cary Cooper, a Manchester University professor who has published extensively on workplace stress, conducted a quick informal survey in 2011 of 100 U.K. business schools to see if *any* of them taught *any* material on employee health, well-being, or engagement in *any* of their courses. The answer, unfortunately, was no (Pfeffer 2018).

We cannot expect business leaders to pay attention to topics that are noticeable by their absence in the courses they take, both in degree and executive education programs. What is taught, and what is ignored, sends an important signal about what business leaders are supposed to attend to and value. Simply put, if we want human sustainability considerations to affect companies' and governments' response to the challenges posed by artificial intelligence, we need more and different measures and much more educational emphasis on human sustainability.

## 4.7 What Sort of Future Will Companies and Their Leaders Create?

As the Cornell economic historian, Louis Hyman (2018), has written, "The history of labor shows that technology does not usually drive social change. On the contrary, social change is typically driven by *decisions* we make about how to organize our world." Strategic choice, driven by values as well as social pressures, matter. This statement is as true for artificial intelligence as it was for the creation of factory technology.

Artificial intelligence could be used to make workplaces and work better for people. To take one example, AI programs could monitor prescription drug use, people's social media postings, and interactions with the health system to quickly identify work environments that are causing harm. AI could help companies evaluate the effects of changes to improve employee well-being. Simply put, AI can be employed in the relentless pursuit of economic efficiency, even at the expense of people, or, alternatively, to help create more humane workplaces and societies.

In the end, whether companies create healthy workplaces where people thrive or toxic work environments that harm people's physical and mental health depends on whether companies get serious about building a culture of health. And no, I am not talking about gyms and wellness programs. The idea of "encouraging sleep-deprived employees to grab 40 winks during the workday" (Channick 2018) by providing places for people to nap seems bizarre. If people didn't have schedules that left them sleep-deprived in the first place, workplaces would not need the ubiquitous coffee bars and ever-increasing nap pods.

Healthy workplaces are ones that prevent stress in the first place, by having people work reasonable hours, in a supportive environment, where they have control over their work, sufficient time off to relax, and can work free from bullying and harassment. There are companies that are committed to these objectives. But many others see employee health as some sort of "nice to have," fine for when times are good, but ignored at the first sign of economic stringency. No wonder health care costs are high and employees disaffected—businesses and governments have given too little attention to the work environments that so profoundly affect people's well-being.

For much of human history, progress along multiple dimensions was readily discernible. Literacy increased and more people stayed in school longer and presumably acquired more skills and knowledge. Medical science extended lifespans dramatically, first through progress against many infectious diseases and more recently in advancements in treating heart disease and cancer. Productivity gains and global economic integration vastly reduced poverty and dramatically increased the comfort and standard of living for many people throughout the world. And technological advances have profoundly affected people's ability to travel, communicate, feed themselves, and numerous other aspects of everyday life.

But there are no guarantees that progress will continue easily and on the same trajectory into the future. There are numerous indications that work environments are getting worse along multiple dimensions ranging from work hours to work–family conflict to aspects of economic insecurity. Work environments profoundly matter for people's well-being. People spend a considerable proportion of their time at work. Social identities derive, in part, from people's occupations and the status of their employer, assuming they have one. People's lifestyles, economic security, and their ability to provide for their families depend on their earnings, often derived from having a job. People often have and find friends at work, meet their romantic partners in the workplace, and enjoy—or not—social support in and from their work environments. Workplaces matter for people's physical and mental health and well-being.

Consequently, the leaders who oversee—who construct—workplaces and work arrangements have a profound responsibility whether or not they realize it and act accordingly. Robert Chapman, the CEO of the manufacturing company Barry-Wehmiller, has said that according to the Mayo clinic, a person's supervisor is more important for their health than their family doctor (Pfeffer 2018). Consequently, Chapman argues, leaders have a responsibility to create workplaces where people go home at the end of the day in better condition than when they arrived in the morning. One of the things Chapman discovered when he began the transformation of the management system and culture at Barry-Wehmiller is the many spillover effects on people's health and on their families. Those effects have reinforced Chapman's determination to be a good steward of the lives entrusted to him—his employees and their family members.

As I have noted (Pfeffer 2018), there are companies—Collective Health, Patagonia, Zillow, SAS Institute, Landmark Health, and others—that have senior leaders who are concerned for the well-being of their workforce. These examples illustrate the obvious but important point that the effects of AI or any other workplace change depend in part on the values and decisions of general managers. But there are not nearly enough such companies or leaders who care about employee well-being, which is why levels of employee engagement and trust in leaders is so low, and why health care costs are so high, as life expectancy in the U.S. has begun to fall. Ironically, many of the management practices that create ill-health do not benefit companies' productivity or profits either, as leaders create truly lose-lose situations.

The interesting challenge arises when company profits do come at the expense of human well-being. What choices will leaders and the societies in which they live make then? Countries have outlawed slavery and child labor, believing that some workplace conditions are morally intolerable regardless of their economic consequences. Yet reading the Universal Declaration of Human Rights adopted by the United Nations General Assembly in 1948 and subsequently embodied in many treaties and agreements reminds us of how far we have yet to go to fulfill the mandates promulgated—and how many workplaces have imposed policies and practices inimical to the fundamental sanctity of human life.

Through my research I have come to believe that many of the choices leaders make, including choices about saving people from technology dysfunctions and the worst consequences of automation and artificial intelligence, are decisions that cause harm, in part because those making the choices have inadequate information and frameworks. But values and priorities matter as well. As long as we place economic objectives so far ahead of human life and well-being, it is hard to see how the implementation of artificial intelligence and other aspects of technological change in the workplace will make things better for the people who exist in such workplaces.

**Acknowledgements** The comments of Jordi Canals and Fabrizio Ferraro on an earlier draft of this paper are gratefully acknowledged.

# References

Bagley, C.B., and K.L. Page. 1999. The Devil Made Me Do It: Replacing Corporate Directors' Veil of Secrecy with the Mantle of Stewardship. *San Diego Law Review* 36: 897–945.

Bauman, D. 2018. Who Foots Most of the Bill for Public Colleges? In 28 States, It's Students. *The Chronicle of Higher Education*. https://www.chronicle.com/article/Who-Foots-Most-of-the-Bill-for/242959.

Belluz, J. 2018. What the Dip in US Life Expectancy Is Really About: Inequality. https://www.vox.com/science-and-health-2018/1/9/16860994/life-expectancy-us-income-inequality.

Benjamin, J. 2018. Business Class. https://newrepublic.com/articles/148368/ideology-business-school.

Benmelech, E., N. Bergman, and H. Kim. 2018. Strong Employers and Weak Employees: How Does Employer Concentration Affect Wages? NBER Working Paper No. 24307, February.

Brynjolfsson, E., and T. Mitchell. 2017. What Can Machine Learning Do? Workforce Implications. *Science* 358 (6370): 1530–1534.

Burton, W.N., G. Pransky, D.J. Conti, C.-Y. Chen, and D.W. Edington. 1999. The Role of Health Risk Factors and Disease on Worker Productivity. *Journal of Occupational and Environmental Medicine* 46 (6): S38–S45.

Canals, J. 2010. Rethinking the Firm's Mission and Purpose. *European Management Review* 7 (4): 195–204.

Catalano, R., R.W. Novaco, and W. McConnell. 2002. Layoffs and Violence Revisited. *Aggressive Behavior* 28 (3): 233–247.

Channick, R. 2018. Office Napping Climbs out from Under the Desk and into High-Tech Pods. *Chicago Tribune*, July 5.

Chirumbolo, A., and J. Hellgren. 2003. Individual and Organizational Consequences of Job Insecurity: A European Study. *Economic and Industrial Democracy* 24 (2): 217–240.

Clarke, Thomas. 2005. Accounting for Enron: Shareholder Value and Stakeholder Interests. *Corporate Governance* 13 (5): 598–612.

Coleman, D., and R. Rowthorn. 2011. Who's Afraid of Population Decline? A Critical Examination of Its Consequences. *Population and Development Review* 37 (Suppl.): 217–248.

Conference Board. 2017. More Than Half of US Workers Are Satisfied with Their Jobs. https://www.conference-board.org/press/pressdetail.cfm?pressid=7184.

Crabtree, S. 2017. *Good Jobs, Great Workplaces Change the World*. Lincoln, NE: Gallup, December 19.

Dahl, M.S. 2011. Organizational Change and Employee Stress. *Management Science* 57 (2): 240–256.

Dahl, M.S., J. Nielsen, and R. Mojtabai. 2010. The Effects of Becoming an Entrepreneur on the Use of Psychotropics Among Entrepreneurs and Their Spouses. *Scandinavian Journal of Social Medicine* 38 (8): 857–863.

Datamation. (2018). Top 25 Artificial Intelligence Companies. https://www.datamation.com/applications/top-25-artificial-intelligence-companies.html.

Davis, G.F. 2009. *Managed by the Markets: How Finance Reshaped America*. Oxford, UK: Oxford University Press.

DeVoe, S.E., and J. House. 2012. Time, Money and Happiness: How Does Putting a Price on Time Affect Our Ability to Smell the Roses? *Journal of Experimental Social Psychology* 48 (2): 466–474.

Docherty, T. 2013. Margaret Thatcher's Legacy Divides British Higher Education. https://www.chronicle.com/blogs/worldwise/margaret-thatchers-legacy-divides-british-higher-educaton/32157.

Dunn, M., and J. Walker. 2016. Union Membership in the United States. https://www.bls.gov/spotlight/2016/union-membership-in-the-united-states/pdf/union-membership-in-the-united-states.pdf.

Dwyer-Lindgren, L., A. Bertozzi-Villa, R.W. Stubbs, C. Morozoff, J.P. Mackenbach, F.J. van Lenthe, A.H. Mokdad, and C.J.L. Murray. 2017. Inequalities in Life Expectancy Among US Counties, 1980 to 2014: Temporal Trends and Key Drivers. *JAMA Internal Medicine* 177 (7): 1003–1011.

Edelman. 2017. 2017 Edelman Trust Barometer Reveals Global Implosion of Trust. https://www.edelman.com/news/2017-edelman-trust-barometer-reveals-global-implosion.

Eliason, Marcus, and Donald Storrie. 2010. Job Loss is Bad for Your Health. Swedish Evidence on Cause-Specific Hospitalization Following Involuntary Job Loss. *Social Science and Medicine* 68 (8): 1396–1406.

Ferraro, F., J. Pfeffer, and R.I. Sutton. 2005. Economics Language and Assumptions: How Theories Can Become Self-Fulfilling. *Academy of Management Review* 30 (1): 8–24.

Freeman, R.E., K. Martin, and B. Parmar. 2007. Stakeholder Capitalism. *Journal of Business Ethics* 74 (4): 303–314.

Frey, C.B., and M. Osborne. (2013). The Future of Employment: How Susceptible Are Jobs to Computerization? Working Paper, Oxford Martin Programme on Technology and Employment, Oxford Martin School, University of Oxford, Oxford.

Ghoshal, S. 2005. Bad Management Theories Are Destroying Good Management Practices. *Academy of Management Learning and Education* 4 (1): 75–91.

Goh, J., J. Pfeffer, and S.A. Zenios. 2015a. Workplace Stressors and Health Outcomes: Health Policy for the Workplace. *Behavioral Science and Policy* 1 (1): 33–42.

Goh, J., J. Pfeffer, and S.A. Zenios. 2015b. Exposure to Harmful Workplace Practices Could Account for Inequality in Life Spans Across Different Demographic Groups. *Health Affairs* 34 (10): 1761–1768.

Goh, J., J. Pfeffer, and S.A. Zenios. 2016. The Relationship Between Workplace Stressors and Mortality and Health Costs in the United States. *Management Science* 62 (2): 608–628.

Golden, L. 2015. *Irregular Work Scheduling and Its Consequences*. Washington, DC: Economic Policy Institute.

Grandy, A.A., and R. Cropanzano. 1999. The Conservation of Resources Model Applied to Work-Family Conflict and Strain. *Journal of Vocational Behavior* 54 (2): 350–370.

Grunberg, L., S. Moore, and E.S. Greenerg. 2006. Managers' Reactions to Implementing Layoffs: Relationship to Health Problems and Withdrawal Behavior. *Human Resource Management* 45 (2): 159–178.

Gumbrell-McCormick, R., and R. Hyman. 2013. *Trade Unions in Western Europe: Hard Times, Hard Choices*. Oxford: Oxford University Press.

Hamilton Project. 2014. Labor Market Training Expenditures as a Percent of GDP in OECD Countries, 2011. http://www.hamiltonproject.org/cjarts/labor_market_training_expenditures_as_a_percent_of_gdp_in_oecd_countries_20#.

Harter, Jim. 2018. Dismal Employee Engagement Is a Sign of Global Mismanagement. http://www.gallup.com/workplace/231668/dismal-employee-engagement-sign-global-mismanagement.aspx.

Hyman, L. 2018. It's Not Technology That's Disrupting Our Jobs. https://www.nytimes.com/2018/08/18/opinion/technology/technology-gig-economy.html.

International Labour Organization. 2015. The Labour Share in G20 Economies. Report prepared for the G20 Employment Working Group, Antalya, Turkey, February 26–27.

Janlert, U., and A. Hammarstrom. 1992. Alcohol Consumption Among Unemployed Youths: Results from a Prospective Study. *British Journal of Addiction* 87 (5): 703–714.

Katz, L.F., and A.B. Krueger. 2016. The Rise and Nature of Alternative Work Arrangements in the United States, 1995–2015. NBER Working Paper No. 22667, March.

Kivimaki, M., J. Vahtera, J. Pentti, and J.E. Ferrie. 2000. Factors Underlying the Effect of Organisational Downsizing on Health of Employees: Longitudinal Cohort Study. *British Medical Journal* 320 (7240): 971–975.

Kochan, T.A., H.C. Katz, and R.B. McKersie. 1994. *The Transformation of American Industrial Relations*, 2nd ed. Ithaca, NY: ILR Press.

Krippner, G.R. 2005. The Financialization of the American Economy. *Socio-Economic Review* 3 (2): 173–208.

Leigh, J.P., and R. DeVogli. 2016. Low Wages as Occupational Health Hazards. *Journal of Occupational and Environmental Medicine* 58 (5): 444–447.

Mackey, J., and R. Sisodia. 2013. *Conscious Capitalism: Liberating the Heroic Spirit of Business*. Boston: Harvard Business Review Press.

Marmot, M. 2004. *The Status Syndrome: How Social Standing Affects Our Health and Longevity*. New York: Times Books.

McKinsey Global Institute. 2017. *Jobs Lost, Jobs Gained: What the Future of Work Will Mean for Jobs, Skills and Wages*. Washington, DC.

Mishel, L., E. Gould, and J. Rivens. 2015. *Wage Stagnation in Nine Charts*. Washington, DC: Economic Policy Institute.

Mortenson, T.G. 2012. *State Funding: A Race to the Bottom*. Washington, DC: American Council on Education. http://www.acenet.edu/the-presidency/columns-and-features/Pages/state-funding-a-race-to-the-bottom.aspx.

Pfeffer, J. 1998. *The Human Equation: Building Profits by Putting People First*. Boston: Harvard Business School Press.

Pfeffer, J. 2018. *Dying for a Paycheck: How Modern Management Harms Employee Health and Company Performance—And What We Can Do About It*. New York: Harper Business.

Pfeffer, J., and D.R. Carney. 2018. The Economic Evaluation of Time Can Cause Stress. *Academy of Management Discoveries* 4 (1): 74–93.

Piketty, Thomas. 2014. *Capital in the Twenty-First Century*. Cambridge, MA: Harvard University Press.

Ray, J. 2016. Fewer Than 200 Million Worldwide Have Great Jobs. http://news.gallup.com/opinion/gallup/191129/fewer0200-million-great-jobs.aspx.

Reich, R. 2014. The Rebirth of Stakeholder Capitalism? https://www.socialeurope.eu/stakeholder-capitallism.

Rojas, R. 2018. "Totally Preventable": How a Sick Woman Lost Electricity, and Her Life. https://nytimes.com/2018/07/13/nyregion/woman-dies-oxygen-machine-electricity-linda-daniels.html.

Schecter, A. 2017. UN Study Warns: Growing Economic Concentration Leads to "Rentier Capitalism." https://promarket.org/un-study-warns-growing-economic-centration-leads-rentier-capitalism/.

Schultz, A.B., and D.W. Edington. 2007. Employee Health and Presenteeism: A Systematic Review. *Journal of Occupational Rehabilitation* 17 (3): 547–579.

Strully, K.W. 2009. Job Loss and Health in the U.S. Labor Market. *Demography* 46 (2): 221–246.

*The Economist*. 2016. Automation and Anxiety: The Impact on Jobs. https://www.economist.com/news/special-report/06/25/automation-and-anxiety.

Thompson, D. 2013. Corporate Profits Are Eating the Economy. *The Atlantic*, March 4.

Tully, S. 2017. Corporate Profits Are Soaring, Here's Why It Can't Last. http://fortune.com/2017/12/07/corporate-earning-profit-boom-end/.

Wilkinson, R.G., and K.E. Pickett. 2006. Income Inequality and Population Health: A Review and Explanation of the Evidence. *Social Science and Medicine* 62 (7): 1768–1784.

Willis Towers Watson. 2017. *Health and Well-Being: 2017/2018 Global Benefits Attitudes Survey*. http://www.willistowerswatson.com.

Witters, Dan. 2018. *Record 21 States See Decline in Well-Being in 2017*. http://www.news.gallup.com.

World Economic Forum. 2010. *Enhancing Corporate Performance by Tackling Chronic Disease*. Geneva.

World Economic Forum. 2017. Future of Retail—Operating Models of the Future. https://www.weforum.org/projects/future-of-retail.

World Health Organization. 2018. Ageing and Health. http://www.who.int/news-room/fact-sheets/detail/ageing-and-health.

# 5

# Can Data Science Change Human Resources?

**Peter Cappelli, Prasanna Tambe and Valery Yakubovich**

## 5.1 Introduction

The fascination with technology, especially in business, belies the fact that the most important developments have been about ideas. As this relates to employees, the rise of scientific management and related developments such as the assembly line transformed business, and reactions to it, including the Human Relations movement, had powerful effects on the field of management. The development of industrial engineering after WWII and the associated effects on practices such as organization design and, through industrial psychology, on virtually all aspects of employment were profound. That led to another pushback against many of these new developments through fields like organizational development and quality of work life-programs.

The rise of the shareholder value approach to corporate governance turned human resource practices of all kinds into cost centers, and their inability to defend those practices on a cost-benefit basis led to sharp cutbacks in the hiring, training and development, and related practices. Even in many large organizations, employment practices have become decentralized and

P. Cappelli (✉) · P. Tambe
The Wharton School, University of Pennsylvania, Philadelphia, PA, USA
e-mail: cappelli@wharton.upenn.edu

V. Yakubovich
ESSEC Business School, Cergy-Pontoise, France

© The Author(s) 2020
J. Canals and F. Heukamp (eds.), *The Future of Management in an AI World*,
IESE Business Collection, https://doi.org/10.1007/978-3-030-20680-2_5

informal. For example, only about a third of US corporations check to see if their hiring practices produce good hires (Cappelli 2017). At the same time as practices have become less structured, there is increasing concern about bias in them, particularly against women but also against protected minorities.

Into this context sweeps the promise of artificial intelligence (AI) and the assertion that algorithms in particular can produce optimal decisions that eliminate human error and bias. The rhetoric mirrors almost exactly that of scientific management from the 1920s and its promise of objective, science-based processes for business that would be both more efficient and unbiased. The speed with which the business rhetoric in management moved from big data (BD) to machine learning (ML) to AI is staggering. So far, companies are struggling to make progress building data analytics capabilities: 41% of CEOs report that they are not at all prepared to make use of new data analytic tools, and only 4% say that they are "to a large extent" prepared (IBM 2018).

AI refers to a broad class of technologies that allow a computer to perform tasks that normally require human cognition. The focus here is narrower and on technologies that already exist, the sub-class of algorithms within AI that rely principally on the increased availability of data for prediction tasks. In the workforce and with respect to human resources, the appeal of more rational, objective decisions is strong because HR performs so many operations and so much money is spent on them. In the US economy as a whole, roughly 60% of all spending is on labor. In service industries, the figure is much higher (MLR 2017).

Around HR topics, interest in AI is almost all with data analytics and the ability to build algorithms, or decision rules, from data. Data analytics is making more progress in fields like marketing than others in business: While there are many questions to be answered there, they tend to be distinguished by their relative clarity, such as, what predicts who will buy a product or how changes in its presentation affect its sales. Outcomes are easily measured, are often already collected electronically by the sales process, and the number of observations—sales of a particular item across the country over time, e.g.—is very large, making the application of BD techniques feasible. Although marketing is not without its ethical conundrums, the idea that companies should be trying to sell more of their products is well-accepted as is the idea that business will attempt to influence customers to buy more.

The application of data science to human resources problems presents very different challenges. They range from practical to conceptual, including the fact that the nature of data science analyses when applied to people has serious conflicts with criteria societies typically see as important for making consequential decisions about individuals. All the ways in which management of employees is unlike marketing and other applications of analytics are relevant here.

A first problem is that HR outcomes are not straight-forward and maybe difficult to measure even if we had the willingness to do so. Consider what constitutes being a "good employee." There are many dimensions to that construct—do they do what they are told, do they act appropriately when not told what to do, are they creative when it is not clear what to do—and measuring all that with precision for most jobs is quite difficult. Performance appraisal scores, the most widely-used metric, have been roundly criticized for problems of validity and reliability as well as for bias, and many employers are giving them up altogether (Cappelli and Tavis 2017). Any reasonably complex job is interdependent with other jobs and therefore individual performance is hard to disentangle from group performance. It is possible to advance outcomes in your own job at the expense of the organization and other employees, for example (Pfeffer and Sutton 2006). It is possible to measure several aspects of job performance, but what it not possible is to create decision rules or algorithms that optimize several aspects of performance at once.

A second concern is that unlike many other organizational decisions, the outcomes of human resource decisions (such as who gets hired and fired) have such serious consequences for individuals and society that concerns about fairness—both procedural and distributive justice—are paramount. Elaborate legal frameworks constrain how employers must go about making those decisions. The decisions not only have to meet whatever criteria of optimization that data science might generate, they also must pass muster both as to the process and the outcomes with respect to fairness concerns.

A third set of concerns stems from the fact that employees are not machines, as the early human relations movement tried to teach scientific management optimizers. Employment outcomes lead to a range of complex socio-psychological concerns that exist among employees, such as personal worth and status, perceived fairness, and contractual and relational expectations, that affect organizational and individual performance. A decision that may be optimal for an algorithm that is perceived by employees as unfair can well lead to behavior that is suboptimal.

We consider these and other problems associated with the optimization approach and data science-based algorithms in the discussion below. To see them, it may be best to contrast the traditional approach to making HR decisions with the data science approach currently being advocated by many supporters of AI.

## 5.2    The New and the Old Approach to HR Decisions

What are now seen as "best practice" approaches to making human resource decisions comes from the post-WWII practices created by industrial psychologists and fitted to large, bureaucratic organizations where planning was a defining element. Although human resources contains an incredibly broad range of practices and procedures—everything from dress codes to compensation structures—we focus here on the smaller set of decisions where after the fact it is possible to observe whether the decision was right or wrong: did our recruiting practices turn up good candidates, did our selection practices produce good hires, and so forth. Table 5.1 includes the set of such common decisions.

In the traditional approach to a topic such as selection, arguably the central HR task today, human resource leaders would begin as a natural scientist might, by consulting the existing literature for hypotheses. They might find, for example, that prior success doing similar work, IQ, and a conscientious personality were associated with candidates who performed well on the job. They would then develop surveys and other tools to measure

**Table 5.1**   HR functions and prediction tasks

| HR operation | Prediction task |
| --- | --- |
| Recruiting—identifying possible candidates and persuading them to apply | Are we securing good candidates? |
| Selection—choosing which candidate should receive job offers | Are we offering jobs to those who will be the best employees? |
| On-boarding—bringing an employee into an organization | Which practices cause new hires to become useful faster? |
| Training | What interventions make sense for which individuals, and do they improve performance? |
| Performance management—identifying good and bad performance | Do our practices improve job performance? |
| Advancement—determining who gets promoted | Can we predict who will perform best in new roles? |
| Retention | Can we predict who is likely to leave and manage the level of retention? |
| Employee benefits | Can we identify which benefits matter most to employees to know what to give them and what to recommend when there are choices, and what are the effects of those benefits (e.g., do they improve recruiting and retention)? |

those attributes among candidates, collect the data, and make job offers to candidates who scored highest on those dimensions. In practice, many other factors would enter into the decision, and human judgment would inevitably be involved, e.g., how should we rate their past performance, given varying circumstances.

If we were thorough, we would not use the measures we created for at least the first round of hiring—that is, not hire on the basis of those measures—then see how the scores on those measures related to the actual performance of the people who were hired, typically using performance appraisal scores as a measure. If we were extremely thorough, we might then adjust our selection practices to rely more on the ones that performed best.

The contemporary world of data science comes at the topic of selection quite differently. It would begin at the end, with measures of the outcome desired. That might be a performance appraisal score as well. Then they would see what information we have on applicants who were hired. We would use as much of it as possible in a ML model: We cut the sample in half, let the model build an algorithm where the attributes of the applicants explained as much as possible about the variation in appraisal scores. Then we would try it out on the other half of the data to see how well our algorithm performed overall as a predictor of being a good employee.

The data science approach offers several advantages. It does not require waiting until after candidates are hired to see their job performance before seeing how well the algorithm predicts who will be a good hire. Unlike the traditional approach, which tells us how well individual measures predict, the data science algorithm gives us an overall assessment of how well everything taken together predicts a good hire. That overall fit is likely to be much better than what we achieved before using only a handful of criteria, and it may well turn up something that predicts well and that we did not use before.

Many observers have suggested that the use of algorithms eliminates much of the bias that otherwise exists in the hiring process. That is a fair statement at least to the extent that the measures used to build the algorithm, including the outcome measures, do not involve human judgment, more so if hiring managers are not given discretion as to how to use the algorithm's scores for candidates.

A limitation of the data science approach is that it requires a great many observations to build an accurate algorithm. ML techniques require a great deal of data, on many employees and a lot of measures about them, to produce an algorithm that predicts well. Many and perhaps most employers do not have enough observations to build sensible algorithms. The ML literature has shown that it takes larger data to improve predictions (Junqué de Fortuny et al. 2013). Smaller employers are unlikely to hire enough candidates to build an effective ML model. At least initially, the data scientists are also limited to the data already collected on applicants.

Other limitations have real teeth behind them. By law, for example, hiring, promotion, and other employment decisions in most countries cannot have an adverse impact (e.g., giving lower scores to women, minorities, or other protected groups) without showing that they predict actual job performance: even then they have to predict better than other practices that do not have an adverse impact. With the traditional approach, we could include gender, race, and other relevant factors in our models relating specific candidate attributes to job performance to see not only whether our practice overall had an adverse impact but also where it occurred. In the data science algorithms, it is extremely difficult to identify the effects of any one variable.

In 2018, Amazon discovered that its algorithm for hiring was having an adverse impact on women candidates (Meyer 2018). Even when the sex of applicants was not used as a criterion, attributes associated with women candidates, such as courses in "Women's Studies" caused them to be ruled out. Understanding exactly what specific measures were causing the lower scores for women was not immediately obvious, and the company stopped using its algorithm. Even if we could demonstrate a causal relationship between sex and job performance, we might well not trust an algorithm that says hire more white men because job performance itself may be a biased indicator, the attributes of the current workforce may be distorted by how we hired in the past (e.g., we hired few women), and both the legal system and social norms would create substantial problems for us if we did act on it.

## 5.3    Data and Its Limitations

One of the developments arguing for a data science approach to HR issues is the availability of new data. HR operations involve lots of separate tasks affecting the performance of the organization in important ways, and each includes specific offices, job roles, written instructions and guidelines to execute as well as the actual activities and interactions of all parties. These operations produce volumes of data, in the form of texts, recordings, and other artifacts. As operations move to the virtual space, many of these outputs are in the form of "digital exhaust," which is trace data on digital activities (e.g., online job applications, skills assessment) that may be used to build recruiting algorithms.

The downside of all this new data begins with extracting it from multiple databases, converted to a common format, and joined together before analysis can take place. This can represent an extraordinary amount of work and an enormous hurdle before one can perform the simplest calculations.

The complexity of HR phenomena created another problem in the form of specialized vendors who address only one task. It is very common for an employer to have a system from one vendor to track employee performance scores, from another for applicant tracking software, from a third for compensation and payroll data, and so forth. Arguably the biggest practical challenge in using data in human resources is simply database management, aggregating existing data so that it can be examined because the systems are rarely compatible.

To illustrate how rudimentary most of the existing database management efforts still are with HR operations, anecdotal evidence suggests that the majority of practitioners use Excel spreadsheets to organize and manage their HR data. Very few used more purpose-built tools such as Tableau that are common in data analytics. Software for bridging datasets and "data lakes" that can archive and access different data sets easily clearly represent a way forward, but they are costly to set up and make sense only for large data operations. So they remain under-used in the HR world.

The complexity inherent in many HR phenomena manifests itself in another data problem, and that is the validity and reliability of data. The most important source of complexity may be the fact that it is not easy to measure what constitutes a "good employee," given that job requirements are broad, monitoring of work outcomes is poor, and biases associated with assessing individual performance are legion. Moreover, complex jobs are interdependent with one another and thus one employee's performance is often inextricable from the performance of the group (Pfeffer and Sutton 2006). Without a clear definition of what it means to be a good employee, a great many HR operations face considerable difficulty in measuring performance, which is the outcome of driving many HR decisions.

If the data itself is not objective, the outcomes of the algorithms will not be objective, either. There is no list of "standard" variables that employers choose to gather and to retain through their HR operations as there might be in fields like accounting. Behavioral measures from attitudinal surveys, for example, vary considerably across organizations, measures of job performance differ, differences in cost accounting mean that the detail that employers have on the costs of different operations differs enormously (e.g., are training costs tracked, and if so, are they aggregated in ways that limit the ability to examine them?), and so forth.

When tackling the challenge of objective data, employers can benefit from the lessons drawn from fields like performance management:

Do not expect perfect measures of performance as they do not exist. It is better to choose reasonable measures and stick with them to see patterns and changes in results than to keep tinkering with systems to find the perfect measure.

- Aggregate information from multiple perspectives and over time. Digital HR tools allow for rapid real-time evaluations among colleagues using mobile devices, for example.
- Objective measures of performance outcomes based on ex ante determined goals and Key Performance Indicators are best, but they are never complete. Complement them with measures to capture less tangible outcomes, such as whether the employee fits into the company's culture, even if those measures are subjective, to prevent a situation where employees optimize on the few objective measures at the expense of everything else.
- Integrate HR data with the company's business and financial data to analyze the effects of HR practices and outcomes on business unit performance.

As noted above, employers rarely if ever have "big data" large enough to require specialized software to handle them. At the same time, not every problem requires a ML algorithm. There is usually more than enough data to address most practical questions, such as whether recruiting from the CEO's Alma Mater really produces better hires. The challenge is in designing an effective system of data management. This is why the Russian vendor IBS developed a product called "The diagnostic of a data ecosystem" whose goal is a comprehensive audit of all company data relevant to individual and team performance. The outcomes of the diagnostic are quantitative and qualitative evaluations of the available data sources and an action plan to make them available for data extraction, transfer, and load (ETL), which is the critical first step of any AI-assisted management.

The management literature has an important advantage over data science in articulating causal relationships, as opposed to predictions from correlations among observed variables in ML. The less data we have, the less we can learn from data analytics, and the more we need from theory and prior research to identify causal predictors of the outcome of interest. Building algorithms should require that our assumptions about what to include in the models are on the table for everyone to see and to persuade the other stakeholders in their accuracy, ultimately by using data and empirical analysis. The formulation of such assumptions often turns into a contest among stakeholders. This is a place where process formalization that presumes contributions from stakeholders is required.

Where a formal process reveals large disagreements as to causal factors, a way forward might include generating additional data from randomized experiments in order to test causal assumptions. Google became known for running experiments for all kinds of HR phenomena, from the optimal number of interviews per job candidate to the optimal size of the dinner plate in the cafeteria (Bock 2015). If discussions, experiments, and leadership's persuasion do not lead to a reasonable consensus on the causal model that generates the outcome of interest, AI-analyses are likely to be counterproductive and thus should be avoided until more or better data can be collected.

One attraction of using vendors is their ability to combine data from many employers, producing large enough data sets to generate their algorithms. Such approaches have long been used with standard paper-and-pencil selection tests, or as they are sometimes known now, pre-employment tests, such as those for sales roles. For instance, the company ADP, which handles outsourced payroll operations for thousands of companies, has been able to harness this scale to build predictive models of compensation and churn. Client companies are willing to make their data available for this exercise in return for access to the predictive models and benchmarked comparisons.

## 5.4   Can We Trust Employee Data?

In many and perhaps most areas of business and organizational life, we have reasonably high confidence that we can trust the validity of the data we produce: we trust our internal accounting numbers and our manufacturing quality figures. When it comes to human responses, however, that is not the case. Employees and candidates can shape or bias their responses in strategic ways depending on how they think the data will be used. Applicants, for example, are almost expected to tell employers what they think the employer wants to hear.

To get more valid data, organizations now search for alternative sources that might be viewed as more authentic, such as social media where they believe individuals are being more authentic. That data is now commonly used in hiring (e.g., looking for evidence of bad behavior, looking for evidence of fit) and to assess "flight risk" or retention problems (e.g., identifying updated LinkedIn profiles). The vendor Vibe, for example, uses natural language processing tools to gauge the tone of comments that employees post on internal chat boards, thereby helping to predict employee flight risk. Banks have tighter regulations requiring oversight of employees and have long analyzed email data for evidence of fraudulent behavior. They are now using it as well to identify other problems. For example, the appearance of terms like "harassment" in email traffic may well trigger an internal investigation to spot problems in the workplace.

Whether social media posts are more authentic than other sources of information is far from clear, of course. (Does the average person spend as much time on vacation as their Facebook posts would suggest?) The nature of such data will change quickly as soon as individuals recognize that employers are monitoring those entries: Once I believe potential employers will see my social media posts, down go the photos of Spring Break parties and up go those of me tutoring students. Efforts to use computer games to assess candidates is yet another effort to obtain authentic data in this case where the candidates do not necessarily know how to spin their responses. But they are already getting help from businesses like the JobTestPrep company that helps potential candidates for jobs at Lloyds Bank figure out how to score well on Lloyds' selection game.[1] Getting authentic data on applicants will remain a challenge because of the ability of candidates to game such efforts.

Then we have issues of privacy. Some employers see no problem in analyzing data from their own systems, such as email; others see that as appropriate as long as the results are anonymized, for example, generating average assessments across the workforce as a whole. Data persistence (how long will my survey responses be retained), data repurposing (will my job preferences be used as part of an algorithm to assess promotion prospects), and data spillovers (will my message about a colleague affect her performance assessment) (Tucker 2017). Here employers have to account for governments' regulations of privacy issues, such as "the right to be forgotten" or the EU's General Data Protection Regulation (GDPR). The former states that business has to satisfy individuals' demands to delete their digital traces after some period of time; the latter is a comprehensive treatment of all the aspects of data privacy in the digital age (www.eugdpr.org). Whether the general public and job candidates will be as tolerant of employer monitoring as the employers are is also an open question.

---

[1]See, e.g., https://www.jobtestprep.co.uk/lloydsbank.

In terms of technological solutions to the issue of data privacy, computer scientists are actively working on privacy-preserving data analytic methods that rely on the notion of differential privacy in building algorithms. Here, data is randomized during the collection process, which leads to "learning nothing about an individual while learning useful information about the population" (Dwork and Roth 2014: 5). Noise can be added to responses to make them hard to trace back to individuals, and while analysts do not know whose data are used in the analysis and whose data are replaced by noise, but they do know the noise generating procedure and thus can estimate the model anyway.

## 5.5   Building Algorithms

As noted above, algorithms in data science are typically generated by ML where software finding patterns in data where information we know is used to make a prediction about something we do not know. When we refer to ML in this context, it means that the software is observing patterns in the data from the past that humans could not easily find. In traditional forecasting, the statistician would use theory and prior research to identify the variables used in an equation to explain past occurrences and then extrapolate from that to the future. In ML, the software itself takes whatever variables are available and arranges them in whatever ways best map onto past occurrences. Unlike forecasting, the predictions are more tightly bound around yes/no questions—will the candidate be a good employee, will they leave this year, and so forth. Then new observations are "scored" or judged by the algorithm as to the probability they will be associated with the occurrence.

"Algorithmic management" goes a step further in using algorithms to guide incentives and other tools to nudge—incentivize or persuade—workers in the direction their client (Lee et al. 2015) or employer (e.g., Netessine and Yakubovich 2012) wants them to act. IBM, for example, uses algorithms to advise employees on what training makes sense for them to take, based on the experiences of similar employees; the vendor Quine uses the career progression of previous employees to make recommendations to client's employees about which career moves make sense for them. Vendors such as Benefitfocus develop customized recommendations for employee benefits, much in the same way that Netflix recommends content based on consumer preferences or Amazon recommends products based on purchasing or browsing behavior.

An ML algorithm for predicting which candidates to hire may well perform better than anything an employer has used before because building a good overall prediction is precisely and only what it is designed to do. This is in contrast to traditional social science-based models, which were designed to apply knowledge about established predictors, such as IQ, to decisions about who to hire and do so one predictor at a time. A typical validity exercise for current hiring practices is designed simply to find whether there is a statistically significant relationship between each measure being used as a selection criterion and the relevant outcome measure. A reasonable complaint about traditional HR is that it has not improved much at all in the advice it offers employers over time, and the advice in absolute terms is not that good. On hiring, for example, the predictors advocated in that research, such as personality and IQ scores, predict so little of job performance (a typical validity coefficient of 0.30, for example, translates to explaining nine percent of the variance in performance) that it created an enormous opportunity for data analytics to do better. It will because its goal is just to predict and to build one overall model using everything available to do so. It is not limited to a small number of one-at-a-time results based on prior research findings.

Because clients rarely have data on employee performance in which they feel confident, because they often discard data on applicants not hired, and because they want to save time, a common approach in the vendor community is to build an algorithm based on the attributes of a client firm's "best performers" rather than looking at the variation across all employees on the performance measure. Consider, for example, the vendor HireVue that helps clients conduct video interviews. Part of its offering now includes controversial algorithms based on facial expressions captured on those videos. The algorithms are developed or "trained" on data from the facial expressions of the top performers at the client firm, and job candidates are assessed based on how similar their expressions are to those of the algorithm.

Is it possible that facial expressions actually predict job performance? Social scientists may find examples like this absurd because there is no reason to expect such a relationship. The ML models and the data scientists behind them, of course, do not care whether we know what the reason might be for such a relationship or whether it corresponds with what we know from research on humans. They only care if there is such a statistical relationship.

The fundamental problem with this approach, though, is that it "selects on the dependent variable" by examining only the attributes of those who are successful, not what differentiates good performers from less good. The algorithm may well capture attributes of good performers accurately, but it is not identifying whether those attributes are truly distinct from those of other performers. Good performers and bad performers may have the same facial expressions, but the algorithm will never know that because it never examined the bad performers.

A different problem is that using an algorithm or indeed any criteria in hiring makes it difficult to tell going forward whether that criteria or decision rule is still generating the desired outcome because of the sample selection problem it generates: We have ruled out candidates who do not fit the algorithm, so we cannot see whether they might now perform better, say under a different company strategy. The only way to avoid this problem is to on occasion turn of the algorithm, to not use it to hire at least for a time, in order to hire some candidates that do not fit its criteria and see if now they perhaps perform better.

This problem that selection based on the hiring criteria prevents learning about that criteria holds for any criterion, of course. With the more standard hiring practice of using only a few selection criteria, it is possible to turn them off one-at-a-time to see the effect, for example, of recruiting from a different set of schools. An algorithm generated by ML operates as one entity rolling many variables together into an overall model. As a result, it is much more difficult to turn off just one criterion.

Selection based on algorithms or any consistent set of criteria can also induce a type of spurious relationship among workers' characteristics called the collider effect in epidemiology and now in data science (Pearl 2018). It occurs when samples are selected in ways that restrict the range of the variables, sometimes known as "range restriction" in psychology. An employer who selects new hires based on college grades and conscientiousness tests, for example, might well find that candidates who have neither good grades nor good scores on conscientious tests are not hired. So when the employer looks for a relationship between college grades and conscientiousness among its employees, it finds the relationship is negative, even though in the broader population the relationship is positive.

More generally, this selection process can reduce the range on variables of interest, making it more difficult to find true effects. For example, if we only hire candidates with good college grades, it may be difficult to identify a true, positive relationship between grades and job performance because the variance of grades in the sample is too limited to identify that relationship. Range restriction also happens when applicants self-select into a firm's pool of applicants, the first step in the well-known "attraction-selection-attrition" framework (Schneider 1987). Algorithms that are based solely on data from the current workforce create this phenomenon, which is not a problem if properly understood.

For example, when the largest Russian bank "Sberbank" introduced SAP's Success Factors, it made a major effort to build a predictive model of a high-performing employee. Despite the availability of detailed records of employees' performance evaluations, training and education records, career moves, socio-demographic characteristics, and so on, a reliable model did not materialize (Fukolova 2018). Instead of continually searching for better data and model, one might consider whether the current selection process correctly filters out potentially low-performers and thus the remaining range of the observed performance factors is restricted and non-predictive.

Several aspects of the modeling process per se can also be challenging. For instance, there is more than one measure of "fit" with the data. A well-known case of this problem concerned the use of a ML algorithm by judges in Broward County, Florida to determine whether a person charged with a crime should be released on bail. The algorithm was trained based on data about whether parolees violated the terms of their parole. The challenge in the data is that the majority of the individuals in the dataset were white, and so the algorithm was driven largely by information about whites. The algorithm predicted the rate of recidivism correctly at an equal rate for whites and blacks, but when it did not predict accurately, it was far more likely to over predict for blacks than for whites (Spielkamp 2017). The problem is that the algorithm cannot optimize more than one measure of fit.

## 5.6   What to Do: Identifying and Addressing Challenges

Much of the improvement we can expect from data science-based algorithms in the workplace is simply that they structure the decision-making process. We know that when hiring managers use their own judgment, they make worse decisions (Hoffman et al. 2015), which is not surprising as they rarely are trained on how to hire. It does not require using algorithms to make this happen, of course. Evidence suggests, though, the algorithms can do a better job of assessing who will advance through the hiring process than do hiring managers (Cowgill 2017). How much of that is the result of simply standardizing the process is not clear.

One possible selection instrument of a standardized hiring process is job simulation. Because of complex logistics and high costs, it has been traditionally reserved for strategic high-stakes jobs and administered by specialized evaluation centers. AI and related technologies, such as virtual reality, make job simulations more realistic, less expensive, and highly scalable. Their use in hiring would yield some measure of potential performance for all job candidates and thus drastically reduce, if not eliminate completely, the collider (range restriction) effect.

An alternative way to eliminate the collider effect is by using selection algorithms trained on larger pool of candidates for related jobs in the same industry. Such algorithms take into account candidates' labor market opportunities: where they applied, what offers they received, and in principle, how they performed on the job. EdGE (https://edgenetworks.in) implemented this approach for large Indian IT companies using extensive data from Indian recruitment firms. Tokyo-based Institution for a Global Society (IGS: www.i-globalsociety.com) assembled its own BD on thousands of students from Japanese universities who apply for positions at IGS's clients, major corporations of Japan. We are not aware of a similar solution for the US.

Within the HR context, there are numerous questions related to fairness. One of the most obvious of these is the recognition that any algorithm is likely to be backward looking. The presence of past discrimination in the data used to build a hiring algorithm, for example, is likely to lead to a model that may disproportionately select on white males. Actions using those algorithms risk reproducing the demographic diversity—or lack thereof—that exists in the historical data. The biased outcomes of the Amazon hiring algorithm noted above was caused by exactly this common problem: because fewer women were hired in the past and because men had higher performance scores, the algorithm was selecting out women—even when sex is not in the candidate dataset, selecting out attributes of women, such as taking "women's studies" courses.

In the HR context, there is a wide-spread belief that evaluations of candidates and employees are shaped heavily by the biases of the evaluator, most commonly as related to demographics. Algorithms can reduce that bias by standardizing the application of criteria to outcomes and by removing information that is irrelevant to performance but that might influence hiring manager decisions, such as the race and sex of candidates (Cowgill 2018). Factors that may seem inappropriate may nonetheless improve the predictive power of the algorithms, such as the social status of one's alma mater. How we balance the trade-off between appropriateness and predictive power is an open question.

The fact that employment decisions are so important to individual candidates/employees and to broader society has led to an extensive legal framework designed to guide those decisions. While the regulations differ by country, it is not uncommon for a large percentage of the labor force to be protected by them. Discrimination refers to actions taken based on one's demographic attributes, and in practice that is measured by "adverse impact," evidence that any employer's decisions have a lower incidence of good outcomes (e.g., hires and promotions) and/or a higher incidence of bad outcomes (e.g., dismissals) than the base rate we would expect from their distribution in the relevant population (see Walsh 2013 Part II for details on the relevant US legal requirements).

With respect to the actions that could be based on algorithms—those that attempt to predict future outcomes—the only defense against evidence of adverse impact is first to show that the decisions taken actually do predict the desired outcomes and second to show that no other process for making decisions would produce at least as accurate predictions with less adverse impact. It is a considerable analytic task for most algorithms simply to know which attributes might be generating adverse impact, which is necessary in order to tell whether that impact can be defended.

As noted above, structuring decisions like hiring and promotion the way algorithms do and taking decision-making away from hiring managers may well reduce bias in those processes. But because algorithms reduce the process to one criterion with little in the way of judgment calls, it is also easier to see any bias that does exist. Will employers find it worthwhile to take on the possible greater risk of legal action in order to reduce total bias? So far, we have no evidence to tell.

If we return to the parole violation example above, it would seem that a better approach to building an algorithm to predict parole violations would be to generate a separate one for blacks and for whites. In the context of HR decisions, that might seem appealing as well, to generate separate hiring algorithms, for example, for men and women. While there may be challenges in using such algorithms (e.g., how do we compare the scores of these two different models), the legal frameworks will not allow us to treat these demographic groups differently.

These examples raise the more general concern about fundamental tradeoffs between accuracy and fairness that must be confronted in any HR machine learning implementation (Loftus et al. 2018). Consider how the role of context changes our judgments. It seems perfectly acceptable to use algorithms to make decisions that essentially reward employees—who to promote, who to hire in the first place. But what about the inevitable use of algorithms to punish employees? An algorithm that predicts future contributions will most certainly be available at some point to make layoff decisions. How about one that predicts who will steal from the company and should be let go before they do?

Here we face a dilemma. The Utilitarian notion of advancing the collective good might well argue for using predictive algorithms to weed out problems and costly employees. When the goal is simply optimizing the success of a business, making decisions about employees based on the probability of their actions seems sensible. The Kantian deontological position, on the other hand, suggests that individuals should be judged based on their own actions. Western societies and their legal systems all value this approach. It can be highly objectionable using this framework to make decisions that reward or punish individuals based on attributes that are only associated with desired behaviors especially if those attributes are simply probabilistic forecasts of future behavior. Firing an employee because they have attributes associated with those who have embezzled in the past, for example, would generally be seen as objectionable.

We see two approaches that can make progress on at least some of the above issues. The first and arguably most comprehensive approach is causal discovery, that is, identifying in the data those variables that cause the outcome of interest, such as good job performance, rather than those that might simply be associated with it. Consider the question as to whether the social status of an applicant's alma mater predicts their job performance if they were hired. From the perspective of generating algorithms, it is enough if the social status measure contributes to the overall accuracy of an algorithm predicting job performance. Traditional statistics, on the other hand, might ask whether the relationship between social status and job performance is true on its own—not just as part of a more complex algorithm—and whether it was causal. Establishing causation is a much more difficult exercise.

Demonstrably causal algorithms are more defendable in the court of law and thus address at least some legal constraints discussed above. They are fairer due to the explicit specification of causal paths from socio-demographic characteristics to performance, which allows individuals to be acknowledged for their performance-enhancing characteristics (e.g., grit or intrinsic motivation) independently of group membership (e.g., the alma mater status) and to intervene in order to compensate for their socio-demographic disadvantages (e.g., to create a strong support network that graduates from top schools get by default). As a result, employees "minimize or eliminate the causal dependence on factors outside an individual's control, such as their perceived race or where they were born" (Loftus et al. 2018: 7) and thus are treated as individuals rather than group members. Individual fairness, in this case, replaces group fairness.

Computer algorithms can assist in causal discovery by searching for causal diagrams that fit the available data. Such algorithms are being actively developed; their interpretation does not require advanced training but does require data about possible causes and their confounders (Malinsky and Dansk 2017). When data are incomplete, one can test for the causality of specific factors in ways common to traditional social science research, such as field experiments.

## 5.7    The Limits to Optimization

Our second approach takes a different tact than trying to produce more accurate outcomes. Instead of boosting the low predictive power of many HR algorithms with measures that are not related causally to the outcomes, we propose acknowledging that these outcomes are essentially random (Denrell et al. 2015; Liu and Denrell 2018). When we have great difficulty determining which candidates will succeed in promotions, for example, rather than asserting that the process is objective (even if we cannot explain why), we might instead take a random draw among candidates with the relevant prerequisites.

Research shows that employees perceive random processes as fair in determining complex and thus uncertain outcomes (Lind and Van den Bos 2002). "Flipping a coin" has a long history as a device for settling disputes, from ties in election outcomes to allocating fishing rights (see Stone 2011). Randomization is especially attractive where there are "losers" in the outcomes and when they remain in the organization or relationship, such as employees who are not selected for promotion. Telling them that the decision literally was made on a coin toss is much easier to bear than either telling them it was a close choice (you were almost as good, on the one hand, but something small could have changed the outcome) or that it was not close (you were not almost as good, but there is nothing you could have done that would have mattered).

Closely related to the notion of fairness is explainability, in this case the extent to which employees understand the criteria used for data analytics-based decisions. A simple seniority decision rule—more senior workers get preference over less senior ones—is easy to understand and feels objective even if we do not always like its implications. A ML algorithm based on a weighted combination of 10 performance-related factors is much more difficult to understand, especially when employees make inevitable comparisons with each other and cannot see the basis of different outcomes. (Professors who have to explain to students why their grade is different than that of their friend who they believe wrote a similar answer are familiar with this problem.) Algorithms get more accurate the more complicated they are, but they also become more difficult to understand and explain.

A well-known example of the importance of explainability to users comes from the Oncology application of IBM Watson. This application met considerable resistance from oncologists because it was difficult to understand how the system was arriving at its decisions. When the application disagreed with the doctor's assessment, this lack of transparency made it difficult for medical experts to accept and act upon the recommendations that the system produced (Bloomberg 2018). Especially in "high stakes" contexts, such as those that affect people's lives—or their careers—explainability is likely to become imperative for the successful use of ML technologies. We expect major progress in this area in the coming years, due to a wave of investment from the commercial and government sectors geared toward explainable AI. For instance, the US Defense Advanced Research Projects Agency (DARPA), known for its successful funding of path-breaking research in IT, has just launched a major initiative on explainable artificial intelligence (XAI) with deliverables, software toolkits, and computational models, expected by 2021 (https://www.darpa.mil/program/explainable-artificial-intelligence).

Having decisions made by an algorithm, even if it is more objective than a decision by a human, has its own drawbacks. To illustrate, it is widely believed that the relationship with one's supervisor is crucial to the performance of their subordinates and that the quality of that relationship depends on social exchange: "I as supervisor look after you, and you as subordinate perform your job well." Even when employees have little commitment to their employer as an organization, they may feel commitment to their supervisor. How is this exchange affected when decisions that had been made by the supervisor are now made by or even largely informed by an algorithm rather than a supervisor?

If my supervisor assigns me to work another weekend this month, something I very much do not want to do, I might do it without complaint if I think my supervisor has otherwise been fair to me. I might even empathize with the bind my supervisor is in when having to fill the weekend shift. If not, I might well go complain to her and expect some better treatment in the future. When my work schedule is generated by software, on the other hand, I have no goodwill built up with that program, and I cannot empathize with it. Nor can I complain to it, and I may well feel that I will not catch a break in scheduling in the future. When retailer Belk's workers raised such concerns, the company allowed store managers to edit computer-generated schedules in order to accommodate workers' personal and social needs. Surprisingly, the schedules' efficiency increased together with workers' satisfaction (Bernstein et al. 2014). More generally, this example shows that introducing ML algorithms as enabling rather than controlling managers and workers is a preferred path, in particular, while the challenges to their use identified in the paper remain salient.

On the other hand, there may be occasions where decisions are easier to accept when made by an algorithm than when made by a human, especially when those decisions have negative consequences for us. Uber riders, for example, respond negatively to surge pricing increases when they perceive that they are set by a human (trying to exploit them) as opposed to by an algorithm. Experimental evidence suggests that willingness to accept and use algorithms depends in part on how they update to deal with mistakes (Dietvorst et al. 2014).

Related to these issues is the engagement in decisions that individuals have that is otherwise lost with the shift to algorithms. If algorithms take over hiring and supervisors play no role in the process, for example, will they be as committed to the new hires as if they had made the hiring decisions?

## 5.8    Discussion and Conclusions

While general-purpose AI is still a long shot in any domain of human activity, the speed of progress toward specialized AI systems in health care, automobile industry, social media, advertising, and marketing is considerable. Far less progress has been made in issues around the management of employees even on the first step of the AI path, which is decisions guided by algorithms. While the challenges identified in this paper persist, we advocate a gradual implementation of new technologies that starts with evaluating, experimenting, and changing HR and general management processes rather than looking for workers' characteristics that magically identify best performers. Reducing costs through the elimination of ineffective instruments and automating others can be a realistic short-term target while substantial gains in hires' quality or employees' performance should be pursued more long-term.

To what extent the changes we suggest require a restructuring of the HR function is an important question. Certainly, HR leaders need to understand and facilitate the Data Generation and ML stages of the AI Life Cycle. The integration of HR data with business and financial data should allow an HR Department to quantify in monetary terms its contribution to the company's bottom line.

Line managers will have to refresh their skill set as well. For them, AI should imply "augmented intelligence," an informed use of workforce analytics' insights in decision-making. The literature on evidence-based management proposes a Bayesian approach to systematically updating managerial beliefs with new information (Barends and Rousseau 2018). We consider it a helpful departure point for AI-management as well.

Our takeaways would have been incomplete without some speculation about the future of management research. At the first glance, it appears to be under multiple threats from computer and data scientists, stringent privacy and confidentiality regulations, and companies' and numerous consultants' homegrown expertise in data analytics. We believe that the rumors of management research's demise are grossly exaggerated for a few reasons: First, if we are right about the unavoidable return to causal modeling, the domain and theory expertise will become critical again. Second, external consultants and even companies' own data scientists have financial and career stakes in building highly-predictive models whether the data warrant them or not. Academic research is not immune to various methods of "massaging" data to get publishable results, such as p-hacking (rerunning various models until some statistically significant effects appear even though they might be just a noise) and HARKing (proposing hypotheses after the results are obtained) (e.g., Shrout and Rodgers 2018; Spellman 2015). This said, researchers are not under pressure to maximize their models' predictive power; in fact, our models of people's behavior in organizations rarely explain more than 50% of the observed variance. If we also keep in mind that papers in top journal have to meet some rigorous theoretical standards and companies get the results for free, academic research looks like a useful component of an emerging system of checks and balances around the quest for AI in HR management.

The tension between the logic of efficiency and of appropriateness affects most organizational action (March and Simon 1993). In the case of HR, the drive for efficiency and concerns about fairness do not always align. We hope that the conceptual and practical insights in this paper will move AI-management in HR forward on both counts, those of efficiency and appropriateness.

# References

Barends, Eric, and Denise M. Rousseau. 2018. *Evidence-Based Management: How to Use Evidence to Make Better Organizational Decisions*. London: Kogan Page.

Bernstein, Ethan, Saravanan Kesavan, and Bradley Staats. 2014. How to Manage Scheduling Software Fairly. *Harvard Business Review*, December. https://hbr.org/2014/09/how-to-manage-scheduling-software-fairly.

Bloomberg, J. 2018. Don't Trust Artificial Intelligence? Time to Open the AI Black Box. *Forbes*, November 27. Last accessed at https://www.forbes.com/sites/jasonbloomberg/2018/09/16/dont-trust-artificial-intelligence-time-to-open-the-ai-black-box/#577a14153b4a.

Bock, Laslo. 2015. *Work Rules! Insights from Inside Google That Will Transform How You Live and Lead.* London: Hachette Book Group.

Cappelli, Peter. 2017. There's No Such Thing as Big Data in HR. *Harvard Business Review*, June.

Cappelli, Peter, and Anna Tavis. 2017. The Performance Management Revolution. *Harvard Business Review*, November.

Denrell, Jerker, Christina Fang, and Chengwei Liu. 2015. Change Explanations in Management Science. *Organization Science* 26 (3): 923–940.

Cowgill, Bo. 2017. The Labor Market Effects of Hiring Through Machine Learning. Working Paper.

Cowgill, Bo. 2018. Bias and Productivity in Humans and Algorithms: Theory and Evidence from Résumé Screening. Working Paper.

Dietvorst, Berkeley, Joseph P. Simmons, and Cade Massey. 2014. Algorithm Aversion: People Erroneously Avoid Algorithms After Seeing Them Err. *Journal of Experimental Psychology: General* 144 (1): 114.

Dwork, Cynthia, and Aaron Roth. 2014. The Algorithmic Foundations of Differential Privacy. *Foundations and Trends in Theoretical Computer Science* 9 (3–4): 211–407.

Fukolova, Julia. 2018. Frames Under the Numbers. *Harvard Business Review*, Russian edition. https://hbr-russia.ru/management/upravlenie-personalom/776169.

Hoffman, Mitchell, Lisa B. Kahn, and Danielle Li. 2015. Discretion in Hiring. NBER Working Paper 21709. http://www.nber.org/papers/w21709.

IBM. 2018. Unplug from the Past. 19th Global C-Suite Study. IBM Institute for Business Value.

Junqué de Fortuny, E., D. Martens, and F. Provost. 2013. Predictive Modeling with Big Data: Is Bigger Really Better? *Big Data* 1 (4): 215–226.

Lee, M.K., D. Kusbit, E. Metsky, and L. Dabbish. 2015. Working with Machines: The Impact of Algorithmic, Data-Driven Management on Human Workers. In *Proceedings of the 33rd Annual ACM SIGCHI Conference: 1603–1612*, ed. B. Begole, J. Kim, K. Inkpen, and W. Wood, ACM Press, New York, NY.

Lind, E. Allan, and Kees Van den Bos. 2002. When Fairness Works: Toward a General Theory of Uncertainty Management. *Research in Organizational Behavior* 24: 181–223.

Liu, Chengwei, and Jerker Denrell. 2018. Performance Persistence Through the Lens of Chance Models: When Strong Effects of Regression to the Mean Lead to Non-Monotonic Performance Associations. Working paper.

Loftus, Joshua R., Chris Russel, Matt J. Kusner, and Ricardo Silva. 2018. Causal Reasoning for Algorithmic Fareness. arXiv:1805.05859.

Malinsky, Daniel, and David Danks. 2017. Causal Discovery Algorithms: A Practical Guide. *Philosophy Compass*. https://doi.org/10.1111/phc3.12470.

March, James, and Herbert Simon. 1993. *Organizations*. Oxford: Blackwell.

Meyer, David. 2018. Amazon Reportedly Killed an AI Recruitment System Because It Couldn't Stop the Tool from Discriminating Against Women. *Fortune*, October 10. http://fortune.com/2018/10/10/amazon-ai-recruitment-bias-women-sexist.

Monthly Labor Review. 2017. Estimating the U.S. Labor Share. *Bureau of Labor Statistics*, February. https://www.bls.gov/opub/mlr/2017/article/estimating-the-us-share.htm.

Netessine, Serguei, and Valery Yakubovich. 2012. The Darwinian Workplace. *Harvard Business Review* 90 (5): 25–28.

Pearl, Judea. 2018. *The Book of Why: The New Science of Cause and Effect*. New York: Basic Books.

Pfeffer, Jeffrey, and Robert I. Sutton. 2006. *Hard Facts, Dangerous Half-Truths and Total Nonsense: Profiting from Evidence-Based Management*. Boston: Harvard Business Review Press.

Schneider, Benjamin. 1987. The People Make the Place. *Personnel Psychology* 40 (3): 437–453.

Shrout, P.E., and J.L. Rodgers. 2018. Psychology, Science and Knowledge Construction: Broadening Perspectives from the Replication Crisis. *Annual Review of Psychology* 69: 487–510.

Spellman, B. 2015. A Short (Personal) Future History of Revolution 2.0. *Perspectives on Psychological Science* 10: 886–899.

Spielkamp, Michael. 2017. Inspecting Algorithms for Bias. *MIT Technology Review*, June 12. https://www.technologyreview.com/s/607955/inspecting-algorithms-for-bias/.

Stone, Peter. 2011. *The Luck of the Draw: The Role of Lotteries in Decision Making*. Oxford: Oxford University Press.

Tucker, Catherine. 2017. Privacy, Algorithms, and Artificial Intelligence. In *The Economics of Artificial Intelligence: An Agenda*, ed. Ajay K. Agrawal, Joshua Gans, and Avi Goldfarb, 423–437. Chicago: University of Chicago Press. http://www.nber.org/chapters/c14011.

Walsh, David J. 2013. *Employment Law for Human Resource Practice*. Mason, OH: South-Western CENGAGE Learning.

# 6

# University, Education, Technology, and the Future of Work

## Bernard Yeung

## 6.1  Introduction

In the second decade of the twenty-first century, people face a future that is filled with unpredictable volatility and disruption of work, which some have called the Fourth Industrial Revolution. On the one hand, we are excited about the potential in efficiency gains and economic growth. On the other, we are feeling widespread economic anxiety that surpasses previous rounds of Industrial Revolutions. The economic anxiety raises doubts about the value of university education, particularly the value of business school.

Historically, institutions of higher learning played a critical role in society's development from pre-Renaissance to the Industrial Revolution. Universities promoted critical thinking and scholastic values. They bred advancements in science, applied science, and technologies. They trained students to meet society's needs. Industrialization and universities developed overtime a symbiotic relationship: industrialization raised universities' market value and universities developed research and trained students to support industrialization. Even in the era of the Fourth Industrial Revolution, the fundamental role of universities—advance values, research, and train students—should remain.

In this age of rapid technological evolution, universities and business schools need to stick to the basic more than ever: advance useful research

B. Yeung (✉)
National University of Singapore, Singapore, Singapore
e-mail: byeung@nus.edu.sg

© The Author(s) 2020
J. Canals and F. Heukamp (eds.), *The Future of Management in an AI World*,
IESE Business Collection, https://doi.org/10.1007/978-3-030-20680-2_6

and develop students who can meet society's needs while keeping a sense of purpose in serving people. Still, there are some needed tweaking. In the future of work, technology creates a fusion of people and intelligent machines like in futuristic movies. Universities may need to train all students like doctoral students. We need to emphasize in our education principle literacy, data literacy, technology literacy, and humanistic literacy (see Aoun 2017). We also now need to emphasize the inclination to ask meaningful questions and to practice critical thinking as well as life-long learning. Moreover, we need to inculcate in them a sense of constructive dissatisfaction—see that the world could be better and take up the responsibility to make good things happen.

The next section discusses universities' role in development, focusing on that industrialization and rapid growth in universities went hand in hand in the twentieth century. The value of universities education might have inadvertently shifted more from its intrinsic component toward its transactional component. Section 6.3 describes two trends resulting from the rounds of Industrial Revolutions—aging and digitalization—which have led to a high level of economic anxiety for all age classes. The result is some justified doubts about the value of education. In Sect. 6.4, we propose responses in facing the future. Conclusions to follow.

## 6.2   Development, the Modern World and Universities' Pursuits

Human beings' curiosity and relentless effort to defy constraints drive development. Yet, economic growth, as measured by per capita GDP, was visibly flat for thousands of years and did not take off until the eighteenth century (e.g., see Fig. 6.1). This puzzling long journey would not have a simple answer. Still, as an academic, my belief is that accumulation of knowledge and widespread education forms the backbone of our development; we did not grow before that happened.

### 6.2.1   The Renaissance and Being Educated in Universities

Our development journey might have started with the Renaissance period, which started at the beginning of the fourteenth century and lasted till the end of the sixteenth century. History.com describes the Renaissance as:

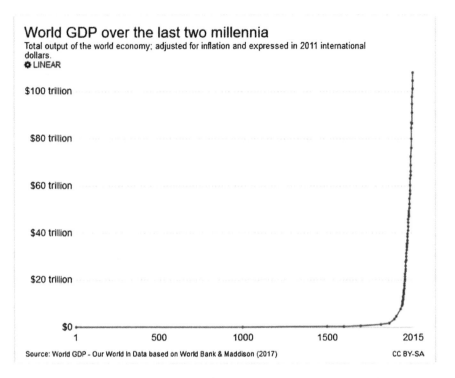

**World GDP over the last two millennia**
Total output of the world economy; adjusted for inflation and expressed in 2011 international dollars.
✿ LINEAR

Source: World GDP - Our World In Data based on World Bank & Maddison (2017)                CC BY-SA

**Fig. 6.1** Economic growth (*Note* This figure was originally published open access under a CC-BY Creative Commons Attribution 4.0 license. *Source* Max Roser [2018])

a fervent period of European cultural, artistic, political and economic "rebirth" following the Middle Ages…. It promoted the rediscovery of classical philosophy, literature and art. Some of the greatest thinkers, authors, statesmen, scientists and artists in human history thrived during this era, while global exploration opened up new lands and cultures to European commerce.[1]

During the Renaissance period, the spread of printing devices helped the accumulation and spreading of knowledge. Reportedly, China started printing in the seventh century and paper printing took off in the ninth century. Printing capability spread around the world. Block printing was common in Europe by 1300, the beginning of the Renaissance period. As the ability to print spread, so did education.[2]

---

[1]See https://www.history.com/topics/renaissance/renaissance.

[2]"Printing" is not a one-time innovation; it developed over time and probably originated from multiple locations. It is, however, quite widely recognized that the invention of the Gutenberg printing press in 1450, allowed for improved communication throughout Europe and for ideas to spread more quickly. See https://www.history.com/topics/renaissance/renaissance.

While the Renaissance was in progress, the Black Death spread around the world in the fourteenth century. The awful disease reportedly killed 30–60% of Europe's population and slashed an estimated world population from 450 million to 350–375 million in the fourteenth century. This caused labor shortage and raised commoners' wages as well as social status. At the same time, the widespread calamity led to collective soul searching. Educated commoners spread critical thinking.

That era had many famous scientists, mathematicians, philosophers, and thinkers; people fondly remember their contributions for centuries; interestingly, they were students and faculty of famous universities.[3] Since the founding of the University of Karueein in 859 AD in Fez, Morocco and the University of Bologna in 1099 in Italy, universities bred science, scientists, and profound scholars. Similar experiences could be found in countries like China, India, Egypt, and Greece. By design, higher education is intimately connected with human development. In Latin, *universitas* refers to "*a number of persons associated into one body, a society, company, community, guild, or corporation*". The association is created for the purpose of having like-minded people to engage in stimulating dialogue—enlightenment for humankind and solving difficult questions.

## 6.2.2   The Industrial Revolution, Matching Institutions and Universities

The development of knowledge and spread of education continued from the Renaissance to the Age of Enlightenment and to various rounds of the Industrial Revolution. During the Industrial Revolution, educated people developed institutions that enabled large scale specialized investments and market exchanges to embrace technological progress stemming from scientific discovery. Economic development took off accordingly. Cotton gins were just a start. What followed were scalable and spreadable general-purpose inventions, like steam power, iron works, machine tools, trains and railways, electricity, cable communication, etc. These innovations allowed people to do many things they never thought they could. People produced

---

[3]These centuries bred great scientists who made invaluable and fundamental contributions in our advancement in science—Nicolaus Copernicus (1473–1543), William Gilbert (1544–1604), Galileo Galilei (1563–1642), Johannes Kepler (1571–1630), William Harvey (1578–1657), Christiaan Huygens (1629–1695), and Isaac Newton (1643–1727), just to name a few. Indeed, these centuries featured an almost endless list of great scientists, thinkers, and philosophers who fundamentally shaped the modern world as we know now.

more, traveled more, communicated more, consumed more and many migrated from farming to urban factories. Industrialization changed our world for good.

The prime driving force of these changes was the previously unthinkably large-scale and efficient mass production. Business organizations emerged to allow people to benefit from specialization and cooperation, which Adam Smith (1776) called the division of labor.[4] Those who took risks to experiment and had good outcomes became rich early industrialists. Matching supportive institutions also emerged. For instance, large-scale companies running assembly lines needed the trust of savers, employees, and buyers. Financial intermediary institutions evolved to support industrialists, not just nobles and royalty, while joint-stock arrangements became an acceptable practice. Professionals and their associations emerged with defined and enforced acceptable standards and behavioral norms. Reliable governance standards emerged and continued to improve, often after a financial crisis. And governments stipulated rules and regulations that aimed to protect the less informed and those with less economic power. While the world was not perfect, these "market institutions" helped establish some reasonable level of trust between savers and users of funds, between customers and suppliers, and between employers and employees. Together, they allowed large-scale specialization and cooperation, grounded on mutual trust the institutions brought forth.

This sustained a virtuous cycle of "industrialization $\rightarrow$ market development $\rightarrow$ growth $\rightarrow$ further industrialization", which is still ongoing. Economic specialization and cooperation created redundant workers and great wealth. The former faced economic anxiety and got angry; they became Luddites, which refers to groups of displaced workers resorting to force to stop mechanization of their manual labor work. However, newly created wealth raised consumption demands and elicited further innovation attempts. The social trust described above allowed industrialists to raise finance to commercialize the innovations and create new jobs. For example, Henry Ford developed assembly lines and model T in 1908. The unemployed found meaningful new employment in his factories, in gas stations, in road constructions and maintenance, car repair shops, in motels, etc., and

---

[4]Technology allows large scale production, which is fruitful only if there is cooperative exchange which allows markets to grow. Adam Smith (1776, Ch. 3) states the following: "As it is the power of exchanging that gives occasion to the division of labor, … When the market is very small, no person can have any encouragement to dedicate himself entirely to one employment, for want of the power to exchange all that surplus part of the produce of his own labor, which is over and above his own consumption."

cars became household goods that expanded ordinary people's reach. The virtuous cycle propelled economic development, e.g., measured by GDP per capita, and changed our lives whether we liked it or not.

The movement led to rapid growth in university education. Industrialization raised the demand for intellectual output and suitably trained minds. Universities became a central contributor receiving both public and private sector money. Faculty members became well-paid specialists producing pure science to meet curiosity, medical science to treat the sick, and applied research to advance new products and production processes. Universities also produced students who supported and indeed led developments. Faculty and their trained graduates, who took up various leadership roles, served up fundamental questions on important social issues—like fairness, equality, and righteous social policies.

At the risk of exaggeration, we thus argue that top-tier universities played an important role in the virtuous cycle of development from the Renaissance to the Age of Enlightenment and to industrialization from the nineteenth century onward. Their roles have evolved from being the training grounds for people who served governments, or churches, to developing people to be thinkers, scientists, and people with skills that met the market. For society, universities have the responsibility to be the brain trust: produce knowledge and solve problems. Yet, their social esteem fundamentally stemmed from the values embedded in what scholarship is about. Indeed, from Scholarship to Virtue (*bo wen yue li*) is Confucius' theme for advanced education; Confucius is known as the educator of all generations in China.

### 6.2.3 The Twentieth Century and Universities

While traditionally universities develop knowledge and human capital as well as enlighten minds, their role shifted toward meeting demands derived from the rapid industrialization in the twentieth century. Also, after WWII, the arrival of baby boomers raised the demand for university education. Correspondingly, university activities might have become transaction value oriented.

Firstly, growing with large scale and rapid industrialization were complicated corporations and organizations; they needed talent. Universities served as a sieve. University graduates bore the sign that, having passed admissions and then graduating, they were above others and thus more employable.

Furthermore, the workplace needed talent with specific skills. Universities responded: they taught marketable skills, e.g., engineering and various functional business skills. Business Schools, while born earlier, grew like mushrooms. We now have functional specializations: accounting, finance, marketing, human resources, operation, strategy, etc.

As economies grew and baby boomers were growing up, the demand for university education rose. University degrees were perceived to be a safe ticket to middle-class status with life-long comfort.

The provision of university education thusly grew with economic prosperity and the resultant derived demand for talents. Competition, however, drove up the cost of university education; elite universities' tuitions went up and so did elite faculty's salaries. The driver was that earnings of graduates from prestigious universities rose, perhaps because they had been tracked to be "well above others", or that they had got into a network of "above average" talent, or they had been exposed to better faculty. In economies where university education was more privatized, more families borrowed a lot of money to put their kids through prestigious private universities.

University education increasingly became a "market-transaction". Wholesale marketization of education led universities to intensify their focus on marketable skills, an equilibrium deal between buyers and sellers: the students paid and the universities they enrolled in had to deliver. Traditional components of university education—enlightenment and inculcation of values—made way for the passing on of marketable skills.

In this period, business schools had their heyday: enrolment, tuition, and faculty salaries shot up. At the same time, faculty members strived to gain respect as scientists. Journals got established and faculty members did their best to assert that they were "scientists", often overlooking the infant status of their disciplines. Over-confidence led to under-recognition of what they might not know. Some business school faculty members might have inadvertently promoted the pursuit of market results without developing for students a grasp of holistic implications of such a pursuit.

Indeed, after the Great Financial Crisis, many lamented that "transaction value focused" business school teaching might lead otherwise good people to have a collapse in moral judgment. When enough of them did that, the market overlooked its moral responsibility—maintaining trust among players and serving society. Business schools might have gone too far.

Not that business education has lost its soul, just that we need to strike a balance.

## 6.3 Fast Changing World Challenges the Value of Business Education

The Industrial Revolution continues. Toward the end of the twentieth century and in the past two decades, two trends have been developing as a natural consequence of global economic development. They are "ageing population" and the exponential rate of development in science and technology, which the World Economic Forum has coined as the "Fourth Industrial Revolution." These trends have hugely significant implications for our future economic evolution.

### 6.3.1 Aging

The first significant trend, aging population, is driven by lowered birth rate and extended life span of the aged. The phenomenon has causal roots deeply linked to industrialization.

Women's participation in the job market has hugely increased, particularly in the last quarter of the twentieth century. This probably has a lot to do with the large-scale adoption of electrical household appliances which reduces the time and effort needed to run a household. Surplus household labor then joins the marketplace to earn tangible income. Also, mandatory education raises women's readiness to advance in the workplace. At the same time, the job market expands its readiness for women, e.g., in service industries, and mechanization reduces the need for sheer brute strength in many jobs. There are probably many other reasons for the huge increase in female job participation. The upshot is that many women find not just a good fit in the job market, but also many fulfilling career options and financial independence. They thus want to advance their own careers and cherish their independence. Getting married, bearing and raising children becomes a competing option, and not necessarily the most preferred.

At the same time, inter-generational wealth transfer is a lot more significant now than in the mid-twentieth century for all advanced countries and even developing countries, e.g., those in Asia. Baby boomers are richer than their parents; they can invest and transfer more wealth to their children. The wealth effect enhances millennial's choice set; they have a life goal of more than just work and raising a family. The outcome is that more do not get married and those who do are less inclined to have a large family.

While birth rate declines, people live longer. Advancements in medical science, sanitary condition, hygiene practice, and general health knowledge obviously prolong people's life expectancy. The two factors together lead to the aging phenomenon in many countries, e.g., South Korea, Japan, China, Canada, Germany, Spain, and France (see https://data.oecd.org/pop/elderly-population.htm or Faraz Haider, WorldAtlas.com updated on April 25, 2017). In Asian countries, the decline in birth rates is aggravated by the challenge of raising kids in a hyper exam-driven competitive environment and the low level of supportive government policies (e.g., short maternity leave).

The aged will have economic anxiety. For the older generation, extended life expectancy in recent years would mean a greater than expected need for retirement money and possibly higher medical care costs. The reduced birth rate will mean simply that there are less working bodies supporting the total population. It is natural that aging baby boomers develop economic anxiety. How can they protect their living standards in their extended future lives? The young, on the other hand, are nervous about their share of the rising national health care bill as their parents' generation ages.

## 6.3.2  The Fourth Industrial Revolution and Economic Anxiety

After centuries of development, basic science, applied science and technology are all advancing at an exponential speed. Material science, additive manufacturing, genome, nanotechnology, bio-tech, new batteries, all push up our capabilities in providing goods and services. Still, the most influential is digitalization. This leads us to the "*Fourth Industrial Revolution,*" a term coined by Dr. Klaus Schwab for the World Economic Forum in his 2015 article and 2016 book.

> The First Industrial Revolution used water and steam power to mechanize production. The Second used electric power to create mass production. The Third used electronics and information technology to automate production. Now a Fourth Industrial Revolution is building on the Third, the digital revolution that has been occurring since the middle of the last century. It is characterized by a fusion of technologies that is blurring the lines between the physical, digital, and biological spheres.[5]

---

[5]Excerpts from *The Fourth Industrial Revolution*, by Klaus Schwab (2016).

The fusion of technologies forming a cyber-physical system is based on the quantum advancement in Computing, Communication, Sensors, and Data Storage technologies. Data analytics, cloud computing, sensors, robots, machine learning, and artificial intelligence allow machines to automatically recognize, store, and process huge amounts of data and conduct real-time optimizing predictions and judgments. The cyber-physical system carries out some human functions, e.g., image and language recognition as well as cognitive judgment, faster and better than people.

Consequently, people have incredibly expanded capabilities to communicate, to connect, to work without actual physical involvement or real contact. We now have driverless vehicles and drones, which help in more than moving people and goods, they assist us in farming, in pollution control, and much more; we have machine-aided surgery; and we have smart cities, smart contracts, account-tech, fin-tech, marketing-tech, legal-tech, policy-tech, and all the other "x-techs". We have extended well beyond Da Vinci's imagination and realized capabilities in science fiction and futuristic movies.

These capabilities' impact comes at incredible speed, scale, and scope. There are several well-known important consequences.

Firstly, they have changed our lives, continuing a trend in previous rounds of Industrial Revolutions. Smartphones, connected with huge computing power, change the way we decide on traveling, entertaining, purchasing, or connecting with friends. Our day-to-day behavior and decisions are seriously affected by and dependent on the digital networks we are connected to.

Secondly, digitalization leads to disruptions in companies and business models, often from unexpected corners. Virtual companies replace brick and mortar companies, like Uber disrupts taxi companies and Airbnb affects hotel business. Platform economics allow platform owners like Google, Amazon, Tencent, and Alibaba to be value heavy, asset-light, and to stimulate innovation for platform users. Data analytics have transformed logistics management. Block-chain creates trustless trust: people do not trust one another but they trust a faceless machine system. Various forms of data analytics and fin-tech thus disrupt traditional finance practices. More will come.

Thirdly, machines more than substitute for people in routine jobs; they can even take over some jobs that require cognitive functions. For example, high-speed algorithm trading programs replace many human traders. Real-time analytic algorithms are tremendously helpful to auditors and analysts and yet reduce the hiring of them. Machine-search changes the life of lawyers, as machines are better than people in coming up with precedents.

Intelligent drones inspect buildings and bridges; computers aid architectural and structural designs; so, engineers and architects have to seek new ways to contribute. The fast progress in machine-human-capital substitution means that experts need to seek new competitive advantages, this time against intelligent machines.

Finally, digitalization has huge room for expansion in scale and scope because the capability is non-rivalry. This creates a winner-takes-all phenomenon that skews corporate earnings and income distribution. Besides creating disruptive production processes, services, and business models, it intensifies competition among peers. Digitalization allows real-time connection between people and market information to attain real-time prediction and optimization. Hayek (1945) posits that the market is an information processor where firms are agents processing their market experiences to act accordingly in pursuing results. Firms mastering digitalization are more agile "market information processors" which more efficiently outcompete other firms. Employees who understand the interactions between customer journey and worker journey are valuable in this competition; they help employers to outcompete peers. Investors equipped with powerful analytics are better than others in picking investment prospects.

The upshot is faster business churning, greater individual business volatility, and shortened horizon of usefulness in skill-sets as capital-labor substitution has become capital-human capital substitution. All of this raises economic anxiety. Companies have a reduced sense of security, for sure. People's prospect of a long-tenured secured job dims. The millennials worry about being displaced at the age of mid-40 or mid-50, something like a decade from now, and having to start a new career path from scratch. Those born after 2000 are entering universities now. They worry about whether they are learning the right skills; their parents' past experiences provide only limited guidance in preparing for the rapidly moving world.

### 6.3.3 Doubts About the Value of Education

Universities, while significant contributors to the trends, are experiencing their own ups-and-downs in this journey. In the twentieth century, Industrial Revolution raised the demand for education. In the twenty-first century, the new trends raise doubts about the value of university education. The implication, however, is that universities should be more valuable than ever. Still, momentarily, let us focus on the concerns.

Firstly, university enrolments are bound to shrink as the reduced birth rate reduces the cohort size of university-age students.[6]

Secondly, value always declines with risks. Job uncertainty will no doubt, ex-ante, dampen people's valuation of education, perhaps particularly business education. Going for an MBA can be a very expensive proposition. The cost is more than just tuition fees, but also the opportunity cost of leaving a fast-moving job market temporarily; these costs are not declining.

There is a related factor which dampens the value of a university degree. As stated above, the current trend of fast innovations coincides with very skewed income distribution—a winner-takes-all phenomenon. While the phenomenon is complicated, it is real; many observe an increasingly polarized income distribution in recent years—median income does not track per capita GDP in the past decade. Digitalization allows the more skilled to scale up and spread out their earning power, leaving the less-skilled with diminished opportunities and earnings. Worse, the displaced middle-skill group will flock to the lower-skill jobs and further depress earnings at the lower end of the skill spectrum. In the current era, it is harder to be in the middle class. Previously, a university degree almost guaranteed middle-class status; now, even a post-graduate degree may not be enough.

Thirdly, with all the internet capabilities, quasi-knowledge can be obtained at our figure tips. Searching the internet, one can find many very informative videos and lectures. Why go to school?

Lastly, technology nowadays can help us to screen people much better than before. Do employers still need universities to do screening? Technological advancement has begun to allow companies to search beyond traditional avenues, e.g., seeking MBAs for finance or consultant positions. The future world of talent management may well be based on highly effective attitude and personality tests, aided by AI, and continuous monitoring, again aided by AI and a batch of similar devices. HR-Tech may allow companies to directly identify and train talent better than universities.

### 6.3.4  Larger Implications

These factors together create a tension mounted atmosphere. The aged worry about life in their prolonged sunset phase. The middle-age worry about job security. The young worry about the uncertain future. Both the middle-age

---

[6]Developed economies feature stronger universities. There is no denial that they could side-step the concern by accepting more students from developing economies.

group and the young worry about their burdens in maintaining the lifestyle of the aged. While technological progress has a lot of potentials in raising productivity, it has yet to delivery real productivity growth other than creating economic anxiety. People and countries have been turning self-centered which fuels international geopolitical conflicts. Universities are a major contributor of advancement in science and technology and supporters of industrial revolutions that lead us to the current tension mounted world. Yet, they are not impressing the world in helping us to navigate and resolve the tensions.

## 6.4    Facing the Future

The concerns are there, but universities' value will be intact if we do the right things. Since inception, universities have always been a breeding ground for talent and leaders, a source of scientific advancement, a problem solver via applied and translational research, and a source of enlightenment. Many traditional faculty and schools have been delivering the above all along. The following is for business schools more than for others. We focus on adjustments needed: in preparing current students, in engineering life-long learning, and in problem-solving-oriented research.

### 6.4.1  Equip the Students

A burning question is how to prepare graduates for the future economy. There are two features in the future economy which we need to equip our students to face.

First, with data analytics, machine learning, artificial intelligence, and rapid technological transformation, the future world will comprise talented people working with intelligent and human-like machines. A lot of data will be fed into a system within which intelligent machines serve core roles: they often take a lot of action without human intervention, or, the system's machines direct people to take action. Yet, people create and oversee the system, including reflecting on the outcomes driven by machines as well as seeking opportunities to extend the services machines can provide.

Second, it is a no-brainer that the future economy will evolve rapidly and unpredictably.

The implication of these two features is that we need to develop in our students basic skills complementary to thinking and learning machines and to prepare them to be effective life-long learners. We make five suggestions on student training below. We focus on life-long learning in the next subsection.

First, students need to be able to function in the future world which operates based on data analytics and technology to let people work with machines, e.g., robots and artificial intelligence. Employees cannot survive the workplace without data literacy and technology literacy, the higher up they are in an organization hierarchy the more so. Indeed, corporations now emphasize developing a rigorous data analytics and artificial intelligence culture. Our education system needs to meet the trend.

Second, we need to strengthen our students' literacy in principles in some fundamental disciplines. Basic principles are the foundation of self-learning. For example, in the rapidly evolving field of economics, we develop in our students a firm grasp of basic economic principles and technical skills in statistics and mathematics. We then make them learn about contemporary economics on their own. Thus, in economics, nothing is new under the sun but each "economic crisis" is a new learning experience. The learning process starts with identifying a curious puzzle, transforming it into intellectual or empirical tension, and resolving the tension using economic principles and a bit of technical analytical skills. Students accumulate economic intuition from the effort. In this way, we train our students to be life-long self-learners. In a nutshell, we need to inspire our students to develop curiosity, the ability to identify intellectual tensions, and a solid grasp of scientific principles.

Third, machines cannot grasp as we do human contexts and experiences. Machines' understanding of the real world can be shallow and fragmented, e.g., a machine trained to visually recognize hot-dogs and bananas would not know that they are linked (as food for humans) while a two-year-old readily would. Humans understand the world in a seamlessly connected manner, in which each concept is linked to the other in some form of a causal or associative relation. Machines, on the other hand, are not able to make a commonsense-based judgment or cannot be empathetic. Machines cannot yet motivate human passions and development of social skills—e.g., they cannot coach a team to have pride in losing a game honorably.

That machines have no hearts and feelings means we need to keep the human-machine system "humanistic" ourselves. For example, an insurance company's data analytics may lead to a risk-premium program that raises its bottom line but ends up practicing statistical discrimination against the aged with high probability of getting chronic illness in near terms. This breaks apart the meaning of insurance—pooling of fortune and cooperating to make a better life for all. The way to counter that is to develop caring humans who reflect with a kind heart on the impact of our acts on people.

Only with caring reflection can we can stop machines from doing the unthinkable to humanity.

Thus, we need to train our students to develop humanistic literacy so that they can use their hearts to work with analytical machines. Studying human beings, e.g., history and culture, enhances our ability to link the connected and be empathetic and caring.

Fourth, in our training, we need to emphasize critical thinking which means identification of causality and assumptions behind the causality. For our students to complement intelligent machines, they need to be aware of the current bugs in machines. I can think of two and there may be more. (i) Machine predictions and optimization often are developed in a black box; human beings do not know the details. (ii) Furthermore, machines do not see biases, missing variables, over-fitting, and out of sample human behavior. Humans have the responsibility to catch them because, in the real world, what goes wrong will be on the individual's or the organization's shoulder, not machines'. To overcome these machine bugs, our students need to develop inquisitiveness and critical thinking. That is, they need to always question how they know an answer is right, to challenge assumptions, and differentiate endogenous correlations from causal correlations.

A deliberately simple-minded story helps to illustrate the importance of delineating correlations from causality. Let say a Dean wants to nurture the development of a happy campus life. She uses facial recognition and machine learning to track their students' smiling time. She finds that students smile and laugh the most when they are drinking together. Should the dean then build more bars to enhance student life? Without denying that alcohol affects drinkers' mood and behavior, the correlation between drinking together and smiling and laughing is endogenous and non-causal—students get together and drink because they have something to celebrate or they want to have a happy time together with their friends. Any causal statement running from drinking together to happiness and using that to make policy decisions would be a bit simple-minded, possibly leading to unintended nasty consequence: having too many drunkards on campus. At the same time, the correlation can fruitfully lead to careful thinking on the "why, what, and how" of nurturing enjoyable and joyful campus life.

Fifth, machines cannot "connect the dots", a form of divergent thinking stemming from curiosity and intuition. Currently, machines are programmed. They can solve problems given to them, but they cannot yet find on their own problems to which their solutions can apply. Furthermore, machines are good at synthesis but weak in unstructured creation. In the foreseeable future, machines specialize in analytics while humans specialize in imagination and divergent thinking: humans ask questions, machines help to seek answers and in turn stimulate humans to ask more questions. Thus, we need to train students to ask meaningful questions.

Let us illustrate. Imagine that we were Prof. Isaac Newton. An apple fell onto our heads. We ask the question, "Why out of an infinitely uncountable number of angles, the apple always falls at only one angle"? Machines calculated, simulated, and produced refined analytical answers so that we thoroughly understood gravitational force. Clearly, the drivers in the learning are humans' enlightening question, their imagination about gravitational force, and the conceptual analytical tools, e.g., calculus, they develop. Thus, the challenge is to train students to ask good questions and develop imagination. While we do not have a programmatic approach, we surely know that encouraging people to ask questions can lead a crowd of people to stimulate one another to ask increasingly interesting questions.

To ask a meaningful question is to question with a sense of purpose. The fruit in the Newton-machine exercise is the application of physics to shoot satellites to the sky, and so on. That is, we need to also raise our students' entrepreneurial spirit. Machines are not able to see additional worthy applications of their algorithms or analytics. Human entrepreneurs are dreamers doing the bridging. Good entrepreneurs are those who see dissatisfaction and find (or borrow) a constructive solution. It is worth emphasizing that here entrepreneurship is not about development of new businesses, it is about seeing that things "should not be that way" and taking the responsibility to make positive changes. We call that constructive dissatisfaction.

In summary, to train our students to be valued contributors in the future human-machine world, we need to emphasize principle literacy, data literacy, technology literacy, and humanistic literacy. We also need to step up our effort in developing our students' curiosity, critical thinking, entrepreneurial thinking, and leadership thinking with a deep-seated care for human lives.

## 6.4.2 Life-Long Learning

Universities should take a very explicit role in developing life-long learning.

In a rapidly changing world, it is impossible to stay current without life-long learning. Life-long learning, however, is a human choice. Yet, a person's preference is shaped by her education. A great high school teacher once impressed upon me that a person who has stopped learning is a person the world has left behind; that is particularly true in the rapidly evolving economy. Educators need to inculcate in our students the desire to conduct life-long learning.

A good way to do so is to put real actions behind our teaching. In business education, MBA and executive education students practice life-long learning. We can expand the practice: every student who passes through a university becomes a member of a life-long learning community and is entitled to take additional courses for free or at marginal cost. That has been the NUS Business School's practice for more than a decade. We are also doing the right thing in welcoming alumni back to share their perspectives, to identify trends, and to work together to meet the future. There are many ways to do so. Details do not matter; the belief and the actual action are real—we should "just do it".

We should expand our call for life-long learning to the currently employed, whether they are our alumni or not. Economic anxiety stems from facing an unpredictable future. Life-long learning is about tooling up continually to move with the frontier. Life-long learning should be an expanded attempt to study emerging trends, themes, and to acquire emerging skills in all fields: computing, engineering, healthcare, urban planning, construction, service, etc. Universities should open their doors to help all past graduates to proactively engineer control of their career destiny, rather than react to imminent retrenchment threats.

### 6.4.3 Research

Since industrialization, business organizations are the main conduits to implementing innovations that improve human lives. Currently, and in the future, business organizations are on turbocharge to deliver. To be relevant, researchers in business schools need to be at the frontier.

Our concern is that business school faculties' incentives are affected by the half-century-old system which amplifies the burden of knowledge. The publication system tends to encourage incremental knowledge development. We sometimes wonder if the journal-referee system and the tenure process for many schools are in tune with the business world which is changing at exponential speed and scope. In the Fourth Industrial Revolution, digitalization and computing power allows a fusion of technologies, which merges multiple disciplines of science and behavioral science, to create interactions between human and machines to overcome barriers in improving our lives. A "smart" city design is one such example. We need to encourage cross-disciplinary thematic research that is rigorous, practical, and relevant.

As an example, let us consider attempts to help the aging population. The work involves more than research in medicine, or system design, or behavioral science, each segmented according to disciplinary boundaries and aimed at "curing" more than "preventing". Our desire is to deliver translational research that connects biological science, medical science, behavioral science, data analytics, and system design to help people age gracefully with reduced medical bills. Data analytics and artificial intelligence can be combined to deliver smart homes and an intelligent advanced warning system to deliver timely healthcare attention as well as inducing the aged to change their behavior. Furthermore, combining these with intelligent financial product innovation can offer low-cost health and life insurance. These are expected results of thematic research, which business schools can participate, because business is the organizer of effective cross-discipline delivery. Business schools could be the effective conduit in these cross-discipline efforts for a noble cause.

The requirement is the inculcation in faculty and students, the recognition that society supports our comfortable living and we have to make a positive difference in people in return. Many great university leaders would share the statement by the first president of Johns Hopkins University, Daniel Coit Gilman, made in his inaugural address in 1876: higher education should aim "…. for less misery among the poor, less ignorance in schools, less bigotry in the temple, less suffering in the hospital, less fraud in business, less folly in politics".

## 6.5   Conclusions

Higher-learning institutions, since inception, promote knowledge development grounded on curiosity, critical thinking, and a desire to enhance quality of life. Universities were the key contributors to knowledge development from the Renaissance period to the Age of Enlightenment. Continual advancement in science and applied science led to the development of general-purpose technologies, which fueled rounds of Industrial Revolution. In the process, universities are the breeding ground for thinkers, leaders, and scientists, who serve society based on "scholarship"—a term that combines striving for excellence, integrity, innovations, teamwork, and care to serve. This echoes the old Confucius teaching—from scholarship to virtue. The contribution of research and teaching in universities has been beyond economic development, they are one of the critical drivers for advancement of value and civilization.

It is not easy to stay on the right course all the time. Industrialization in the twentieth century raised the market value of university education, particularly business schools' education. Universities respond by producing students with marketable skill-sets that meet the needs of large-scale industrialization. The marketization of education might have inadvertently created the impression, or indeed the reality, that universities have reduced the emphasis on character-building. Some have suggested that this contributed to a collective collapse of moral judgment which led to the Great Financial Crisis.

The latest round of industrialization, based on digitalization, is creating rapid and unpredictable job disruption and business churning. Digitalization is scalable, spread-able, and empowers numerous "recombination", as Schumpeter (1934) would put it in his *Theory of Economic Development*, which invigorates creative destruction. With the churning of businesses and an increase in machines replacing manual labor, intelligent machines may even take away some jobs that require cognitive capabilities. The sentiment is that, in the rapidly changing future, job skills will have short lifespans in the marketplace. This will lead to a high level of economic anxiety among the old, the young and the currently employed, and the value of university education could be in doubt. Adding fuel to fire is the recognition that digitalization can reduce the instrumental role of formal university education in obtaining information (or even knowledge) and in signaling talent.

However, the doubt is healthy. This guides us to stay on the right direction. Universities' and business schools' proper response is to meet society needs and to reiterate the intrinsic purpose of higher education. In the future world, intelligent people will work alongside intelligent machines in a complementary manner. Thus, business schools, and generally universities, will need to think hard about students' needs.

This essay suggests that students will need to be more inquisitive and more critical and analytical in their thinking. They need more than ever to have the capability to be continual self-learners. That also means that they need to develop principle, data, technology, and humanistic literacies, as first explained in Aoun (2017) and reiterated here.

Moreover, in the new world of intelligent people working with intelligent machines, the human role is less about routine solution finding, but more about finding problems in which solutions apply. We connect the dots for powerful machines which can analyze and optimize. Thus, we need to stimulate students to have imagination and recognize commonality across disciplines. (The stimulating book by McAfee and Brynjolfsson [2017] offers comprehensive in-depth analysis.)

Business organizations are the most prevalent human organization to bring capabilities from multiple disciplines to address human needs. Thus, business schools particularly need to emphasize cross-discipline thematic applied research to address pressing issues like aging and environmental stresses. Hence, faculties and students will need to bear the syntheses in mind.

Indeed, all of this is for a purpose. Machines do not (yet) have empathy and can ruthlessly be single-minded. We need to emphasize in students a sense of care and the tendency to reflect. Life needs a purpose. The inculcation of the mentality to serve and care for people is particularly important in the era of intelligent machines work with people—people provide the hearts which machines do not have.

The above has always been the forte of good universities. We develop science, applied science, social science, humanities, all for the purpose of bringing good to society. We pursue not only market value, but the purity of intellectual pursuits and a sense of purpose. Indeed, one fundamental responsibility of universities is to promote values embedded in good scholarships. Reiterating the intrinsic value of education is the right thing to do.

**Acknowledgements** I am most grateful to Jordi Canals, for his encouragement and his many helpful comments in improving the essay.

# References

Aoun, Joseph E. Robot-Proof. 2017. *Higher Education in the Age of Artificial Intelligence*. Cambridge, MA: MIT Press.

Faraz Haider. WorldAtlas.com.

Hayek, Frederick. A. 1945. The Use of Knowledge in Society. *American Economic Review* 35 (4): 519–530.

McAfee, Andrew, and Erik Brynjolfsson. 2017. *Machine, Platform, Crow. Harnessing Our Digital Future*. New York: W. W. Norton.

Roser, Max. 2018. Economic Growth. Published online at OurWorldInData.org. Retrieved from https://ourworldindata.org/economic-growth.

Schumpeter, Joseph A. 1934. *Theory of Economic Development*. Transaction Publishers, 5th ed., 1997 (Originally published: Cambridge, MA: Harvard University Press, 1934).

Schwab, Klaus. 2015. The Fourth Industrial Revolution: What It Means and How to Respond. *Foreign Affairs,* December.

Schwab, Klaus. 2016. *The Fourth Industrial Revolution*. New York: Crown Business.

Smith, Adam. 1776. *An Inquiry into the Nature and Causes of the Wealth of Nations*. London: W. Strahan and T. Cadell.

# 7

# AI and the Leadership Development of the Future

Franz Heukamp

## 7.1 Introduction

Artificial Intelligence (AI) is seen today by many as strong force of change. It affects many parts of society: how people make decisions as consumers, how organizations manufacture goods and provide services and how people work, among others (McAfee and Brynjolfsson 2017).

What exactly constitutes AI is debated among specialists (Boden 2018) and further discussed in other chapters of this book. For all practical purposes, the term AI refers to the set of analytical tools that have been developed over the past decades which have resulted in extreme performance increases in many tasks compared to human levels or in entering domains that were up to now "reserved" for humans, such as driving.

The advances in AI have been well publicized by using tasks that have high visibility such as the Jeopardy TV show in which IBM's Watson prevailed over the best human players in 2011; or the defeat of chess world champion Garry Kasparov by Deep Blue in 1997; or AlphaGo beating the worlds arguably best Go players Lee Se-dol in 2016 and Ke Jie in 2017.

Besides, the daily use of AI-assisted tools such as GPS navigation software and other similar applications have created an everyday experience and presence in most people's lives. In addition, some of the most successful

F. Heukamp (✉)
IESE Business School, University of Navarra, Barcelona, Spain
e-mail: fheukamp@iese.edu

© The Author(s) 2020
J. Canals and F. Heukamp (eds.), *The Future of Management in an AI World*,
IESE Business Collection, https://doi.org/10.1007/978-3-030-20680-2_7

companies of the past few years in terms of growth and sheer company size such as Amazon, Google or Microsoft have based their success on the application of AI in their products and services and have embraced an "AI first" strategy which has given additional credibility to the general claim that AI's impact on all aspects of life is already strong and only going to grow further.

Even though the speed of AI's further development and its potential limits, if any, are still being debated (Ford 2018; Domingos 2015), there is seems to be a consensus that the effect of AI on virtually all aspects of life is potentially more profound than any other technological change in human history so far.

Not surprisingly, this technological change is being felt in all parts of society and while the adoption of technology driven mass market products and services has been quick and virtually universal, there is also fear in society about the negative effects of automation and digital technology. Job losses potentially at a scale of millions and a loss of privacy are only two of the topics that are being discussed among specialists and the larger public.

Many organizations are in the process of adapting their business models, organizational structures, policies etc. as they are trying to harness the possibilities that AI is offering. Around this business and organizational transformation, new demands on management and leadership capabilities arise as decisions are being taken about shifts in strategy, adoption of technology and the organizational change needs to be managed that these decisions create.

The purpose of this chapter is to explore what those management and leadership attributes are that are becoming more relevant in an era of AI and how they can be consistently developed. We will distinguish, first, what kind of additional knowledge leaders of the AI era will need, second, what kind of skills they need to preferentially develop and third, what kind of personal attributes they need to have as leaders in order to succeed.

## 7.2   The Impact of AI on Management and Leadership

Using technology to increase productivity or reduce the exposure to dangerous processes is not new. The use of robots in manufacturing goes back many decades and visiting a shop floor of a car manufacturer today leads to an encounter with heavily automatized production processes. In general, automatization has taken place to reduce tasks that were "dirty, dull and dangerous" (Davenport and Kirby 2016). Accordingly, automatization has been seen as positive for workers, facilitating difficult types of jobs and has led to increases in productivity which have generally counted on abroad consensus in society regarding its necessity and virtue.

The new wave of automatization brought by AI is somewhat different. It is broader in scope because in principal it is limited only by the question whether a task can be described by an algorithm. If this is the case, automation is likely to happen eventually (Davenport and Kirby 2016).

This opens up a large domain of jobs and entire new sectors to this type of change. No single sector will be excluded and the extent of the change that is to be expected has been described, for example, for the professions, predicting profound changes as most of their standard tasks would be automated soon (Susskind and Susskind 2015).

For many industrial sectors, McKinsey (2017) predicts that around 50% of current work activities are technically automatable with technologies that already exist today and 60% of current occupations have more than 30% of activities that are technically automatable.

It may be difficult to pinpoint exact numbers for each industry and occupation but what seems foreseeable is that virtually all will somehow be affected, thus making the impact of AI on how people and organizations work very profound. In addition, the time frame for this change is short: 10–15 years are what McKinsey (2017) estimates.

Concrete applications of AI in different industries consists so far mostly in tools that are used to accomplish a specific task, aimed at realizing a level of performance that was impossible to reach up to now. In that sense, the "intelligence" shown by these AI applications is narrow even though the impact on productivity can be very powerful.

To organize the discussion around the impact of AI on the need for specific leadership capabilities, we distinguish between the three areas of *knowing*, *doing* and *being* (Hesslebein and Shinseki 2004). Using this parsimonious framework for leadership we ask the following three questions: As AI is gaining ground, in order to be successful, what does a leader need to know? What must they be able to do? And what kind of person must they be, in terms of character, identity and world view?

## 7.2.1 What Do Leaders Need to Know?

Current AI applications can be considered tools to improve the prediction capacity (Agrawal et al. 2018). They generate insight and information about some kind of issue that is of interest. For example, this insight can concern the evolution of a potentially malignant tumor based on the analysis of an image, combined with a scientific model. Or it could be a prediction about the potentially fraudulent nature of a wire transfer.

## Business leaders will have to know the basics about AI models

Most AI applications today use machine learning and specifically neural networks of different layers (= deep neural networks) in order to have a machine learn from some data the relationship between different variables of interest (Boden 2018). Once an algorithm has learned, from training data, it can be used to make predictions based on the data of interest.

The scientist's adage "garbage in, garbage out" reflects insight about the impact that the quality of the data has on a prediction model in terms of accuracy, level of bias etc. Correspondingly, for a manager, understanding and controlling the process that generates the data, creating a strategy to collect data in an efficient manner and the ability to analyze this data appropriately are important in terms of effectiveness of using AI and managing the data collection effort from an organizational and economic perspective.

Moreover, being knowledgeable in basic aspects of analytics so as to know which questions to ask and how to interpret the output are basic aspects of knowledge for leaders in an AI era without which they will have difficulties to take appropriate decisions in their work.

Another specific aspect to consider is the knowledge about potential data bias which has been shown to be quite relevant in a good number of important AI applications and which have been discussed in the press on several occasions. For example, in a hiring project at Amazon (Hill 2019) which attempted to predict the quality of candidates by analyzing the performance of past candidates, data is never neutral and can be biased. In the case of Amazon, the current dominance of male employees lead the algorithm to downgrade potential applications from female candidates, perpetuating an undesired lack of diversity and potentially missing out on great female talent. The tool was never put to work.

## Business Leaders Will Have to Know About Organizational Transformation

AI tools act (so far) mostly on a specific single task. This may stem from the fact that AI solutions are often context dependent and in that sense narrow. Algorithms for voice recognition can be very different from algorithms that analyze images. Also, companies that develop AI solutions are often startups that need to focus on a single task that they want to improve.

The tasks that are affected by AI-powered solutions are typically part of a larger work flow which will be changed through the adoption of a new AI tool. In a first step of analysis, managers will have to decide, task by task, which changes to AI tools make sense for an organization. However, drawing from the experience in organizations on how the introduction of PCs changed them, it is likely that the full power of automation in terms of efficiency gains will only be realized once the work flows as a whole are re-engineered.

This strong link between AI-driven automation and the impact on an existing organization makes it very useful to understand the basics of organizational transformations.

## 7.2.2  What Must Leaders Be Able to Do?

AI Leaders need to be good decision makers and specifically be good in judgment and learning. Among other aspects, management consists of taking decisions in an uncertain environment. In decision under uncertainty, a decision maker (or a group) considers different alternative options, evaluates how uncertainty (risk) affects possible outcomes and connects the outcomes to the preferences of the decision maker. This process requires a prediction about how the observed reality (data) is linked to possible outcomes, often quantifying the risk. Moreover, the decision-making process has two additional important parts: judgment and learning.

Judgment is here understood as the process of evaluating how the predicted outcomes link to the preferences of the decision maker. To give an example, in medical decision making, a given treatment may lead to the reduction in the size of a tumor, with a given probability and implying a certain economic cost and maybe some other side effects. The judgment of the medical doctor consists in evaluating the outcome for the patient in terms of improved health, accounting for possible side effects, the economic costs and other potentially relevant factors.

In general, judgment can include the willingness and ability to take risks, the interaction between different types of risks and more generally a deep understanding of what is good and acceptable as an outcome for an organization, thus connecting with how it sees itself and the values it wants to reflect

Learning in decision making is about improving the quality of a decision and its prediction and judgment elements, based on the observed outcomes of prior decisions. The ability to learn defines the potential of a decision maker and puts a limit on the effectiveness of a leader.

As AI will offer a greatly enhanced capacity to predict and will make it cheaper, using machines, it is very likely to be used much more often in many different business processes. This is what the rise of analytics is about that we broadly observe in business models, both of recently started and more traditional businesses. Prediction will become a commodity, and this will shift the value in decision making to judgment and learning. Both will gain in importance.

A third aspect of decision making that is particularly relevant in the context of AI is the *enhancement* of human decision making through machines. The interaction between humans and machines requires collaboration in a new way. For example, if a company is considering the acquisition of some other entity, it will be analyzing the different alternative targets with respect to their growth potential, different types of risks etc. IBM has suggested that Watson could be used to support this type of analysis, providing predictions about a range of different outcomes. Besides making a judgment about which, if any, of the alternative takeover targets is appropriate for the company, given its strategy, risk appetite etc. there is also a specific skill in knowing how to use the abilities of the machine, which questions to ask, how to interpret the answers etc.

## Some Specific Analytical Skills

Not only will decision making based on analytical insights that are enhanced by AI be more ubiquitous because of their quality and affordability. They will also draw to the forefront specific analytical skills that are becoming more relevant.

The distinction between correlation and causality has always been critical in drawing actionable conclusions from data. Contemporary econometric analysis, for example, spends considerable effort in finding ways to distinguish between the two in a variety of ways. In each case there is an explicit reasoning that links a mathematical model with the observed reality (data) which can be explained in words and which has to withstand the scrutiny critical analysis.

Deep learning algorithms which power the currently most popular and relevant AI tools, offer difficulties in this respect (Boden 2018). The algorithm learns from data, in principle without much prior orientation and an optimized model can at times be very difficult or even impossible to understand in its structure. The analyst may observe which variables are deemed relevant by the model to explain the data but there may be a complete lack of actual understanding of the real-world phenomena behind it. In other words, these algorithms can lead to black box solutions.

If, for example, a financial institution analyzes customer credit risk with such a model it may not be able to justify the credit decision other than by saying that "the model said so," which is certainly dissatisfying and which may also run into regulatory problems as financial supervision authorities require reasoned decisions.

## Critical Thinking

In the context of understanding the implications of the underlying assumptions of AI models and how they relate to real business situations, another skill that stands out is critical thinking. Critical thinking is the objective analysis of a problem at hand in view of making a judgment. This may require testing the assumptions behind the description of the problem, questioning the criteria that are considered relevant for the judgment and checking on the quality of the analysis itself. Critical thinking is among the most priced skills that education can produce. In line with the enhanced value of judgment mentioned before, it will be of increased importance going forward.

## Driving Organizational Change: People Development and Orchestrating Collaboration

Before, we discussed that many AI tools are point solutions that improve pieces of currently existing work flows. Powerful improvements in productivity or new product advances will require re-engineering current processes to realize those gains and redefining the jobs that people in an organization do.

Correspondingly, managerial work will include more often the analysis of current work flows, the forecast of gains in efficiency through AI tools and the redesign of processes. In terms of types of jobs in a company, new ones may be created through the use of more technology, for example in the area of software development, data analytics etc. Other jobs may be augmented in their scope, changing, for example, clerical jobs to have a stronger component of advisory or consulting as their analytical aspects become more powerful and mundane at the same time.

Arranging this type of change can be complex and in order to be successful it needs to be accompanied by a lot of attention toward the people who will be affected. Pfeffer (2018) has shown that in many organizations, a large number of employees are already disengaged today and the wave of automation that can be expected in the coming years will require a lot of focus on people management in order to avoid further slide in negative sentiment toward work and the organization.

Hence, the most critical part will be driving the necessary organizational change which implies developing people and orchestrating collaboration.

In developing people, senior managers work in order to guarantee that people have the right set of capabilities in order to succeed in the new context of an organization and at the same time they work in order to create a solid pipeline of candidates to succeed the senior management in the future. In addition, it is also a way to help individuals grow personally and to discover deeper fulfillment through their work.

The changes in jobs and work flows that will be brought about by the use of technology require a lot of change from employees in terms of their capabilities and attitudes and therefore need a strong commitment to people development. Senior executives will need to create a framework to guarantee the acquisition of the capabilities outlined in the prior sections such as the critical technical skills required, in addition to the change management related capabilities, the capabilities to interact skillfully with machines and the reinforcement of leadership traits such as coaching etc. In fact, as technology becomes more powerful and generally more widely available, the development of talent has become for many organizations the single most important strategic advantage (Charan et al. 2018).

A specific challenge for senior executives is the need to establish a culture of collaboration around AI-driven projects (Davenport and Foutty 2018). The nature of AI-driven solution as mostly single task applications may suggest in the beginning that it relates to a reduced number of people and functions in a team. However, the transversal nature of these technologies which often quickly affect all aspects of a business, such as operations, HR, IT, marketing and others require the creation and sustenance of a collaborative culture in order to obtain good results. A consequence of this is the rapid uptake in the use of agile development methods for a whole range of tasks which many leading companies in the adoption of AI-driven technologies show (Denning 2018). Interestingly, as a working culture, this then also applies to cases where technology is only a side topic. A case in point is the bank BBVA which has been identified as a leader among financial institutions in providing digital services and which has extended the agile work techniques to more than 30,000 employees (out of a total of approximately 130,000) at the end of 2018.

## 7.2.3  What Kind of Person Must They Be?

The third dimension of leadership capabilities relates to character and world view that a leader needs to show. Leadership studies have established that behavioral attributes and the personality it reflects are important aspects of leadership (Snook et al. 2012). AI is producing powerful tools that can change entire companies and entire sectors. As with all forceful change, the direction of this change that the leadership of an organization needs to determine is crucial. We can quickly identify that in the context of AI, we will need leaders who are deeply concerned about ethics, who are humble and approachable and who are flexible and adaptable to changing circumstances.

### Deeply Concerned About Ethics: Trust and Privacy

With the more intensive use of AI by leading technological companies such as Facebook or Google, trust and privacy have emerged as critical themes in the perception by the larger public about technology. These and many other companies that use AI process large amounts of data in order to provide their services. Leaders need to balance in their work the rights and needs of personal privacy with the desire to provide high-quality services and be economically viable. This kind of tradeoffs require ethical leadership and a profound interest in the people that the organization is serving. Based on a set of policies and actions that provide transparency, trust can be maintained and increased which is many times the fundamental value that makes a difference between organizations. Leaders need to understand this and act accordingly.

### Personal Traits: Humility and Adaptability

In addition to specific tasks that the senior leadership in an organization is faced with, there are also questions on *how* they should approach leadership in the context of technological change through AI in terms of behaviors that are shown, and which reflect specific leadership traits.

In the context of change through AI-driven technology, humility and adaptability have emerged as two important leadership traits (Chamorro-Prezumic et al. 2018; Neubauer et al. 2017). Jim Collins concluded already some time ago in his study on the success of certain types of companies over time that "the x-factor of leadership is not personality, it's humility" (Collins 2001), but in the context of fast change which is induced by technology and which is likely to accelerate, there is even more weight that we need to place on it.

Humility specifically refers to the ability of a leader to recognize that in the fast-changing environment provoked by AI, no one, not even the most senior person of an organization, will have all the answers. This leads to the insight that in order to advance, they need help and advocate a common search for the best solution. Quite naturally, a more inclusive, collegial leadership style emerges which puts weight on the opinion of others. Hierarchies tend to get flatter and there is an emphasis in organizations on transparency and communications so as to receive the input from the organization that is needed (Siilasmaa 2018).

Similarly, rapid change requires the ability to adapt to new realities and lead the organization through it. The rapid pace of change is reflected in the increase of speed in technology uptake, in the exponential growth of data that is being produced and for many executives it translates into always quicker changes in strategy and approach which more and more become "work in progress."

In this situation of swift change and adaptation to new realities, being able to develop and communicate a compelling vision about what the purpose of an organization is and how it can achieve it, is critical. When change is fast, nobody should move with superfluous items that weigh them down. Leaders need to distil from the history and present of a company the essential elements—and only those—that point to its reason to exist and that all stakeholders find compelling to take along as change and adaptation occur. This will increase engagement of all in the organization.

## 7.3   Conclusions

AI is driving profound change in organizations and businesses. A part of the change has to do with how people will work, which kinds of jobs will exist in the future etc. For senior leaders, these changes will affect the kind of issues they have to work on and where and how they need to lead people. Table 7.1 summarizes the different leadership attributes that we have discussed. I think it is fair to say that in the era of AI, leadership work will become more demanding. There is more complexity in the many tasks that need to be handled, there is uncertainty about where things are going,

**Table 7.1** Key leadership attributes in the era of AI

| Know | Do | Be |
|------|-----|-----|
| Technology | Data analysis | Ethical, unbiased |
| Analytics | Judgment | Humility |
| Machine learning | Learning | Adaptability |
| Organizational models | Critical thinking | Vision—purpose |
|  | Augmented work | Engagement |
|  | Process reengineering | Trust |
|  | Strategy setting | Privacy |
|  | People development |  |
|  | Orchestrating collaboration |  |

and in times of change the direction in which things have to go need to be spelled out more clearly. AI will replace some jobs and change all, for managers there will be a lot more to do.

# References

Agrawal, A., J. Gans, and A. Goldfarb. 2018. *Prediction Machines*. Boston: Harvard Business Review Press.

Boden, M. 2018. *Artificial Intelligence: A Very Short Introduction*. Oxford: Oxford University Press.

Chamorro-Premuzic, T., Michael Wade, and Jennifer Jordan. 2018. As AI Makes More Decisions, the Nature of Leadership Will Change. *Harvard Business Review*. https://hbr.org/2018/01/as-ai-makes-more-decisions-the-nature-of-leadership-will-change.

Charan, R., D. Barton, and D. Carey. 2018. *Talent Wins*. Boston: Harvard Business Review Press.

Collins, J. 2001. *From Good to Great*. New York: HarperBusiness.

Davenport, T., and J. Kirby. 2016. *Only humans need apply*. New York: HarperCollins.

Davenport, T., and J. Foutty. 2018. AI-Driven Leadership. *MITSloan Management Review*. https://sloanreview.mit.edu/article/ai-driven-leadership/.

Denning, S. 2018. *The Age of Agile*. New York: AMACOM.

Domingos, P. 2015. *The Master Algorithm*. New York: Basic Books.

Ford, M. 2018. *Architects of Intelligence*. Birmingham: Packt Publishing.

Hesslebein, F., and E. Shinseki. 2004. *Introduction to 'Be, Know, Do: Leadership the Army Way'*. San Francisco: Jossey-Bass.

Hill, A. 2019. Amazon Offers Cautionary Tale of AI-Assisted Hiring. *Financial Times*. https://www.ft.com/content/5039715c-14f9-11e9-a168-d45595ad076d.

McAfee, A., and E. Brynjolfsson. 2017. *Machine, Platform, Crowd: Harnessing Our Digital Future*. New York: Norton.

McKinsey Global Institute Report. 2017. *Jobs Lost, Jobs Gained: What the Future of Work Will Mean for Jobs, Skills and Wages*.

Neubauer, R., A. Tarling, and M. Wade. 2017. *Redefining Leadership for a Digital Age*. IMD and metaBeratung GmbH.

Pfeffer, J. 2018. *Dying for a Paycheck*. New York: HarperCollins.

Siilasmaa, R. 2018. *Transforming Nokia*. New York: McGraw-Hill.

Snook, S., N. Nohria, and R. Khurana. 2012. *The Handbook for Teaching Leadership*. London: Sage.

Susskind, R., and D. Susskind. 2015. *The Future of the Professions*. Oxford: Oxford University Press.

# Part IV

## Some Key Managerial, Interdisciplinary Challenges

# 8

# AI, Marketing Science and Sustainable Profit Growth

Dominique M. Hanssens

## 8.1 Introduction

The digital age is living up to its promise of radicalizing the practice of marketing for businesses large and small. Easily available price and product quality comparisons are enhancing the information used by consumers when they make brand choices. New digital advertising media are vastly superior in their ability to target the right customer at the right time. Online retailing is gaining ground on traditional retailing in a number of sectors. Some argue that the most important of digital marketing changes is yet to come, in the form of network-enabled *smart* devices often referred to as the *Internet of Things* (IOT). When that happens, digital marketing will have invaded all four pillars of marketing activity, the so-called *four Ps* (product, price, place and promotion).[1]

These and other digital marketing actions create a vast array of high-precision data on consumer purchases and the circumstances surrounding these purchases. Some companies and consulting firms have developed a sophisticated ability to *mine* these data for the purpose of improving the effectiveness of their marketing. As a simple example, a consumer whose

---

[1] In what follows I use the term *product* broadly, i.e. a physical product or a service.

---

D. M. Hanssens (✉)
UCLA Anderson School of Management, University of
California, Los Angeles, CA, USA
e-mail: dominique.hanssens@anderson.ucla.edu

© The Author(s) 2020
J. Canals and F. Heukamp (eds.), *The Future of Management in an AI World*,
IESE Business Collection, https://doi.org/10.1007/978-3-030-20680-2_8

past behavior indicates a tendency to buy products "on sale" may be a more lucrative target for promotional offers than another consumer who is brand loyal regardless of price point. The power of developing this capability is well illustrated by the rapid growth of online retailer Amazon.com and the corresponding decline in business performance for a number of traditional retailers.

Perhaps less visible to the outside world has been a parallel development of *quantitative marketing knowledge,* i.e. insights into the impact on business performance of various marketing *actions,* including product, price, distribution and promotion initiatives, and marketing *assets,* including brand equity and customer relationships. These advances were made primarily in the academic world, specifically in research business schools around the world. For example, as early as in 1964 an important econometric study quantified the advertising effects for a health care product (Palda 1964). This discipline, often called *marketing science,* preceded the emergence of the digital economy by several decades, so that a substantial knowledge base was already available and could only be improved upon by the arrival of these new digital data sources. In particular, a number of important *empirical generalizations*—"laws" if you wish—about marketing impact were derived based on hundreds of scientific studies published in the major academic and professional journals. These lessons learned are important as we try to understand which AI initiatives are likely to add value and become successful. In this chapter I will highlight the most fundamental of these generalizations and then discuss their extension and adaptation into the digital age. A more comprehensive review may be found in a Relevant Knowledge publication of the *Marketing Science Institute* (Hanssens 2015).

Quantitative marketing impact assessment is important because, without it, there can be no verifiable connection between marketing investments and business results, so marketing is largely a guessing game. For example, since advertising is costly, an advertiser needs to know by what amount a planned campaign will increase revenue. Then, this additional revenue, multiplied by the brand's gross profit margin, should exceed the advertising cost in order to realize a positive return. But how should one tackle this, given that different industries have vastly different metrics for business performance? For example, a hotel chain may use a "revenue per available room" metric, a bank may look at newly generated customer assets, an industrial firm may look at contract values, etc.

One powerful answer lies in the use of *percent change* as a focal metric, which by definition removes the problem of different measures for different industries. Economists have long used so-called *elasticity* metrics to quantify,

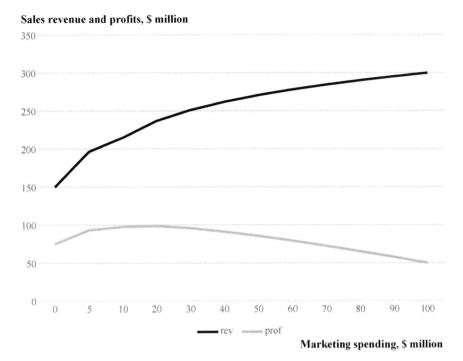

**Sales revenue and profits, $ million**

Marketing spending, $ million

**Fig. 8.1** Illustration of the marketing → sales and marketing → profit relationship (*Notes* In this illustration, sales revenue [in $ millions] is $150 with no marketing support. The response elasticity is 0.15 and the gross margin is 50% of revenue. Sales rev ["rev"] is shown in solid line, and profit [contribution to overhead] is shown in grey line)

for example, the impact of price or income changes on demand. We can do the same thing for the marketing mix, for example an advertising elasticity of 0.12 means that, if you increase advertising spending by 10%, your revenue increases by $0.12 * 10\% = 1.2\%$. Notice that elasticities less than 1 in absolute value imply *diminishing returns* to marketing, a phenomenon that has long been understood in marketing practice. Figure 8.1 shows graphically what a marketing elasticity curve of, say, 0.15 looks like. The more is spent, the higher sales, but these increases happen at a diminishing rate. Since costs are linear, that also implies that, at some level of marketing spending, the additional net revenue no longer covers its marginal cost, so profits start to decline. Thus, from a profit perspective, there is some optimal level of marketing spending, which depends critically on the productivity of that spending (i.e. the response elasticity) *and* the gross margin (contribution to overhead) on sales or revenue. Figure 8.1 illustrates the different shape of the curves connecting marketing spending to sales revenue vs. gross profits.

Now that we have a comparable metric of marketing effectiveness, let's review what thousands of studies have revealed about its quantification. Naturally, individual studies may generate different numbers, depending on the specific circumstances of each project. In what follows, I will describe average or *benchmark* results, along with the conditions under which the elasticities are either higher or lower than the benchmark. I will first review benchmarks for individual marketing *actions* (mainly short-term impacts) and then address benchmarks for marketing *assets* (mainly long-term impacts). A more complete description may be found in Hanssens (2015).

## 8.2 Impact of Marketing Actions

### 8.2.1 Impact of Pricing

In competitive markets, the average price elasticity is around **−2.6**. That is very strong, indicating that consumers are price takers for the most part. However, strong brands benefit from lower up-elasticities (i.e. when a strong brand increases its price, it suffers a smaller decline in volume than when a weaker brand does the same), and higher down-elasticities (i.e. when a strong brand cuts its price, the effects are more pronounced). Furthermore, the digital age makes these price sensitivities a bit stronger, as consumers now find it easier to make price comparisons across brands. The net conclusion is that, in the digital age, *price management* becomes one of the most important challenges for marketing executives, as the effects of price changes are major. In the theatrical and sports worlds, for example, ticket pricing has become quite sophisticated and computerized, including artificial intelligence algorithms, as prices not only reflect the quality of the seat in the theater or stadium, but also the audience appeal of the upcoming performance, as well as the "remaining time until the event."

A special case of price effects is that of **temporary price cuts**, i.e. sales promotions. These are known to be even more impactful than regular price changes, with elasticities of **−4.0** or higher. Thus offering a 25% temporary price reduction can readily *double* sales volumes ($4 * 25\% = 100\%$). There is an important caveat, though: these dramatic demand effects are short lived. In virtually all cases, when product prices return to their pre-promotion levels, so do demand levels. In my own research on this topic, I could find only about 3% of incidences where price promotions resulted in long-lasting benefits for the brand. Since price promotions necessarily involve margin reductions, they can be hazardous to profitability and should be managed carefully. Price promotions are preferably scheduled in an *unpredictable* fashion, so consumers cannot easily build expectations around the next price promotion and postpone their purchasing accordingly. A glaring counterexample of this in the United States is the widely used "January white sale" for linens. Since most consumers are well aware of major discounts on linens in January, why would they buy these products in December?

## 8.2.2   Advertising Effects

In spite of drastic changes in communications technology over the last few decades, advertising elasticities have remained remarkably stable: about **0.1** on average. So, if a brand doubles its ad spend, its sales tend to increase by about ten percent on average, all else equal. That is the smallest elasticity across the marketing mix. There are of course differences in impact across advertising executions. The strongest of those lies in advertising content, i.e. advertising for new products can have an elasticity of up to 0.3, whereas the effects for well-established products can be very small, around 0.01 or even zero. So, advertising when you have something new to say works a lot better than repeating old news. In addition, advertising for durable products (such as automobiles) is generally more elastic than that for frequently purchased products. Indeed, durable products generally involve more purchase deliberation and are riskier to consumers, so they tend to be more sensitive to external information sources, including advertising. On the other hand, so-called advertising *clutter* reduces impact, so the extent to which competitors advertise is another (this time negative) driver of elasticity.

Artificial intelligence has invaded the advertising domain, in particular in improving *targeting*. For example, consumers' online behavior is routinely used to determine what the consumer is currently interested in, leading to more time-targeted advertising messaging. As an illustration, extensive research in the Shanghai subway system has revealed that, the more congested the trains, the higher travelers' responsiveness to mobile ads delivered on smartphones (Andrews et al. 2016). For example, purchase rates from mobile ads are *twice* as high in subway cars with five people per square meter vs. two people. The authors offer an intuitive interpretation of their finding: *mobile immersion*. As increased crowding invades one's physical space, people adaptively turn inwards and become more susceptible to mobile ads. As such, mobile ads can be a welcome relief in a crowded subway environment.

Such empirical findings about consumer behavior, in particular about their use of digital interfaces, are welcome news for artificial intelligence. For example, the finding can be combined with real-time data on crowdedness in various settings in order to determine the optimal time to deliver mobile ad messages. Nevertheless, while the advertising delivery mechanisms (media) continue to evolve, the overall advertising response elasticities on consumer demand have changed little. Not surprisingly, then, after half a century of technology innovations in advertising, the average relative advertising spend in the US economy has remained remarkably stable: around 3% of revenue.

### 8.2.3  Impact of Personal Selling

Sales calls are sometimes viewed as separate from the marketing function of the enterprise, but they shouldn't be. Much like advertising, sales calling represents persuasive information delivery to prospects and customers. However, because of its labor-intensive and personalized nature, sales calls can be expected to be *more impactful* than advertising, and also more expensive (the cost of a typical business-to-business sales call in the US market exceeds $500). The response elasticities support this view, i.e. sales call elasticities average **0.35**, about 3.5 times the advertising effect. We also know that there is an *interaction* effect between the two, i.e. sales call efforts tend to be more productive when the brand or products being sold is supported by advertising. However, both sales calls and advertising are subject to diminishing returns to scale, and must therefore be managed carefully to preserve and enhance profitability, as already illustrated in Fig. 8.1.

Artificial intelligence has begun to impact personal selling, notably through digital delivery channels. For example, using a digital interface, a sales person can deliver a product presentation much more efficiently, thereby reducing the cost of each sales call. Here, too, effective targeting is the key objective, though the task is more challenging, mainly because of organizational buying complexities. However, given the proven magnitude of the sales call elasticities, progress in this area is likely to have a sizeable impact on revenue and profitability alike.

### 8.2.4  Impact of Product Quality

Delivering high-quality products results in positive customer experiences which, in turn, generates customer satisfaction. While this tenet has always been true, it is an area where the internet has made a major difference. Indeed, consumers can now easily track and quantify *product reviews*, as published in various magazines and websites. Do these product reviews matter? We have learned that review *valence* (i.e. the intrinsic goodness or badness of a product review) has a substantial sales elasticity, around **0.69** on average. Thus a ten percent improvement in perceived product quality (as judged by professional reviewers) drives up demand by around 7%! Even the mere *quantity* of product reviews has a positive demand effect, with elasticity around **0.35**. These results demonstrate that the buying public has become much more responsive to objective information about products than about persuasive information (such as advertising).

An excellent illustration of this phenomenon has been provided in the hospitality industry (Hollenbeck 2018). Using a large database of hotel revenues and customer satisfaction ratings in Texas, this research revealed that the relative importance of brand affiliation as a revenue driver has gone down over time, in favor of the perceived quality of an individual hotel. Indeed, travelers now find it much easier to collect quality ratings from individual hotels (say, the Hilton in San Antonio), and these have become stronger determinants of hotel choices than the mere brand affiliation of the hotel (for example, the attractiveness of the Hilton brand name).

## 8.2.5   Impact of product innovation

A somewhat different aspect of product policy is **product innovation.** This is the marketing mix element that carries the most risk because it requires consumers to change existing habits to new ones, especially for major and disruptive innovations such as the all-electric automobile. As can be expected, sales response to product innovation is highly variable, ranging from complete failures to game-changing successes. As such it is difficult to attach a meaningful average response elasticity to innovation. At a qualitative level, we do know that products with an *intermediate* level of newness generally do not fare as well as either *incrementally new* or *radically new* products. Thus the relationship between business performance and product innovation is generally U-shaped.

Going beyond individual sales response effects, extensive research has revealed some remarkable results around innovation effects on investors, i.e. firm value, at least for publicly listed firms. Innovative firms tend to score higher returns than less-innovative firms. The effects are also long-lasting, i.e. one-year window effects of innovation have been shown to be positive, especially for radical innovations. Finally, when a firm shows its confidence in its innovation through aggressive advertising, that enhances the positive effect of the innovation on its stock price.

## 8.2.6  Distribution effects

**Distribution** effects, i.e. how available is the product to the consumer? Research has shown that the sales-to-distribution relationship is S-shaped, whence the need for two elasticities. These elasticities are surprisingly strong, ranging from **0.6** to **1.7**. Importantly, there is a zone of increasing returns to distribution (i.e. elasticity > 1). To explain this, imagine that you are introducing a new frequently purchased product (such as a branded beverage). At low levels of distribution, the product is available only in large supermarkets, where it competes with all other available brands and has a low choice share. However, as distribution improves, the product becomes available in smaller stores, where brand choices are more limited, and thus the product faces less competition. Think about the last time you needed a headache remedy just before boarding a flight. How many analgesic brand choices were available for purchasing at the little store next to the boarding gate?

Distribution impact is also undergoing major change in the digital age. Online retailers offer vastly more choices for consumers compared to their brick-and-mortar counterparts. Painters and other artists whose work was previously viewable only at a local art dealer can now enjoy a global footprint when they list with a digital art store. For individual consumers, distribution is also taking on a new meaning in the form of *apps* on their digital devices. For example, your consumption of financial, real estate, insurance, social media, and many other services is likely to be much higher for providers whose app is downloaded on your smartphone vs. others. Research in marketing science has yet to explore the consequences of these new forms of distribution. However, in light of the high distribution elasticities described earlier, we expect these consequences to be substantial.

## 8.3    Impact of Marketing Assets

The summary above has focused on how commonly used marketing initiatives impact brand sales and revenue, which tend to be the most relevant short-term performance metrics for executives. However, continued marketing actions may also impact two less visible, but potentially more important long-term performance metrics. Unlike sales and profits, which are *flow* metrics, these long-term measures are *stock* metrics. Chief among these are two marketing-driven assets: *brand equity* and *customer equity*. Brand equity refers to the financial value to the firm of customers' perception of the brand. For example, how much more future sales and profit margins can Coca-Cola expect relative to a lesser known competitor brand in the same sector? Customer equity is equivalent to a firm's expected future income streams, but rather than deriving this number from a product perspective, it is derived from a customer perspective. For example, how many new customers can a firm expect to attract and what is the retention rate and profit margin of its existing and new customers?

Since both brand equity and customer equity are critically dependent on various marketing activities, these asset metrics place the marketing function front and center in the economic welfare of a business. In particular, **customer satisfaction** with a brand's offering plays a key role in driving both assets. Perhaps the best way to appreciate this is to study *investor behaviors*, at least for publicly listed firms. It is often assumed that investors (and, therefore, the stock market overall) react only to changes in firm's expected future earnings, which sometimes leads to a perception that "only quarterly earnings reports matter." However, careful empirical research into the determinants of stock prices and stock returns have shown otherwise. For example, Fornell et al. (2016) document that, over a 15-year period (2000–2014), an investment portfolio based on firms' customer satisfaction scores, would have yielded a cumulative return of 518%. By comparison, investing in the S&P 500 would have yielded a cumulative return of 31% over the same time period. Note that this long sample period includes the major financial crisis that started in 2007. The key takeaway is that customer satisfaction movements, even though they are not financial metrics, contain information about the future of a business that is *not* picked up by earnings and other financial data collected at the same time. The marketing profession offers, of course, an intuitive explanation for this phenomenon: satisfied customers are more likely to remain loyal to the brand, to increase their consumption of the brand and/ or to recommend the brand to others, all of which impact future revenue generation in ways that current cash flows may not (yet) reflect.

In technical terms, customer satisfaction strengthens both the *brand equity* and the *customer equity* of the brand. These two brand asset metrics, in turn, have a positive impact on firm value, holding constant other determinants of firm value. This relationship was quantified in a recent empirical generalizations study by Edeling and Fischer (2016). On the basis of nearly 500 estimates from 83 different scientific studies, the authors derive that the average brand strength → firm value elasticity is **0.33**, while the customer relationship → firm value elasticity is **0.72**. Thus marketing actions that strengthen the brand and/or the firm's customer relationships should be viewed as *investments*, not merely expenses as they sometimes are.

Finally, we comment on **market leadership**, an asset that is often pursued by firms. Does market share impact firm value? The answer is "weakly so", according to an empirical generalizations study by Edeling and Himme (2018). Based on 89 prior studies, they estimate the average market share → financial performance elasticity to be **0.13**. This is an interesting result: it confirms, on the one hand, that market leadership (as quantified by market share) matters financially, but on the other hand, the relationship is weaker than that of either brand strength or customer relationship strength. Therefore, *how* a firm obtains a high market share matters, for example is it through brand strength or through low prices? I also note that the market share → financial performance relationship differs across subcategories, for example it is stronger for B2B than for B2C.

### 8.3.1 Impact of AI

The digital age plays an important role in *shifting* the relative importance of the different marketing assets. One of these roles has already been discussed, i.e. providing easy consumer access to plentiful product reviews, which makes consumers more responsive to product information (e.g. the perceived quality of the Hilton Hotel in San Antonio), at the expense of mere brand affiliation (e.g. the Hilton brand name) (Hollenbeck 2018). As a result, *consumer experiential metrics* are becoming increasingly relevant in demand generation and, therefore, firm value. From a societal perspective, the good news is that, going forward, AI can be expected to contribute to a higher overall level of customer satisfaction with products and services.

A careful test of this premise is provided by examining the role of "brand strength" vs. "customer relationship quality" in the prices paid for *mergers and acquisitions*. Indeed, the occurrence of a merger or acquisition is the only instance where *enterprise value* is assessed with real market data. When a merger or acquisition takes place, accounting specialists in "purchase price allocation" determine the fractions of the purchase price that are attributed to "brand" and "customer relations", respectively. For example, in 2012, Kellogg acquired the Pringles (potato chips) business from Procter & Gamble for $2.7 billion. The brand value of Pringles was estimated at 29% of the purchase price (enterprise value), and the customer relations value was estimated at 3%. By contrast, the 2007 acquisition of the Finnish Sampo Bank by Danske Bank resulted in a 1.5% relative brand valuation and 14% customer relations valuation.

Binder and Hanssens (2015) examined the relative importance of brand and customer relationship value for over 5000 mergers and acquisitions between 2003 and 2013. The results are shown in Fig. 8.2. They demonstrate the inverse movement of these two metrics over time. Brand importance declined from about 19% of purchase price to around 9%, whereas customer relationship value increased from about 8 to 17% over the same

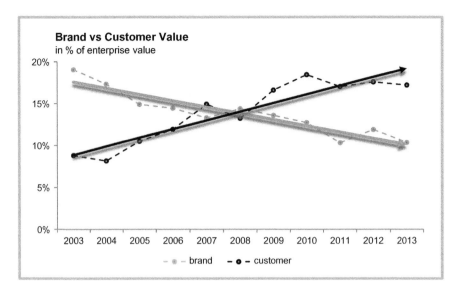

**Fig. 8.2** The evolution of brand value vs. customer relations value in mergers and acquisitions (*Source* Binder and Hanssens 2015)

time period. The authors' interpretation of these trends is that the recent abundance of high-quality customer data enables companies to maintain stronger customer relationships than in the past. While brand remains an important asset, AI on these customer data is increasingly relevant in customer relationship management and, ultimately, in driving firm value.

These insights on AI impact also drive home the important consideration that AI alone cannot build a brand or develop any other important marketing asset for the firm. AI is well suited for enhancing the execution quality of various marketing initiatives, for example through real-time promotional targeting that reaches "the right customer at the right time." However, the response elasticities of such actions are not high enough to create a long-term strategic advantage for firms, *unless* they are accompanied by initiatives that enhance the two key stock metrics for the firm: brand equity and customer equity.

## 8.4    Conclusions

AI has just started to impact decision making in virtually all aspects of business. This chapter has focused on one such business area, acquiring, retaining and growing customers, which has traditionally been the domain of marketing. Even before the advent of the digital economy, a number of *empirical* generalizations about marketing impact had already been established in the young discipline of marketing science. Thus it made logical sense to start with a review of these findings, both with respect to specific marketing actions and with respect to marketing assets. We chose a response metric, elasticity, that enabled us to make comparisons of impact across the marketing mix and we highlighted the difference between top-line and bottom-line impact.

Taken together, we found that the strongest impact of marketing actions results from the *combination* of marketing communications, value to the customer, and distribution. Thus AI initiatives that target prospects with information about a valued product that is easily accessible are likely to be the most successful. That principle is difficult to put into practice, though, because AI by definition requires substantial skill specialization, which tends to create fragmented decision making (*silos*) in the organization. For example, one group focuses on brand marketing, another on social media, a third on dynamic pricing models, but it is challenging to create a unified approach across these specialties. Yet the importance of a *holistic* approach to marketing (in contrast to a silo-ed approach) becomes evident when one considers that the key marketing-generated assets that positively influence firm value are *customer satisfaction, brand equity* and *customer equity*. Making the numerous technological developments in AI serve that purpose is a key challenge for senior management going forward.

At a practical level, the following recommendations for executives follow from these insights:

- Evaluate each AI initiative from a customer benefit perspective. In particular, which of the four marketing pillars are being impacted: product (is the AI creating a better product?), price (is the AI lowering the price for customers?), distribution (is the AI making the product more readily available) or promotion (is the AI providing useful information to customers?).
- Use the known response elasticities to form a preliminary idea about the likely impact of each AI initiative. For example, an AI improvement in sales call effectiveness is likely to have a stronger demand impact than a commensurate improvement in advertising effectiveness. The strongest marketing impact will come from initiatives that *combine* elements of the marketing mix.
- Going forward, expect customers to become more sensitive to documented customer experiences (for example from reliable product reviews), at the expense of overall brand image. Thus the continuous monitoring

of customer satisfaction levels, with rapid intervention when needed, becomes a key managerial priority. AI can play a prominent role in this monitoring.

- Finally, as much as AI can and will contribute to improvements in marketing execution, it will also create more specialty silos in the organization. Each silo will fight for budgets and control, and thus holistic oversight—always focused on the customer experience with the brand— must be provided by senior management.

# References

Andrews, M., X. Luo, Z. Fang, and A. Ghose. 2016. Mobile Ad Effectiveness: Hyper-Contextual Targeting with Crowdedness. *Marketing Science* 25 (2): 218–233.

Binder, C., and D. Hanssens. 2015. Why Strong Customer Relationships Trump Powerful Brands. *Harvard Business Review Online*, April.

Edeling, A., and M. Fischer. 2016. Marketing's Impact on Firm Value: Generalizations from a Meta-Analysis. *Journal of Marketing Research* 53 (4): 515–534.

Edeling, A., and A. Himme. 2018. When Does Market Share Matter? *Journal of Marketing* 82 (3): 1–24.

Fornell, C., F. Morgeson, and G. Hult. 2016. Stock Returns on Customer Satisfaction Do Beat the Market. *Journal of Marketing* 80 (5): 92–107.

Hanssens, D. (ed.). 2015. *Empirical Generalizations About Marketing Impact*, 2nd ed. Cambridge, MA: Marketing Science Institute.

Hollenbeck, B. 2018. Online Reputation Mechanisms and the Decreasing Value of Chain Affiliation. *Journal of Marketing Research* 55 (5): 636–654.

Palda, K. 1964. *The Measurement of Cumulative Advertising Effects*. Englewood Cliffs, NJ: Prentice Hall.

# 9

# How Can Human-Computer "Superminds" Develop Business Strategies?

## Thomas W. Malone

## 9.1 Introduction

To understand the impact of artificial intelligence on management, it's useful to contemplate an obvious but not widely appreciated fact. Virtually all human achievements—from developing written language to making a turkey sandwich—require the work of groups of people, not just individuals working alone. Even the breakthroughs of individual geniuses like Albert Einstein aren't conjured out of thin air; they are erected on vast amounts of prior work by others.

A good one-word term for the human groups that accomplish all these things is *superminds*—groups of individuals acting together in ways that seem intelligent.

Superminds take many forms. They include the hierarchies in businesses and other organizations; the markets that help to create and exchange many kinds of goods and services; the communities that use norms and

---

This chapter is adapted from Thomas W. Malone, *Superminds: The Surprising Power of People and Computers Thinking Together* (New York: Little Brown, 2018; London: Oneworld Publications, 2018) and Thomas W. Malone, "How Human-Computer 'Superminds' Are Redefining the Future of Work". *MIT Sloan Management Review*, 2018, 59 (4): 34–41. Reproduced with permission of the Licensor through PLSclear.

---

T. W. Malone (✉)
MIT Sloan School of Management, Cambridge, MA, USA
e-mail: malone@mit.edu

© The Author(s) 2020
J. Canals and F. Heukamp (eds.), *The Future of Management in an AI World*,
IESE Business Collection, https://doi.org/10.1007/978-3-030-20680-2_9

reputations to guide behavior in many professional, social, and geographical groups; and the democracies that are common in governments and other organizations.

All superminds have a kind of collective intelligence, an ability to do things that the individuals in the groups couldn't have done alone. What's new is that machines can increasingly participate in the intellectual, as well as the physical, activities of these groups. That means we will be able to combine people and machines to create superminds that are smarter than any groups or individuals our planet has ever known.

To do that, we need to understand how people and computers can work together more effectively on tasks that require intelligence. And for that, we need to define intelligence.

## 9.2   What Is Intelligence?

The concept of intelligence is notoriously slippery, and different people have defined it in different ways. For our purposes, let's say that intelligence involves the ability to achieve goals. And since we don't always know what goals an individual or group is trying to achieve, let's say that whether an entity "seems" intelligent depends on what goals an observer attributes to it.

Based on these assumptions, we can define two kinds of intelligence. The first is *specialized intelligence*, the ability to achieve specific goals effectively in a given environment. This means that an intelligent entity will do whatever is most likely to help it achieve its goals, based on everything it knows. Stated even more simply, specialized intelligence is "effectiveness" at achieving specific goals. In this sense, then, specialized collective intelligence is "group effectiveness," and a supermind is an effective group.

The second kind of intelligence is more broadly useful and often more interesting. It is *general intelligence*, the ability to achieve a wide range of different goals effectively in different environments. This means that an intelligent actor needs to be not just good at a specific kind of task but also good at learning how to do a wide range of tasks. In short, this definition of intelligence means roughly the same thing as "versatility" or "adaptability." In this sense, then, general collective intelligence means "group versatility" or "group adaptability," and a supermind is a versatile or adaptable group.

## 9.3    What Kind of Intelligence Do Computers Have?

The distinction between specialized intelligence and general intelligence helps to clarify the difference between human and computer abilities. Some computers are far smarter than people in terms of certain kinds of specialized intelligence, such as arithmetic and certain kinds of pattern recognition. But one of the most important things most people don't realize about AI today is that it is *all* very specialized (Brooks 2014).

Google's search engine is great at retrieving news articles about baseball games, for example, but it can't write an article about your son's Little League game. IBM's Watson program beat the best human players of the game *Jeopardy!*, but the program that played *Jeopardy!* can't play tic-tac-toe, much less chess.[1] Tesla cars can (sort of) drive themselves, but they can't begin to pick something from a warehouse shelf and put it in a box.

Of course, there are computer systems that can do these other things. But the point is that these are all different, specialized programs, not a single general AI that can figure out what to do in each specific situation. In fact, none of today's computers are anywhere close to having the level of general intelligence of any normal human 5-year-old. No single computer today can converse sensibly about the vast number of topics an ordinary 5-year-old can, not to mention the fact that the child can also walk, pick up weirdly shaped objects, and recognize when people are happy, sad, or angry.

How soon, if ever, will this change? Progress in the field of artificial intelligence has been notoriously difficult to predict ever since its early days in the 1950s. For instance, when researchers Stuart Armstrong and Kaj Sotala (2012) analyzed 95 predictions made between 1950 and 2012 about when general AI would be achieved, they found a strong tendency for both experts and nonexperts to predict that it would be achieved between 15 and 25 years in the future—regardless of when the predictions were made (Bostrom 2014). In other words, general AI has seemed about 20 years away for the last 60 years.

More recent surveys and interviews tend to be consistent with this long-term pattern: People still predict that general AI will be here in about 15–25 years. So while we certainly don't know for sure, there is a good reason to be skeptical of confident predictions that general AI will appear in the next

---

[1]David Ferrucci, e-mail to the author, August 24, 2016. Ferrucci led the IBM team that developed Watson.

couple of decades. My own view is that, barring some major societal disasters, it is very likely that general AI will appear *someday*, but probably not until many decades in the future.

All uses of computers will need to involve humans in some way until then. In many cases today, people are doing parts of a task that machines can't do. But even when a computer can do a complete task by itself, people are involved in developing the software and modifying it over time. They also decide when to use different programs in different situations and what to do when things go wrong.

## 9.4   How Can People and Computers Work Together?

One of the most intriguing possibilities for how people and computers can work together comes from an analogy with how the human brain is structured. There are many different parts of the brain that specialize in different kinds of processing, and these parts somehow work together to produce the overall behavior we call intelligence. For instance, one part of the brain is heavily involved in producing language, another in understanding language, and still another in processing visual information. This "society of mind" (Minsky 1988) suggests a surprisingly important idea for how superminds consisting of both people and computers might work: Long before we have general AI, we can create more and more collectively intelligent systems by building societies of mind that include both humans and machines, each doing part of the overall task.

In other words, instead of having computers try to solve a whole problem by themselves, we can create cyber-human systems where multiple people and machines work together on the same problem. In some cases, people may not even know—or care—whether they are interacting with another human or a machine. People can supply general intelligence and other skills that machines don't have. The machines can supply the knowledge and other capabilities that people don't have. And, together, these systems can act more intelligently than any person, group, or computer has done before.

How is this different from current thinking about AI? Many people today assume that computers will eventually do most things by themselves and that we should put "humans in the loop" in situations where people are still needed (Biewald 2015). But it's probably more useful to realize that most things now are done by groups of people, and we should put computers into these groups in situations where that is helpful. In other words, we should move from thinking about *putting humans in the loop to putting computers in the group*.

## 9.5    What Roles Will Computers Play Relative to Humans?

If you want to use computers as part of human groups in your business or other organization, what roles should computers play in those groups? Thinking about the roles that people and machines play today, there are four obvious possibilities. People have the most control when machines act only as *tools*; and machines have successively more control as their roles expand to *assistants*, *peers*, and, finally, *managers*.

### 9.5.1   Tools

A physical tool, like a hammer or a lawn mower, provides some capability that a human doesn't have alone—but the human user is directly in control at all times, guiding its actions and monitoring its progress. Information tools are similar. When you use a spreadsheet, the program is doing what you tell it to do, which often increases your specialized intelligence for a task like the financial analysis.

But many of the most important uses of automated tools in the future won't be to increase individual users' specialized intelligence. Instead, they'll be to increase a group's collective intelligence by helping people communicate more effectively with one other. Even today, computers are largely used as tools to enhance human communication. With e-mail, mobile applications, the web in general, and sites such as Facebook, Google, Wikipedia, Netflix, YouTube, and Twitter, we've created the most massively connected groups the world has ever known. In all these cases, computers are not doing much "intelligent" processing; they are primarily transferring information created by humans to other humans.

While we often overestimate the potential of AI, we often underestimate the potential power of this kind of *hyperconnectivity* among the 7 billion or so amazingly powerful information processors called human brains that are already on our planet.

## 9.5.2  Assistants

A human assistant can work without direct attention and often takes initiative in trying to achieve the general goals someone else has specified. Automated assistants are similar, but the boundary between tools and assistants is not always a sharp one. Text-message platforms, for instance, are mostly tools, but they sometimes take initiative and autocorrect your spelling (occasionally with hilarious results).

Another example of an automated assistant is the software used by the online clothing retailer Stitch Fix Inc. based in San Francisco, California, to help its human stylists recommend items to customers (Wilson et al. 2016). Stitch Fix customers fill out detailed questionnaires about their style, size, and price preferences, which are digested by machine learning algorithms that select promising items of clothing.

The computer in this partnership is able to take into account far more information than human stylists can. For instance, jeans are often notoriously hard to fit, but the algorithms are able to select for each customer a variety of jeans that other customers with similar measurements decided to keep.

And it is the stylists who make the final selection of five items to send to the customer in each shipment. The human stylists are able to take into account information the Stitch Fix computers haven't yet learned to deal with—such as whether the customer wants an outfit for a baby shower or a business meeting. And, of course, they can relate to customers in a more personal way than the computerized assistant does. Together, the combination of people and computers provide better service than either could alone.

## 9.5.3  Peers

Some of the most intriguing uses of computers involve roles in which they operate as human peers more than assistants or tools, even in cases where there isn't much actual artificial intelligence being used. For example, if you are a stock trader, you may already be transacting with an automated program trading system without knowing it.

And if your job is dealing with claims for Lemonade Insurance Agency LLC, based in New York City, you already have an automated peer named AI Jim (Wininger 2016). AI Jim is a chatbot, and Lemonade's customers file claims by exchanging text messages with it. If the claim meets certain parameters, AI Jim pays it automatically and almost instantly. If not, AI Jim refers the claim to one of its human peers, who completes the job.

### 9.5.4  Managers

Human managers delegate tasks, give directions, evaluate work, and coordinate others' efforts. Machines can do all these things, too, and when they do, they are performing as automated managers. Even though some people find the idea of a machine as a manager threatening, we already live with mechanical managers every day: A traffic light directs drivers instead of a police officer; an automated call router delivers work to call center employees instead of a human manager. Most people don't find either situation threatening or problematic.

So if computers can play various roles relative to the people in groups, how can they help the superminds actually be smarter in developing strategies?

## 9.6    How Will Superminds Develop Strategies?

If you want to design a supermind (like a company or a team) that can act intelligently, it needs to have some or all of the five cognitive processes that intelligent entities have—whether they are individuals or groups. Your supermind will need to *create* possibilities for action, *decide* which actions to take, *sense* the external world, *remember* the past, and *learn* from experience (see Fig. 9.1).

Computers can help do all these things in new ways that often—but, of course, not always—make the superminds smarter. To see how, let's consider

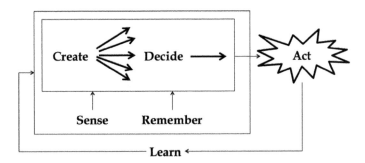

**Fig. 9.1**  The basic cognitive processes needed by any intelligent entity. Entities that act intelligently (such as people, computers, and groups) usually need to do five things: create possibilities for action, decide which actions to take, sense the external world, remember the past, and learn from experience (Reproduced from Malone 2018, *Superminds*)

how a large corporation like Procter & Gamble could develop a new strategic plan. The possibilities we'll discuss are just that: possibilities. I have no reason to believe that P&G is doing these things at present. But I think that P&G and many other companies are likely to do things like this in the future.

### 9.6.1 How Has P&G Done Strategic Planning in the Past?

Before considering how P&G may do strategic planning in the future, let's look at how they did it in the past. According to P&G's former CEO, A. G. Lafley, the strategic planning process the company used under his leadership focused on a series of key questions about the company's overall *goals*, the *markets* it wants to address, the *value for customers* it provides, the *activities* that provide this value, and the ways it can gain strategic *advantages over its competitors* (Lafley and Martin 2013; Lafley et al. 2012).

For example, in the late 1990s, P&G used this process to decide whether to try to become a major player in the global beauty-care sector. A key problem was that P&G didn't have a credible brand in skin care, the largest and most profitable part of that sector. Its only entry was the struggling Oil of Olay[2] brand, which had relatively small sales and an aging customer base. P&G identified several possible strategic options, including: abandoning Oil of Olay and acquiring an established brand from a competitor; keeping Oil of Olay as a low-priced, mass-market brand for older customers and improving its wrinkle-reduction performance; moving Oil of Olay into the higher-priced prestige distribution channel of upscale department stores; or reshaping the brand to be a "masstige" brand sold in special display cases of mass-market retailers at a price point somewhere between mass-market and prestige products.

To evaluate these options, Lafley and his colleagues specified "conditions for success" that would have to be true for each choice to be successful. For instance, they believed that for the innovative "masstige" option to work, the following had to be true: the potential customer segment would need to be big enough to be worth targeting, P&G would need to be able to produce the product at a cost that would allow a lower selling price than the full-on prestige products in the category and mass-market retailers would need to

---

[2]Oil of Olay and all other products named here are trademarks of Procter & Gamble.

be willing to create special display cases for this new product category. A key part of the process was doing research to gauge whether these conditions were true.

According to Lafley, the strategy-development process was organized as a series of meetings with a carefully selected team of people from different parts of the company. For instance, the strategy team didn't just include senior executives and their staff members; it also included promising junior executives and operations managers who would help implement whatever decisions were made. The result of all this work was P&G's decision to revive the Oil of Olay brand by moving it into the new "masstige" category.

Lafley and his collaborators suggest that a similar process was also used to develop strategies at other levels of P&G—not just in specific product categories (like skin care) but also in larger product sectors (like beauty products) as well as for the whole corporation.

Now let's consider how computers could help improve a strategic planning process like this by *involving more people* and by *letting computers do more of the thinking* in the various cognitive processes required.

## 9.6.2  Create

The traditional strategic planning process in P&G and most other large companies involves a relatively small group of people and relies heavily on the time-honored communication technology we call meetings. But imagine what would it look like if companies used online tools to open up the process to anyone in the company who wanted to participate and even to selected others from outside the company, too.

### Contest Webs

One promising approach for doing this is to use a family of related online contests, called a *contest web* (Malone et al. 2017). There could be separate online contests for strategies at different levels of the organization. For example, if P&G used this approach, the company might have separate contests to create strategies for each brand, such as Oil of Olay, Pantene shampoo, and Tide laundry detergent. It could also have separate contests for how to combine the strategies of the brands in each business unit, such as beauty-care and fabric care. And the company could have another contest aimed at combining the strategies for all the business units into a single overall corporate strategy (see Fig. 9.2).

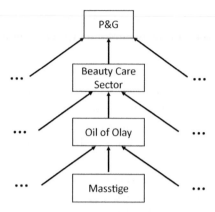

**Fig. 9.2** A "contest web" for developing strategies at different levels of a company. In each contest, people compete to develop good strategies for that part of the company. Contests at higher levels combine strategies from lower levels (Reproduced from Malone 2018, *Superminds*)

In each of these challenges, anyone in the company could propose a strategic option, and others could then comment on or help develop the ideas. Eventually there would be one "winner" in each challenge—the strategy that was eventually chosen—but during the planning process, it would be important to consider a number of different options.

In the *Oil of Olay* challenge, for example, people might propose strategies like the ones we saw above. In each case, they would need to describe key elements of the strategy, such as product characteristics, customers, and competitive advantage. With regard to the "masstige" strategy that P&G eventually chose, for instance, a proposal might say that P&G's labs would give the product broader antiaging effects than its competitors and that it would be advertised and packaged as a prestige brand even though the price would fall somewhere between mass-market and prestige levels.

But by opening the process to lots of people, surprising new options might arise. For instance, if this process was used today for P&G's cosmetics strategy, a group of young, tech-savvy employees—who would probably never have been included in the corporate strategic planning process in the 1990s—might propose a whole new cosmetics concept involving skin and eye makeup specially formulated for each customer based on selfies that customers take off their own faces and questions they answer about their style preferences.

In the challenge at the next level up, for the *global beauty-care sector*, people could propose strategies that included options for Oil of Olay as well as for Cover Girl cosmetics, Pantene shampoos, and other current or potential

P&G brands. In each case, the proposals would need to describe how the strategies for all the brands would fit together into a coherent sector-level plan. For instance, Pantene and Cover Girl might do joint advertising in certain channels, and Pantene and Head & Shoulders shampoos might try to avoid competing too directly with each other.

At the *overall corporate strategy* level, proposals could include combinations of strategies for each sector: beauty, grooming, health care, and so forth. For instance, the overall corporate strategy Lafley described for P&G included elements like using large-scale R&D capabilities to build highly differentiated products with global distribution. So in a coherent corporate strategy, each of the sector and brand strategies should include differentiated global products.

Of course, these are the kinds of questions P&G already thinks about in its strategic planning process, but with more people involved, there would be many more chances for innovative new approaches to emerge and more chances for people with detailed knowledge of, say, specific manufacturing difficulties to bring their expertise to bear on larger corporate strategies. Thus the odds of P&G finding better strategies could be significantly increased.

## Semi-Automated Tools to Help Generate More Possibilities

So far we've talked about relying solely on people to come up with strategic possibilities. But machines can be helpful here, too. In many aspects of strategy, there are generic possibilities that arise over and over again, and machines can automatically prompt people to consider these possibilities in relevant situations.

For instance, Michael Porter articulated three generic strategies that companies in almost any industry can use: *cost leadership* (being the low-cost producer), *differentiation* (being unique on dimensions, like quality, that customers value), and *focus* (tailoring products to a narrow segment of customers) (Porter 1980). P&G generally uses the differentiation strategy, but in other situations it could be useful to have software tools that explicitly remind strategic planners of possibilities to consider. In fact, in addition to just suggesting individual possibilities to consider, software tools that we might call *strategy recombinators* could also suggest new combinations of different strategic possibilities.

For instance, if people created several possible answers to key strategic questions (such as what products to sell, what customer segments to address, and what sources of competitive advantage to use), then it would be easy for a system to automatically generate many possible combinations of these options for people to quickly evaluate. One possible kind of competitive advantage, for example, might be letting customers use smartphones to customize their products. And the system could automatically suggest the possibility of doing this for all P&G's products: cosmetics, shampoos, toothpastes, laundry detergents, potato chips, and others. Of course, many of these combinations would be silly or impractical and could be very quickly eliminated, but some might be surprisingly useful. And even silly options sometimes give people other good ideas.

For instance, in the early 2000s, P&G developed a process for printing entertaining pictures and words on Pringles potato chips. A strategy recombinator might have led to a similar idea that seems promising: using this technology to let customers buy Pringles that are preprinted with images the customers provide themselves.[3]

## 9.6.3 Decide

One benefit of involving more people in generating strategic possibilities is that you get far more possibilities, and this can greatly increase the chances that you have good options to consider. But deciding which possibilities are most promising requires evaluating them all, and this can be extremely time-consuming.

Fortunately, new technologies make it easier to involve far more people and far more kinds of expertise in evaluating these possibilities. For instance, P&G might want its manufacturing engineers to evaluate whether it is technically feasible to make a proposed new product, its operations managers to estimate the manufacturing cost, and perhaps outside market researchers to predict the demand for the product at different price points. Online tools can make it much easier to involve all these kinds of experts.

It's also often possible for people who aren't experts to do some of the work of evaluation. For instance, one aspect of evaluating a strategy is

---

[3]P&G sold the Pringles business to Kellogg in 2012, so this would no longer be a P&G product. For a description of the invention of the process for printing on Pringles, see Larry Huston and Nabil Sakkab, "Connect and Develop: Inside Procter & Gamble's New Model for Innovation." *Harvard Business Review*, March 2006, reprint no. R0603C, https://hbr.org/2006/03/connect-and-develop-inside-procter-gambles-new-model-for-innovation.

figuring out whether the different parts of the strategy are consistent. In P&G's case, its overall corporate strategy involves selling innovative, differentiated products at a global scale. So if someone created a strategic option that involved selling a low-cost, conventional laundry detergent only in Germany, that would *not* be consistent with P&G's overall strategy because it involves a conventional product, not an innovative one, and a local strategy, not a global one. That means this strategy should probably be screened out. And it wouldn't require an expert in marketing or strategy to tell this; even unskilled workers on Amazon's Mechanical Turk online labor market could probably do it.

## Prediction Markets

In some cases, it may also be worth combining many people's opinions about some of these questions. For instance, P&G might use online *prediction markets* to estimate the demand for products they are considering selling. Such markets have already been used to successfully predict movie box office receipts, winners of US Presidential elections, and many other things. Somewhat like futures markets, prediction markets let people buy and sell "shares" of predictions about uncertain future events.

For instance, if you believe that global sales for Pantene shampoo will be between $1.8 billion and $1.9 billion per year, you could buy a share of this prediction. If the prediction is right, then you will get, say, $1 for each share you own of that prediction. But if your predictions are wrong, you will get nothing (Wolfers and Zitzewitz 2004). That means the resulting price in the prediction market is essentially an estimate of the probability that sales will be in this range

Since some products being considered may never be produced, it's also possible to create *conditional prediction markets*, in which people make predictions about what the eventual costs would be if the product is produced. Then, if the product *is* produced, people are paid for the accuracy of their predictions. If the product is *not* produced, everyone just gets his or her money (or points) back.

In many cases, it might also be useful to let people enter detailed arguments online for and against the different points of view, which could inform the people who are participating in the prediction market. Any of these approaches could provide a strong basis for making a final decision, drawing upon the best information available in a vast community of people with a wide range of expertise.

## Using Semi-Automated Tools to Evaluate Possibilities

The hardest—but also potentially the most valuable—thing computers can do in this process is automatically evaluating possibilities. Evaluating ideas about business strategy often requires the kind of soft knowledge that is very hard to formalize in computers because it's related to the kind of general intelligence that people have and computers don't. But if artificially intelligent computers can do automatic evaluation of strategic possibilities, that allows the whole problem-solving process to operate far faster.

Perhaps the most obvious way to automate part of the evaluation process is to use spreadsheets and other kinds of computer software that can simulate real world outcomes. For instance, if the people who submit proposed strategies for all the parts of your business include revenue and expense projections, then spreadsheets (or other simple programs) can do a good job of estimating the consolidated earnings for your whole company. Or if you've already done enough market research to have good automated models of how different customers respond to price changes, then you could use those models to estimate your revenue at different price points.

Another way computers can be helpful is by applying rules experts have previously specified. For instance, if each person who creates a strategy proposal for P&G checks a box to specify what type of generic strategy his or her proposal embodies (e.g., low-cost, differentiated, or niche), then simple programs can check whether a given proposal is consistent with the overall P&G corporate strategy. Even if the people who create proposals don't specify the type of strategy explicitly, today's natural-language-understanding programs could probably do a pretty good job of figuring it out.

Another interesting way of simulating what might happen in the real world is to use what are called Bayesian networks to estimate probabilities for related events.[4] For instance, a major recession in the next two years could affect many of the factors P&G would evaluate for potential new products, including the cost of raw materials and consumer demand. But if

---

[4]For an overview of Bayesian networks written for a general audience, see Pedro Domingos, *The Master Algorithm: How the Quest for the Ultimate Learning Machine Will Remake Our World* (New York: Basic Books, 2015), chapter 6.

Bayesian networks are often difficult to use at large-scale, but there are numerous technical approaches to doing so. One that seems particularly promising for applications like those described here is Markov Learning Networks (MLNs) because they allow people to specify many kinds of rules for the likely logical relationships among events without having to estimate detailed conditional probabilities (see Domingos, *The Master Algorithm*, chapter 9).

purchasing specialists separately estimate whether materials costs would be acceptable with a recession and without one, and if marketers do the same for sales volume, then a Bayesian network could automatically combine all these estimates with separate projections by economists about the probability of a recession. The result would thus be an integrated prediction that draws upon expertise from economists, purchasing specialists, and marketers, all automatically combined by computers.

Of course, we're still a long way from having anything like complete computer models of even a single company, much less the whole economy. Such models would have to take into account the vagaries of human behavior, political changes, market fads, and all the other complexities of the real world. So even though automated simulations can be incredibly helpful for evaluating strategic options, they're not enough. People—who aren't perfect at predicting these things, either—still need to use their best judgment to make final decisions after computer simulations have done what they can.

## 9.6.4   Sense

A key necessity for developing good strategic plans is the ability to effectively sense what is going on in the external world: What do customers want now? What are our competitors doing? What new technologies might change our industry? By far the most visible technology for improving sensing today is big data and data analytics.

For example, P&G might use AI software to analyze the positive and negative comments about its products in online social networks to gauge how customer sentiment about the products is changing. It might conduct online experiments at different prices for the products. And it might be able to obtain early warnings about sales changes by installing video and touch-sensitive floors in retail stores to analyze how much time customers spend looking at P&G's products versus competitors' products.

P&G might even be able to do something Amazon.com Inc. has already done: use vast amounts of data to develop detailed models of many parts of its business, such as customers' responses to prices, ads, and recommendations, and how supply-chain costs vary with inventory policies, delivery methods, and warehouse locations (Granville 2015). With tools like these, computers can take over much of the quantitative work of strategic planning by running the numbers, and people can use their general intelligence to do more qualitative analysis.

## 9.6.5  Remember

We saw above how software tools could help generate new strategic options by suggesting different generic strategies to consider. More broadly, technology can help superminds create better strategic plans by helping them remember a broad range of good ideas that others have previously had in similar situations. For example, software assistants embedded in an application for generating strategy proposals could automatically suggest a much broader range of generic strategies than those we discussed above, including the following:

- Integrating forward by taking on some of the tasks done by your customers, or integrating backward by taking on some of the tasks done by your suppliers;
- Outsourcing more of the things you do internally to freelancers or specialized providers;
- Moving into related market segments, nearby geographical regions, or other markets frequented by your customers.

When you pick one of these options, the system could then automatically provide a template including the kinds of details necessary for that type of strategy. And the system could suggest many different ways of combining different strategic choices for different products and market segments.

## 9.6.6  Learn

If a system is used over time, it can help a supermind learn from its own experience to become more and more effective. For example, it might help recognize strategic ideas that most people wouldn't recognize in their early stages. In the 1970s, when Steve Jobs and Bill Gates were first playing around with what we now call personal computers, most people had no idea that these strange, awkward devices would turn out to be among the most innovative and influential products of the next several decades.

It's certainly not easy to rapidly filter ideas without missing these diamonds in the rough. But perhaps it's possible to identify the unusual people who do have this skill by systematically tracking over time how accurately, and how early, people predict technological advances and other kinds of breakthroughs. Then we could ask these people to take a second look at some of the "crazy" ideas that we might otherwise reject.

Another intriguing possibility is to use "cyber-human learning loops" that begin with human experts evaluating strategies manually and then gradually automate more and more of the work as the machines get better at predicting what human experts would do.

For example, in a company like P&G that generally tries to compete on quality rather than price, experts evaluating product strategies would usually reject strategies that emphasize low price. But instead of programmers writing programs that explicitly filter out low-price strategies, a machine learning program might automatically recognize that experts often reject these types of strategies and then start suggesting this action. If the experts agree with the suggestion enough times, then the program might stop asking and just do the filtering automatically.

## 9.7   A Cyber-Human Strategy Machine

You might call the kind of strategic planning process we've just seen a *cyber-human strategy machine*.[5] Given how complex such a system could be and how generic much of the work would be, it seems unlikely that companies would develop their own proprietary systems for this purpose. Instead, today's consulting firms, or their future competitors, might provide much of this functionality as a service. Such a strategy machine company, for instance, could have a stable of people at many levels of expertise on call who could rapidly generate and evaluate various strategic possibilities, along with software to automate some parts of the process and help manage the rest.

In the long run, such a strategy machine might use a supermind of people and computers to generate and evaluate millions of possible strategies for a single company. Computers would do more and more of the work overtime, but people would still be involved in parts of the process. The result would be a handful of the most promising strategic options from which the human managers of the company would make their final choices.

With a system like this, it could be possible for companies to dynamically revise their strategic plans much more frequently than they do today,

---

[5]Martin Reeves and Daichi Ueda use the term *integrated strategy machine* to describe a somewhat similar idea. But unlike their article, the focus in the present article is more on how large numbers of people throughout the organization and beyond can be involved in the process and on the specific roles people and machines will play. See M. Reeves and D. Ueda, "Designing the Machines That Will Design Strategy," http://hbr.org.

whenever significant new developments occur. And it seems quite possible that the resulting strategies would be much more intelligent than those the companies use today. In fact, it might become harder and harder for companies that don't have a cyber-human strategic planning process like this to compete with those that do.

# References

Armstrong, S., and K. Sotala. 2012. How We're Predicting AI—Or Failing To. In *Beyond AI: Artificial Dreams*, ed. J. Romportl, P. Ircing, E. Zackova, M. Polak, and R. Schuster, 52–75. Pilsen, Czech Republic: University of West Bohemia.

Biewald, L. 2015. Why Human-in-the-Loop Computing Is the Future of Machine Learning. *Data Science* (blog), November 13. www.computerworld.com.

Bostrom, N. 2014. *Superintelligence: Paths, Dangers, Strategies*. Oxford, UK: Oxford University Press.

Brooks, R. 2014. Artificial Intelligence Is a Tool, Not a Threat. *Rethink Robotics* (blog), November 10. www.rethinkrobotics.com.

Granville, V. 2015. 21 Data Science Systems Used by Amazon to Operate Its Business. *Data Science Central* (blog), November 19. www.datasciencecentral.com.

Huston, L., and Nabil Sakkab. 2006. Connect and Develop: Inside Procter & Gamble's New Model for Innovation. *Harvard Business Review*, March. Reprint no. R0603C. https://hbr.org/2006/03/connect-and-develop-inside-procter-gambles-new-model-for-innovation.

Lafley, A.G., and Roger L. Martin. 2013. *Playing to Win: How Strategy Really Works*. Boston, MA: Harvard Business Review Press.

Lafley, A.G., R.L. Martin, J.W. Rivkin, and N. Siggelkow. 2012. Bringing Science to the Art of Strategy. *Harvard Business Review* 90 (9): 3–12. https://hbr.org/2012/09/bringing-science-to-the-art-of-strategy.

Malone, T.W., J.V. Nickerson, R. Laubacher, L.H. Fisher, P. de Boer, Y. Han, and W.B. Towne. 2017. Putting the Pieces Back Together Again: Contest Webs for Large-Scale Problem Solving, March 1. https://ssrn.com.

Malone, T.W., Kevin Crowston, and George A. Herman (eds.). 2003. *Organizing Business Knowledge: The MIT Process Handbook*. Cambridge, MA: MIT Press.

Minsky, M. 1988. *Society of Mind*. New York: Simon and Schuster.

Porter, M.E. 1980. *Competitive Strategy*. New York: Free Press.

Reeves, M., and D. Ueda. 2016. Designing the Machines That Will Design Strategy. *Harvard Business Review*. http://hbr.org.

Wilson, H.J., P. Daugherty, and P. Shukla. 2016. How One Clothing Company Blends AI and Human Expertise. *Harvard Business Review*, November 21. http://hbr.org.

Wininger, S. 2016. The Secret Behind Lemonade's Instant Insurance, November 23. http://stories.lemonade.com.

Wolfers, J., and E. Zitzewitz. 2004. Prediction Markets. *Journal of Economic Perspectives* 18 (2): 107–126.

# 10

# The CEO as a Business Model Innovator in an AI World

Joan E. Ricart

## 10.1 Introduction

This chapter focuses on the business model (BM) innovation associated with Artificial Intelligence (AI). This technology is almost ready for a profound transformation of business models. And this transformation will change radically the organizations as we know them today. It may take some time but it will come. Under this premise, our real interest is on the role, and the changes in that role, of the CEO. Given our interest on the CEO and our belief that a fundamental task of him or her in this century is being a business model innovator, we will focus this chapter on how AI changes BMs.

For this purpose the chapter is organized as follows. After this introduction, we conceptualize the role of the CEO in Sect. 10.2, as based on our study of many CEOs around the world. In Sect. 10.3 we briefly define a business model and try to justify that today we have, thanks to the technology, many ways to innovate on it. In Sect. 10.4 we enter AI into this equation and try to understand what kind of new business models should be emerging thanks to AI. This understanding of the nature of the disruption is important as we go back to the CEO characteristics to understand the nature of the response of CEO in incumbent firms and how the role

J. E. Ricart (✉)
IESE Business School, University of Navarra, Barcelona, Spain
e-mail: jericart@iese.edu

© The Author(s) 2020

J. Canals and F. Heukamp (eds.), *The Future of Management in an AI World*,
IESE Business Collection, https://doi.org/10.1007/978-3-030-20680-2_10

of a CEO is changing as a consequence of AI that we cover these topics in Sect. 10.5.

With this tour starting at the CEO roles and finishing back to these roles, we try to illustrate that managing a firm will be quite different in the forthcoming future but management per se will still be human, not machine-based; management will still be based on purpose, motivation, and values, and therefore, human will still dominate, but the support of machines will make it tremendously different. Definitively, all will change in management so that the essential will keep being the same. A tremendous revolution at the doorsteps of all firms. Are we ready?

## 10.2  The Role of the CEO

To study the role of a CEO is to study the fundamental priorities and responsibilities of a general management function in any organization. The literature on this topic is scarce and mostly empirical, based on the observation on what managers do. We combined different academic sources with empirical observations (Andreu and Ricart 2014)[1] to propose the split of the general management's responsibilities into four basic areas—areas that are independent of one another, yet constitute a system where the whole is greater than the sum of its parts. General managers should approach each of these responsibilities contextually in order to achieve a balanced and effective fit for the four fundamental areas. The major challenge comes in making decisions and implementing them without losing sight of any of them (see Fig. 10.1).

The first area of responsibility is the *institutional configuration*. This includes the company's ownership, corporate governance systems, and the firm's stakeholders. The degree of freedom of action, in relation to the other three roles, that the general manager enjoys in any given scenario (what we generically define as "governance") will vary substantially from one case to another.

The decisions taken by general management and their respective implementation are, of course, also conditioned by the *external environment* in which the company operates, and this corresponds to the second area of

---

[1]Some key works on what CEOs include: what CEOs do (Mintzberg 1973; Kotter 1982; Drucker 2004), the impact they may have on organizations (Finkelstein and Hambrick 1996; Barlett and Ghoshal 2000); how to develop some specific competencies (Bower 2008; Mintzberg 2004). In addition, I have been interviewing with some colleagues more than 200 managers with general management responsibilities. The outcome is reflected in our publications (Ricart et al. 2007; Llopis and Ricart 2013).

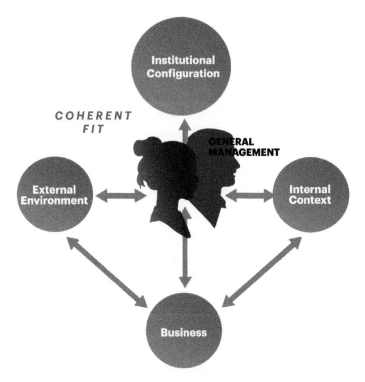

**Fig. 10.1**   The CEO's areas of responsibility (Andreu and Ricart 2014)

responsibility. The general management has to decide on the company's role or external mission (which consists of defining the clients' real needs) within such a competitive environment. Again, the degree of freedom can vary enormously from one context to another.

Management decisions are also shaped by the company's *internal context*, the third area of responsibility. The internal context includes its human talent, business culture, resources, and knowledge. Managers develop the company's internal mission into this framework, including the respect of human dignity and how to develop workers, both personally and professionally.

The fourth area of responsibility is the *business model; it* sets out how value will be created and captured for the different stakeholders involved. As such, it can be viewed as an interactive and dynamic extension of the value chain. The business model is a vital link between the company's strategy and its organization. The responsibility of general management is to establish a business model that follows the company's external and internal missions within an institutional configuration, turning the business strategy into reality through its daily operations.

Managing a system in a balanced way is never easy. It is true that each task has a particular impact and it is relevant by itself, but it's important not to overlook the risk that addressing a challenge in one area may have unintended consequences on another, interdependent area. Therefore, the challenge for general management is the need to manage a *complex, interconnected system*, while the reality is that most of the conceptual models developed to help managers tend to divide the system into its constituent parts rather than dealing with them as a whole. Furthermore, it is also important to reflect these tasks as dynamic, thus we refer these managerial responsibilities as *governing, strategizing, organizing, and business model renewal* (see Fig. 10.2).

Based upon the different cases used to develop this model, we identified three characteristics in which CEOs excel when executing these difficult tasks. These three characteristics are very relevant in difficult times of transformation: *Discipline* understood as rigor and competence, essential

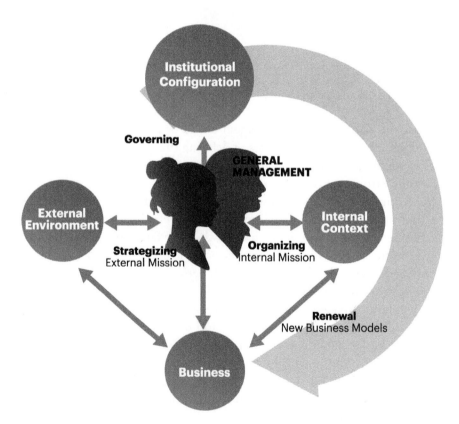

**Fig. 10.2** The key tasks of a CEO (Andreu and Ricart 2014)

elements to manage today realities; *Innovation,* necessary to solve difficult and challenging problems and serve the needs of clients in the future; *Responsibility,* to understand that CEO's decisions have many types of consequences to all stakeholders and the footprints left in the way are extremely important and relevant.

## 10.3 The Impact of Technology on Business Model Innovation

The business model is one of the most widely used terms in both academic and business literature on strategy. Years after the technology bubble burst, leading to the development of many new Internet-based business models, the term continues to be used and reaches top priority in the agenda of senior executives worldwide. Even more importantly, companies who focused their innovation in business models had, on average, operating margin growth over 5% higher than their competitors (calculated as compound annual growth rate in the last five years). The same indicator for companies that innovated in products/markets is positive, but close to zero, and for companies innovating in operations it is even negative (IBM 2012).

There is a growing number of academic papers in this area, including special issues of *Long Range Planning* (2010) and a recent special issue in *Strategic Entrepreneurship Journal* (2015), or *Universia Business Review* (2009) (in Spanish). First, we need to offer a clear definition of what a business model is.

I described it in this way (Ricart 2012):

*A business model* explains *the underlying logic of a business unit,* understood as *how the unit creates and captures value* (Casadesus-Masanell and Ricart 2010). Let us first consider a few terms about this generic definition of the business model on which we find a broad consensus. First, the analysis unit refers to the *business unit* (or, simply, 'the business'). The business refers to a unit that covers specific needs for a group of customers in a given geographical area, and that usually faces an identifiable set of competitive bids. The business unit is therefore identified by external factors (i.e., types of customers, their needs, markets, competitors, etc.). However, this unit is normally identified with a set of activities with which to articulate the value proposition for identified customers. When a firm defines a business unit, it identifies the idiosyncratic factors in which it wishes to compete to serve those needs (or to exploit that opportunity), i.e., the factors of its value proposition. To deliver the corresponding value proposition (and at the same time capture enough value) the company 'designs' its business model. Stated differently, the business model outlines the basic guidelines to follow in order to create value and try to capture enough of the same. Thus, *business models identify the approach for creating and capturing value to exploit business opportunity*, and this approach constitutes *the logic behind the business model.*

The business model is nothing new, as any business had to design business models to exploit the opportunities identified in the environment. The history of the business world is full of inventions and innovations in business models that with the time transform into the standard way of doing things. Innovations can be the result of *technological changes*, like those ushered in by the Industrial Revolution that allowed leveraging incredible economies of scale. One interesting innovation was the development of the commercial radio business model, which offered a free service that was financed through advertising.

Business model innovations sometimes stem from other types of changes, such as the identification of poorly or scarcely covered needs. For example, quick parcel services initially competed with the postal service, which was intended as a public service and did not properly cover some business needs. Similarly, when U-Haul rentals started in the United States there were very few services of this type. As Peter Drucker (2004) noted, "Changes offer opportunities and entrepreneurs design business models, sometimes from scratch, to exploit them more effectively than available alternatives or substitutes."

However, the business model concept is fashionable today and probably for good reasons. One of these reasons is the accelerated emergence of new business models or different ways to compete (create and capture value) popping up in many different fields. Today we are witnessing *an increasing variety of simultaneous competition with different business models in multiple sectors*. There is more room for innovation and, even more importantly, the relevant competition relies less on imitation and more on replacement or, stated otherwise, in the use of disparate business models to address the same needs (i.e., the business unit). Competition today takes the form of substitutive (different) business models instead of the classic imitation of the more successful business models. Furthermore, competing with different business models opens a space to exploit complementary differences and to integrate complements into ecosystems, changing completely the rules of competition.

In other publications, I have elaborated on the drivers of change and the different representations of business models and business model innovation

(Ricart 2015). One of the key drivers of change is no doubt the development of ICT. Javier Zamora (2017; Zamora et al. 2018), has perfectly captured the force of IT change in the concept of *digital density*, the percentage of connected data that is used per unit of activity, a concept that aggregates connections and interactions. As digital density grows, the opportunities and risks of business model innovations increase exponentially.

Before we move into the distinctive impact of AI on business models, let me identify three trends that shape business models today and that interact with AI. First, we see an important move from products into services and solutions. Software can help identify the nature of this change. Software was a very personalized service and most of the effort of software companies were in the direction of industrializing it and having a product they could sell in a massive market. However, more recently, the move (accelerated by cloud) is toward selling software as a service where you pay for use, the software is always updated, and you own the data, but not the software.

The second trend is the growth of ecosystems. Linear value chain is not only fragmented but transformed into a network of complements, suppliers, distributors, customers, and many times actors playing several of these roles. Health or telecom are examples of industries transforming into complex ecosystems. Note also that the previous trend and this one are not independent, just the opposite, they complement each other as each node of the network ecosystem provides some kind of solution to others members of the ecosystem.

Equally related to the previous trends is the third one: the increasing use of (digital) platforms to integrate solutions and coordinate different parts of the ecosystems. Most popular platforms are essentially two-sided where the platform connects suppliers with users many times creating a market or other coordinating mechanisms. But we see increasingly the emergence of complex multisided platforms with extremely complex mechanisms of coordination and value distribution.

## 10.4  Artificial Intelligence in Business Model Innovation: The Case of Platforms

"Artificial Intelligence is that activity devoted to making machines intelligent, and intelligence is that quality that enables an entity to function appropriately and with foresight in its environment" (Nilsson 2010). Operationally, AI refers to a branch of computer science that studies properties of intelligence by synthesizing intelligence (Simon 1995). Fueled by significant improvements in hardware, the trends that drive AI today can be captured, as seen in previous chapters, in the development in many areas, such as large-scale machine learning, deep learning, reinforcement learning, robotics, natural language processing, collaborative systems, crowdsourcing, and human computation, or Internet of things, among others.

### 10.4.1 Business Models and Drivers of Value

AI technologies interact with digital density in a multiplicative way and facilitate the transformation of business models through four key drivers of value (Zamora et al. 2018; Zamora 2019, Chapter 11 in this book):

- *Automation* and process redesign to increase efficiency. As digital density increases it is possible to connect machines and databases with intelligent systems that can control processes with essentially no human interaction: Many retailers online serve clients with automatic systems, and scoring systems are able to negotiate and grant credits without human interaction.
- *Anticipation*, the use of data to predict, is possible today thanks to the new statistics of Big Data. Using it, managers can better decide based on a data-driven diagnostic not possible before. Rolls-Royce uses data to anticipate maintenance decision in their connected airplane engines. We are already seeing many "objects" connected and so controlled "intelligently" at a distance. The use of big data and wearables for medical diagnostic opens a whole new future for medical prevention and treatment.
- *Coordination* can be improved by using remote data together with smart systems overcoming distance, in space and time constraints, for better coordination. Industry 4.0 is all about smart coordination of production systems; the wearable example helps to move sport clothing into health-related services.
- *Personalization* is a further move to the long tail into the one-to-one service, for personal credit, personal insurance, or personal treatment.

### 10.4.2 The Emergence of AI-Based Platforms

AI-based business models can help humans to do particular activities or even full modules in a more efficient way. They can analyze and remember great quantities of data, can uncover new patterns, and can do simple tasks very efficiently. As a consequence incorporating technology can increase the efficiency of our current business models and be a perfect tool or assistant to the humans involved in the process. But technology allows the emergence of novel business models that do things in a different way leveraging the key drivers of AI technologies; by combining the four drivers identified above, new disruptive business models can emerge.

IT and in particular AI technologies allow the invention of disruptive business models in many areas of activities as transportation, home robots, healthcare, education, and public safety, among others In many sectors with high digital density AI technologies (fast learning and smart interaction) have the potential to transform everything. As we see applications in different areas and experimentation in many others, we can identify some common characteristics of the emerging business models. The drivers identified before moving the design of business models from the simple "product" or "service" to satisfy a need to a (personalized) solution provided by a coordinated ecosystem supported by a platform offering. This integrates personalization, coordination, some level of automation and good capacities of anticipation, all packaged in a multisided platform. One common characteristic of these business models is the use of platforms.

A platform business model is a particular way to coordinate different partners in a value creation and value sharing exercise by providing enough value proposition to each partner to get this collaboration going Platforms are therefore tools to coordinate partners in an ecosystem to get enough integration to solve the real problems of the clients. As Malone (2018) points out, platforms use different coordination mechanisms as markets (prices), hierarchies (orders), democracies, (votes), or even just the right incentives or other forms of motivation. We have special interest in the new emerging set of (online) platforms business models that combine human and machine intelligence to create new logics for value creation.

A platform as Uber is a good example. Perhaps the key contribution of Uber is to be able to substitute a hierarchical "regulated taxi" with a market-driven mobility system that can better satisfy both sides of the market. Furthermore, AI is successfully used to "predict" where clients will need to hail a taxi, so creating new sources of value. Thanks to AI we can create an improved market where before regulation used hierarchy to solve "the market failure."

Malone (2018) suggests how we can compare different "platforms" depending on three variables: Cost of group decision-making; benefits of group decision-making; distribution of such benefits. As we apply all these concepts to the business ecosystems and their evolution and try to understand business model innovation and competition, we learn that IT and AI in particular can change in a drastic way the effectiveness of different platforms, by creating opportunities to develop novel business models that try to capture the value created by better forms of coordination in the platform. We do not try to claim any dominance of one form over the other overall, as each one will depend on the particular goals of each business model; however, we can see that new disruptive business models emerge in each different industry.

Transportation is a good example of an industry, perhaps to be called mobility, which has already changed and will drastically change thanks to the technology. Cars are already pretty smart and connected. Most cars incorporate already a GPS system to assists drivers and at the same time to provide very valuable information to technology companies and car manufacturers about transportation patterns. Furthermore, cars are already equipped with a wide range of sensors, again some of them helpful to the drivers but others mostly to capture information. Before self-driving vehicles become a reality, we already count with some automated functionality, including elements such as: Intelligent Parking Assist System, available since 2003; summon parking, available since 2016; lane departure systems, in use in North America since 2004; adaptive cruise control, in use in North America since 2005; blind spot monitoring, available since 2007; and lane changing systems, in highways since 2015 in North America. Not yet self-driving but "these functionalities assist drivers or completely take over well-defined activities for increased safety and comfort" (AI100 2016, p. 19).

Self-driving cars have evolved from 2000 until today and we see a lot of experimentation in progress. Google's and Tesla's semi-autonomous cars are driving on city streets today. Others are following. We still need some technological deployments (as G5 for fast communications) and greater difficulties are associated to security concerns, insurance contracts, or ethical decision-making. All this makes it unclear a broad acceptance soon, but we are at the door of seeing more controlled deployment. As we move into self-driving and the prevalence of sharing systems of all types, we can see a great move from ownership to mobility as a service where community and market mechanisms will substitute hierarchical systems.

Demand transportation systems as Uber, Lyft, Didi, or Cabify have been emerging in different parts of the world. Hierarchical systems as regulated taxis are being substituted by market systems with dynamic pricing. At the same time, these players are collecting so much information on transportation patterns they can be very relevant actors in the learning systems to move into self-driving cars.

The concept of mobility as a service is being developed in many cities around the world. Technology and data help develop better transportation planning systems. Cities use AI methods to optimize services in several ways, such as bus and subway schedules, tracking traffic conditions, dynamically adjusting speed limits and applying smart pricing in highways, bridges, and HOV lanes… The multimodal systems are every time more integrated (hierarchy) in pricing, design, and scheduling; but we also see "voting" systems (as the use of Waze) that provide a lot of information for people to make their own choices, together with market systems as dynamic prices. Large megacities as well as small ones, transform themselves in coordinated communities or complex ecosystems where optimization is possible thanks to smart systems and integration. Sensors in cities and infrastructure are essential for the well running of these systems as well as to collect enough big data that AI machines can "learn" and better predict the necessary actions and recommendations for all this to work fine. A key question is: are systems resilient and foolproof enough?

We do not expect these systems to work without human intervention any time soon; we do expect humans to become partners to self-driving cars and drones in their training, execution, and evaluation. This partnering will happen both helping humans that are collocated with machines, but also virtually. "We predict advances in algorithms to facilitate machine learning from human input. We also expect models and algorithms for modeling of human attention, and to support communication and coordination between humans and machine. This is an integral part of the development of future vehicles" (AI100 2016, p. 24).

Of course transportation industry is just an example of the type of changes we should be expecting relatively soon as the process is already starting in other industries as home robots, health, education, community services, public safety, and security or entertainment.

Airbnb is also an illustrative case. The company was founded in 2009 in San Francisco by providing a solution to two different problems. On the one side, the founders lived in a large apartment in San Francisco and this was increasingly expensive. On the other side, San Francisco had recurrently students and association meetings with a lot of people looking for inexpensive accommodation. The solution was to add some airbeds in their apartment and sell the space to people attending the event with an application. Airbnb was born. It rapidly expanded in the city and moved soon to New York but the value proposition was the same: find hosts with unused space, help them to distribute it to visitors, and offer an alternative accommodation for guests and visitors.

The business grew very fast and soon the listed space incorporated much more than unused space, moving full apartments into short-term renting, full houses with many apartments or many rooms, small hotels, all these offerings were listed in Airbnb sites, creating big conflicts with city officials, especially in large touristic cities. Very fast the platform has been evolving in different dimensions. On the one hand, providing a more collaborative relation with cities and clarifying the offering by additional segmentation of clients and host, using AI systems to match both sides. Overall Airbnb is a multisided platform offering many different services and types of accommodation and creating a new tourist in partnership with the cities (even if this has proven very difficult in some cities).

### 10.4.3 Platforms and Public–Private Collaborations

In addition to Airbnb, the growth of cities today also provides many examples of community-like organizations in megacities where technology has a fundamental key role. IT and in particular AI open new opportunities to create Public–Private Collaboration, even involving large communities of user, not possible without this technology. In fact the role of the public sector is very important to "moderate" these platform business models and to make them acceptable to the citizens while avoiding excessive capture of monopoly rents. Note that integration is key, but of course it makes all members of the ecosystem afraid and the public role in regulating and policing such systems is fundamental.

Beyond C2C and B2C, platform businesses and ecosystems are also emerging in the B2B world. But in this context, the ecosystem members are vulnerable to the excessive exploitation by the technology platform that integrates them. As a consequence, we see more reticence to the development of these new business model of those emerging with the use of some kind of Public–Private organization that plays the role of controlling the platform. Sometimes focused platforms emerge thanks to the reputation and deep relationship of trust already existing. For instance, Hilti was able to develop a business of fleet management, setting a platform to control power tools in construction sites. While the platform has been pretty successful thanks to the established reputation of the company specialized in construction sites and already selling direct, but it faces a lot of difficulties in establishing itself as the platform to serve all types of tools and supplies to construction sites.

While we do not try to forecast winners in each field, Malone (2018) helps us identify three key trends associated to the use of new technologies.

AI technology allows the emergence of very large ecosystems with novel ways to organize and coordinate; and we know that larger ecosystems are smarter as the size is relevant! As the community gets larger we get all kinds of diversity, unusual skills, new forms of knowledge and ideas. AI technologies also decrease the cost of group decision-making in platforms (even with growing size), therefore making possible coordination that before was not possible. We have already seen some key mechanisms in the previous examples.

How can the ecosystems and communities think more intelligently? They get to be smarter as a consequence of the big increase on digital density realized by the combination of: *smarter sensing*, associated to Internet of the Things and the increasing number of sensors everywhere; *smarter remembering*, of course associated to big data; and *smarter learning*, as machine learning or deep learning. Improvements in this front allow machines, with human help or autonomously, to learn at a big speed.

The ideas above show the potential for disruptive business models. And they touch just the surface and leave away novel business models emerging for new combinations of platforms and ecosystems in a way we have not yet imagined. The revolution is already at our door.

What are the barriers to the development of solution-driven ecosystems integrated by platforms and enabled by technology? Of course one limitation is still the development of the technology, but speed is exponentially increasing with the computer power of today and the big growth in data. The real barriers, as we elaborate latter, are security, privacy, reliability, and ethics. And also good management needed to excel in the new forms of competition today, platform competition.

## 10.5   Incumbents Reaction to Disruptive Models

We do not know how the disruptive business models based on AI will look exactly in each particular industry or even when and how they will emerge, however we have shown that the potential is present in almost any economic activity and even to satisfy some needs not well covered today. We have shown that AI enable managers to make distinctive choices in front of difficult problems they try to solve. Choices could be different assets to invest in, different policies or even different governance choices. In fact, the nature of the new technology enables big changes in governance that can have of course drastic consequences. New choices and new consequences generate new business models, some of them quite radical or disruptive.

We tend to relate disruption with new companies and start-ups, as the lack of position and legacies make them more prone to develop and prove new technologies. Therefore, a fair question to ask is what established companies and in particular their CEOs should do as a response to this important threat?

We have characterized the directions of change for novel business models pushed by IT and in particular AI, so-called smart business models. We have highlighted three key directions: solution-focus, ecosystem-building, and platform-integrated. The emergence of such business models represents tremendous movements relative to the capacity of the members to create capture value. Power to capture value shifts very fast with the introduction of these new players. Therefore one way or another incumbents should be active in this new competitive landscape.

As they get active here, they should respond to some fundamental questions about what role to play in this new landscape. First, can they lead an ecosystem, develop an integrative platform and attract members in the ecosystem? If they cannot, should they be members of an ecosystem? How can they assure value creation and capture in this new game? As governance is key, what role should the public sector, the leading organization, and the company itself play in such governance?

We conceptualized the CEO task as managing a complex open and dynamic system that integrates governing, strategizing, organizing, and business model renewal. Furthermore, they should perform these roles with discipline, innovation, and responsibility as described in Sect. 10.2. As a consequence, facing the threat of disruptive AI-based business models, they should be able to leverage in these characteristics to confront this complex future.

**Discipline** in this context requires understanding the potential of AI technologies and how they can impact their area of activity. Of course, we are not saying the all CEO should be experts in all AI technologies; they should be aware of their potential, follow the main trends, have people or partners that can provide them with insights, follow what start-ups and competitors are doing in this front, and have some level of experimentation. They need to understand AI, its possibilities, its drivers of value, its barriers to overcome.

There are many specific steps to be taken to assure that the company deals with the digital transformation in due time and therefore prepares itself with rigor and discipline to the requirements and opportunities of AI. Some companies can find a way to be part of the ecosystem deeply working on this matters for the application in its industry. For instance, in the transportation industry we have developed above, even car manufacturing or transport infrastructure managers or constructors should be part of the development by collecting information from connected cars, studying data or proving algorithms.

Other industries may also deal with these issues either by establishing alliances or joint ventures with specialized technology companies, or even just licensing technology from them. These technologies are specialized enough that there is room for algorithm developments in technology companies. Of course in these cases some key elements are the discussions on intellectual property and in a very special way the ownership of the data used for the machine learning. The algorithm can be generic but the data needed to help the machine learn is another history. Playing in this arena will be difficult.

One way or another it is a key aspect of the necessary discipline of being a good CEO to find the way to assure the digital transformation of the company and be aware of the state of the art of AI as applied in its area of activity. Being late in this front can be extremely dangerous, but being too early also has pioneering costs. Finding the right balance is difficult but it is fundamental.

**Innovation** is the second key characteristic of the CEO task in our complex times. Without an innovation mindset, the needed changes will be close to impossible. Applying technology to do more efficiently the thing we already do, is just one step in automatization, necessary but not sufficient. It is important to understand also the use of AI technologies for better coordination, anticipation, and personalization in addition to efficiency gains, and this requires doing things differently, so business model innovation.

Whatever we focus on the needs of customers we are already covering or in new ones not well covered today or needed in the future, innovative ways to satisfy them are not just possible but necessary. Nurturing these capacities of creativity, innovation, and entrepreneurship are essential to move forward. This requires developing new capabilities in the organization well in advance to the new technologies being ready for use.

As before, the company needs to be embedded in an ecosystem of innovation, in particular technology-based innovation. Should we develop and experiment with pioneering business models, should we be fast second sensing in the environment and either coping or buying to be a fast second? Should we be intrapreneurs or use corporate venturing? In each case it would depend a lot of our own capabilities and the evolution of the right ecosystems, but we should be there to make the right decisions at the right time. As seen in the different examples, the current state of technology in relation to most industries still calls for experimentation and learning.

The most difficult step in this process will come once we realize that we need to morph our business model to a new business model as, perhaps still profitable today, we believe it may not have future tomorrow. Changing large, successful in the past, business models is a very difficult strategic transformation. Then it would be necessary to change the organizational processes from learning and experimenting to a critical transformation.

**Responsibility** is a fundamental characteristic of good CEOs and very essential in the transformation companies will be facing with AI applications. This transformation will have fundamental consequences to all stakeholders and this requires careful decision-making in the key crossroads along the way. Ethical choices cannot be delegated. They can be consulted, discussed, or debated, but the limits between machines and humans and what it is right or not would have to weighted with strong values and clear responsibilities.

In the phase of experimentation and learning, we need to specially work on several dimensions of governance that could be the biggest organizational barrier to overcome when we need to move into the transformation phase. The first is Fairness: AI algorithms can be fundamentally biased mostly due to the poor quality of data used in the learning process. How to deal with this biased in fundamental before we fully deploy such systems. The second is Accountability: Who is responsible for machine-made decisions or actions? Can we protect the system form unanticipated negative consequences? The third is Transparency: Are the algorithm choices clear and transparence or there is a black-box hiding the logic of the system? Can we and everybody understand the logic of machine decisions? The fourth is Ethics: Are the right values embedded into the system? Can we assure the ethical quality of the decisions?

The above points are more important the more we move AI applications from process automation, to cognitive insight, and finally to cognitive engagement (Davenport and Ronanki 2018). In particular most of the responsibility issues highlighted above (but not all) are especially important in cognitive engagement AI applications where chatbots and intelligent agents make choices that affect human stakeholders, be those customers, employees or any other.

Back to our focus on the novel business models that will emerge thanks to IT and in particular AI technologies. How can a CEO use discipline, innovation, and responsibility to sense, think, design, and deploy novel business models?

To do so, we have governance, strategy, and organization around business model renewal. The whole system is important, and therefore the role of the CEO in this transformation is, by itself, the fundamental task of this position. We have discussed before that AI technologies will provide opportunities for radical changes in the business model. This type of change goes beyond simple automatization of some parts of the business model, or even just modular changes in some parts of it. It may radically change the way the business model is governed, the capabilities needed in the organization, and the value proposition to the (perhaps new o different) customers.

This has two related and important consequences. The first one is that the transformation that AI, as evolution of the increasing digital density, is inducing in all industries is a clear responsibility of the CEO and its top management team and governance structure. It is located at the core of a general management responsibility. Second and beyond this point, it is fundamental and perhaps the most important task of the CEO today as we are at the door-step of a profound transformation of society and the CEO cannot escape this responsibility.

Our focus has been the impact of AI on business models. While we are still in the phase of experimentation, we expect soon, and have to be ready for, a profound transformation in business models. Such a transformation will have implications for all the CEO. Generalizing is always very difficult as AI can just automatize something in a very efficient way and transform totally the business model in a very disruptive way, but some reflections can be useful.

Changing the business model requires per se new forms of strategizing as the business model is the reflection of a realized strategy. In a world of fundamental uncertainty and ambiguity, the strategy will have to be sensitive to fast learning and agile responses. Many contingencies, and alternative moves in the complex ecosystem will have to be involved in the strategy. As mentioned, we are still in the phase of learning, but an agile response should be soon ready.

As consequence organizations should move into an agile mode and this is a big change for many companies, especially large successful organizations. Note that there is a kind of a double necessity for agility. Smart business models will require agile organizations able to grow fast in a decentralized way. At the same time, corporate organizations need to be agile if they want to be effective in transforming and morphing their businesses to AI-based business models.

Last, but not least, one should be aware that the nature of the change in the transformation phase may require changes in the governance of the firm. CEOs need to reflect on the stakeholders that should be involved, on the type of regulation and non-market strategy, on the social impact of the business, on the change in vision, or in the form of governance. Everything may require a change as the transformation of the business moves ahead.

As all the genuine responsibilities are affected, will AI replace management itself? Will we see machines managing humans? Will we automatize business models to replace CEOs?

We will surely see mostly machines supporting humans and substituting some activities, and modules by programmed ones, smart objects, smart contracts, perhaps smart business models, but essentially more a complement (augmentation) to management that a substitute. Machine learning may support management but not replace it, at least not yet.

Management will stay the same, but it may also be very different, more data supported, more evidence-based, with more AI support. If we focus on the CEO genuine responsibilities, governing will still involve mechanisms for engaging stakeholders and building trust, but as commented the changes in governance can be very radical; strategizing is still making choices, purpose is still fundamental, imagination, and innovation are still on the human side, again the strategy of the future can be radically different, but the strategist is still a human; organizing represent managing complex trade-offs and building processes to reconcile different viewpoints, making trade-off over time and investments facing high uncertainty and long-term payoffs, or crafting a sense of identity or purpose as well as eliciting discretionary efforts from employees. Humans will still be at the helm but supported by IT to be agile; last but not least, business model renewal and invention still needs imagination, creativity, and a holistic view and machines are far from it.

Discipline, innovation, and responsibility will stay as the key characteristics of CEOs, and these characteristics are still on humans not machines. Machines can take parts of the tasks, provide more discipline, more evidence, and allow faster experimentation, but imagination, purpose, motivation, dealing with humans will still remain human tasks. Dealing with the barriers and challenges associated to technology (and data) requires ethical governance choices and this cannot be delegated, even less delegated to machines. Values are still on the human side.

# References

AI100. 2016. *One Hundred Year Study on Artificial Intelligence.* Stanford University. https://ai100.stanford.edu. Accessed August 1, 2016.

Andreu, R., and J.E. Ricart. 2014. The Genuine Responsibilities of the CEO: A Framework for Managing Today. *IESE Insight* 23 (Fourth Quarter): 15–21.

Bartlett, C.A., and S. Ghoshal. 2000. *The Individualized Corporation: A Fundamentally New Approach to Management.* Chatham, Kent: Random House.

Bower, J.L. 2008. The Teaching of Strategy: From General Manager to Analysis and Back Again. *Journal of Management Inquiry* 17: 269–275.

Casadesus-Masanell, R., and J.E. Ricart. 2010. From Strategy to Business Models and Onto Tactics. *Long Range Planning* 43 (2–3): 195–215.

Casadesus-Masanell, R., and J. E. Ricart. 2011. How to Design a Winning Business Model. *Harvard Business Review* 89 (1/2): 100–107.

Davenport, T. H., and R. Ronanki. 2018. Artificial Intelligence for the Real World. *Harvard Business Review* 96 (1): 108–116.

Drucker, P. 2004. *The Practice of Management.* Oxford: Elsevier Butterworth-Heinemann.

Finkelstein, S., and D. Hambrick. 1996. *Strategic Leadership: Top Executives and Their Effects on Organizations.* Minneapolis/St. Paul: West Pub. Co.

IBM Global Business Services. 2012. Global CEO Study 2006, 2008, 2010, 2012. The 2012 Study. Available at http://www-05.ibm.com/services/es/ceo/ceostudy2012/.

Kotter, J. 1982. *The General Managers.* New York: Free Press.

Llopis, J., and J.E. Ricart. 2013. *Qué hacen los buenos directivos: El reto del Siglo XXI.* Madrid: Pearson Education.

Malone, T. W. 2018. *Superminds: The Surprising Power of People and Computers Thinking Together.* New York: Little, Brown.

Mintzberg, H. 1973. *The Nature of Managerial Work.* New York: Harper Collins.

Mintzberg, H. 2004. *Managers Not MBAs: A Hard Look at the Soft Practice of Managing and Management Development.* San Francisco, CA: Berrett-Koehler.

Nilsson, N.J. 2010. *The Quest for Artificial Intelligence: A History of Ideas and Achievements.* Cambridge: Cambridge University Press.

Ricart, J. E. 2012. Strategy in the 21st Century: Business Model in Action. IESE technical note SMN-685-E.

Ricart, J.E. 2015. The CEO as a Business Model Innovator. In *Shaping Entrepreneurial Mindsets,* ed. J. Canals, 97–115. The Palgrave Macmillan IESE Business Collection. London: Palgrave Macmillan.

Ricart, J.E., J. Llopis, and D. Pastoriza. 2007. *Yo Dirijo: La Dirección del Siglo XXI según sus protagonistas.* Barcelona: Ed. Deusto.

Simon, H.A. 1995. Artificial Intelligence: An Empirical Science. *Artificial Intelligence* 77 (2): 95–127.

Special Issue on Business Models. 2010. *Long Range Planning* 43 (2–3).

Special Issue on Business Models. 2015. *Strategic Entrepreneurship Journal* 9 (1).

Special Issue on Business Models. 2009. *Universia Business Review* 23 (3).

Zamora, J. 2017. Programming Business Models Through Digital Density. *IESE Insight* (Second Quarter): 23–30.

Zamora, J., K. Tatarinov, and S. Sieber. 2018. The Centrifugal and Centripetal Forces Affecting the Digital Transformation of Industries. *Harvard Deusto Business Review* (279). Ref. 018189.

# 11

# Managing AI Within a Digital Density Framework

Javier Zamora

## 11.1 Introduction

The introduction of AI into an organization should not be considered as a new technology in isolation, but coupled together with other new technologies such as social media, mobile, cloud computing, big data, and IoT, among others. Together they constitute mere manifestations of an environment with an exponentially increasing digital density (Zamora 2017), which I defined as the percentage of connected data that is available per unit of activity, being a unit of activity a country, a region, an industry, an organization, or a business unit. In other words, digital density is an indicator of how many of the processes that are conducted in a given unit of activity are based on data that can be accessed remotely (i.e., connected data). In this sense, connected data becomes an abstraction of the physical entity itself, which can be remotely observed, monitored, and/or controlled.

This increase of digital density is often used to gauge an organization's potential to generate new business models. As digital density intensifies, the once sharply defined lines between the digital and the physical worlds begin to fade, forging a new, blended environment, in a process known as digital transformation. Therefore, we should not consider AI as a mere technological infrastructure. AI has an impact on the business model

J. Zamora (✉)
IESE Business School, University of Navarra, Barcelona, Spain
e-mail: jzamora@iese.edu

© The Author(s) 2020
J. Canals and F. Heukamp (eds.), *The Future of Management in an AI World*,
IESE Business Collection, https://doi.org/10.1007/978-3-030-20680-2_11

| Value Propositions based on AI | Automation |
| | Anticipation |
| | Coordination |
| | Personalization |
| AI Challenges | Privacy |
| | Integration |
| | Reliability |
| | Security |
| AI Governance Principles | Fairness |
| | Accountability |
| | Transparency |
| | Ethics |
| | Practical Wisdom |

**Fig. 11.1**  Business model and organizational model dimensions of AI

(Casadesus-Masanell and Ricart 2011) by allowing new value propositions, and on the other hand the impact on the organization in terms of governance, capabilities, and cultural change. Figure 11.1 summarizes the business and organizational dimensions that a manager should take into account when introducing AI technology into an organization.

The scope and timing of the impact of AI vary from industry to industry. For this reason, we will use examples of different sectors (e.g., healthcare, financial, retail public sector, etc.) to emphasize the different degrees of complexity and risk involved when using new value propositions based on AI. We will first review "why" AI is today a reality in those sectors, identifying the new sources of (big) data. Secondly, we will answer "what" kind of new value propositions based on AI are feasible in different sectors. We consider examples of AI in the context of four types of interactions, namely automation, anticipation, coordination and/or personalization of interactions. Finally, we will address the new challenges in terms of privacy, integration, reliability, and security that AI implementation ("how") poses to any organization.

As connected data, as both input and output of AI algorithms, becomes one of the main assets of organizations, we need to understand the best way to incorporate this technology into the firm's business model. More often than not, deploying any new technology in an organization requires a transition period during which two modes coexist: a learning mode through pilots and an earning mode by executing the current business model. During this transition period, the organization should identify the newly required operational capabilities to successfully manage AI technology. In addition, general management (Andreu and Ricart 2014) should be aware of the new managerial challenges they will face as AI becomes more present in their organizations.

Firstly, organizations will face important issues regarding the fairness of AI models depending on the bias introduced by the training data set. Secondly, as AI is going to be integrated in the decision-making process, issues about accountability will have to be faced in the event of undesired outcomes. Thirdly, general managers will trust those AI systems only if those systems are transparent to them instead of becoming a "black box," that is to say, systems that explain themselves on how they reach certain recommendations. Fourthly, AI should take into account any decisions made on ethical issues based on the values (utility function) when those algorithms are designed. Last but not least, the use of AI must also be guided by the good judgment of the general management, who must act on the basis of what is right for all stakeholders, based on a practical wisdom which is aligned with the mission of the organization.

This chapter begins by introducing AI in the context of the digital density framework, that includes three different dimensions: the technology model, the business model, and the organizational model. Then, using examples of several industries, we illustrate the new kind of value propositions using AI that are feasible today. These new value propositions are the result of combining AI technology in one or more of four types of interactions: automation, anticipation, coordination, and personalization. Next, we address the AI challenges in organizations in terms of privacy, integration, reliability, and security that these new value propositions based on AI pose to the organization. Following these challenges, we identify new capabilities needed to implement AI successfully in the firm. Thereafter, we identify the AI governance principles in terms of fairness, accountability, transparency, ethics, and practical wisdom that a general manager should be aware of and act accordingly regarding the externalities of AI beyond its impact on their business models. Finally, general management should manage AI in a holistic way in the organization, not only by leveraging the benefits of AI in the design of new value propositions, but also understanding AI's current limitations to address new challenges and minimize the negative externalities of the use of AI with customers, employees and the society at large.

## 11.2  AI Within the Digital Density Framework

Although the origins of AI (Zamora and Herrera 2018) as a new discipline date back to the year 1956, only recently it has gained its momentum and many industries have started looking at AI as a promising technology. The AI renaissance as a viable technology happened mainly due to the confluence of three factors. The first factor is the increase in computation power and decrease of its cost, as a direct consequence of Moore's Law. The second factor is the availability of huge data sets (big data) derived from a hyperconnected digitized world. And the third factor is the advance in the scalability and performance of AI algorithms.

In the context of the digitalization of organizations, people and even things, we should not consider AI as a technology in isolation, but together with other technologies, such as social media, cloud computing, mobile, big data, IoT, and blockchain, as a manifestation of a world with an exponential increasing digital density (Zamora 2017). In other words, as much more processes of the organizations, people, and things get more and more connected it translates into a growing digital density and begins blurring the frontiers between the physical and digital worlds. This new scenario where the physical and digital world are indistinguishable is the underlying driving force of digital transformation that many organizations are undergoing in recent years. Therefore, AI is also a technology that leverages this scenario of high digital density by turning the connected data into new sources of value creation and capture for the organizations.

Andrew Ng, Adjunct Professor at Stanford University and a worldwide expert in AI, considers AI as a general-purpose technology such as electricity has been. In other words, AI has the potential to redefine many industries, in the same way, electricity redefined industries at the beginning of the twentieth century or more recently the Internet changed the way many companies compete. However, in the same way that a company does not become an Internet company just by creating a web page, a company does not become an AI-organization by the mere acquisition and introduction of AI systems in their IT portfolio. To that extent, AI, as well as, with other new technologies involved in a digital transformation process should be considered in a holistic way when considering its impact in different dimensions (see Fig. 11.2): technology platform, business model, and organizational model.

In the specific context of AI, the Technology Platform refers to the required IT infrastructure, which mainly comprises of a collection of AI algorithms (Zamora and Herrera 2018) that today—more often than

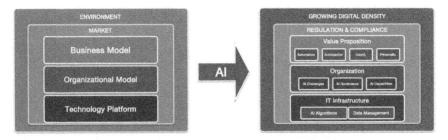

**Fig. 11.2** Framework for digital transformation (left-side) and its application in AI (right-side)

not—are machine learning algorithms performing mainly prediction and/or classification functions. However, the competitive advantage does not reside in owning those algorithms since the majority of them are available to many organizations, but having the data to train and test the algorithm to build and validate a model to be used later with the new data. Consequently, in a world of high digital density, the data (Zamora et al. 2018) becomes one of the fundamental assets of the organization. Therefore, the IT infrastructure comprises also of all the needed information systems to have an efficient data management (i.e., capture, curation, search, protection, etc.).

The next dimension is the Business Model, which refers to the underlying logic and dynamics (Ricart 2012) of a business to create and capture value. One integral component of the business model is the value proposition (Osterwalder and Pigneur 2010), or the products and services that create value for a given customer. In this regard, new value propositions are enabled by using AI technology in four types of interactions:

– *Automation* or using AI to automate existing processes by removing manual steps to achieve cost reductions.
– *Anticipation* or using AI for prediction or recommendation purposes.
– *Coordination* or using AI to coordinate in an intelligent way a multitude of actors who participate in the creation of the value proposition.
– *Personalization* or using AI to customize the value proposition for a given customer.

AI processes data to build the new value proposition (Zamora 2017) using a combination of some of those four types of interactions.

The Organizational Model dimension refers to how AI has an impact inside the organization (Káganer et al. 2013). This includes several aspects. On the one hand, how organizations start using AI in pilots for a learning purpose to explore the potential of the technology, as well as, later scaling successful pilots into production as an integral component of the execution of a given business model. On the other hand, AI calls for new capabilities both at the operational level (e.g., data scientists) and managerial level addressing the new challenges regarding privacy, integration, reliability, and security. Moreover, additional managerial capabilities are required for the governance (Andreu and Ricart 2014) of AI inside an organization given a regulatory and compliance framework where the company develops its activity. Specifically, this governance should address issues related to the fairness, accountability, transparency, ethics, and practical wisdom when an organization offers a new value proposition based on AI.

This chapter will focus on the Business Model and the Organizational Model dimensions.

## 11.3  New Value Propositions Using AI

In Fig. 11.3, we show the digital density architecture, which interconnects the physical world with the digital world together with the business logic. The bottom layer represents the physical world, consisting of organizations, people, and things. Above the physical layer we have the connection layer, which relates the physical world to the digital world. The organizations traditionally have been connected to the digital world by digitizing their processes (e.g., ERP, CRM, etc.), people are connected to the digital world through human-machine interfaces (e.g., web, app, voice, etc.) while things are being connected either through sensors to read their state (e.g., position, temperature, speed, etc.) or through actuators to change their state (e.g., turn it on, accelerate, etc.). On top of this connection layer lies the connected data that represents the physical world (Zamora 2017).

As digital density increases, the data layer better represents the physical world. In this scenario, data is becoming the main asset of the organization, since data has become the raw material for creating new value propositions and in turn for building new business models. Metaphorically speaking, if data is considered the "new oil" of the economy, then AI becomes one of the "engines" which transforms this data into new value propositions.

One example of the increasing digital density in the health sector is the Biobank Data in the UK, where data has been collected from over 500,000 people for the last 30 years, including their medical history, imaging, genetic data via the European Genome-phenome Archive (EGA) and physical and medical activity through mobile monitoring. Health researchers, using AI technology, are working with this data repository to improve the prevention,

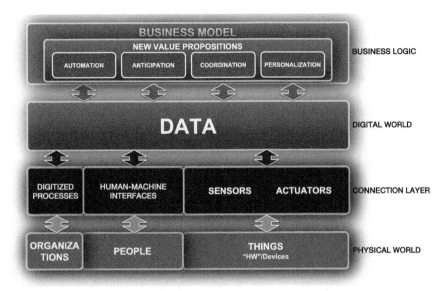

**Fig. 11.3** Digital density architecture

diagnosis, and treatment of a wide range of serious and life-threatening illnesses. Their work is being translated into the deployment of intelligent systems in health care, where doctors can now map a patient's data, including what they eat, how much they exercise, and what is in their genetics; cross-reference that material against a large body of research to make a diagnosis; access the latest research on pharmaceuticals and other treatments; consult machine-learning algorithms that assess alternative courses of action; and create treatment recommendations personalized to the patient.

As we mentioned above, the connected data derived from a high digital density environment can be used to build new value propositions as a combination of one or more of four types of interactions: automation, anticipation, coordination, and/or personalization. Although the majority of the new value propositions are the result of the combination of more than one type of interaction, the following examples are categorized under the type of interaction, which is more prevalent in the value proposition.

## 11.3.1 Automation Using AI

Traditionally, organizations have been connected to the digital world by digitizing their different processes. The majority of these processes could be automated since they could be described by workflows handling limited and well-defined cases that could be implemented in enterprise software applications (e.g., ERP, CRM, etc.). The drastic reduction of computation cost due to Moore's Law has been behind the popularization of this type of software, enabling massive digitalization of companies.

However, some organization's activities require a more sophisticated automation, because they imply an almost infinite number of scenarios (exceptions), that traditional software cannot deal with. In those cases, Robot Process Automation (RPA) or AI "workers" can be used, where AI systems watch/observe the activity of a worker and learn from her/his actions taking advantage of AI systems' large capacity to remember. For instance, AI can be very efficient in the legal world, where traditionally lawyers spent hours searching through documents and looking for evidence (i.e., responsive documents) for a given trial. AI can automate most of the process by pre-classifying the documents into two categories, separating the ones that are not responsive from the ones that might be responsive and should be submitted to a lawyer for a final classification. Similar application of AI can be found during M&A procedures when looking for clauses in all contracts that can imply future liabilities. For instance, clauses in client's contracts that can be terminated in the event of an acquisition.

The previous examples are doable because of the advances in the Natural Language Processing (NLP) techniques for classifying purposes. NLP can be also used to enhance productivity by introducing virtual assistants to automate interactions with customers, which is being increasingly used with chatbots in finance and retail industries. Automation process based on implementing AI in the health sector is represented by algorithms managing data related to medical records, analyzing medical tests, X-Rays, and CT-scans. Sense.ly, a health industry start-up, developed a digital nurse called Molly that helps patients with symptoms that do not require a visit to a physician. Boston Children's Hospital similarly uses the Amazon's virtual assistant Alexa to advise parents about children's treatments or whether symptoms require a visit to a doctor.

Using AI (and other digital technologies) for automation purposes brings the cost down, since less manual work is needed. Frequently automation is the first step that many organizations perform in a context of high digital density as it directly replaces previous manual processes by digitalizing them. However, as technologies spread to more organizations, businesses should focus on other interactions beyond automation (e.g., anticipation, coordination and/or personalization) to maintain a competitive advantage.

## 11.3.2 Anticipation Using AI

As digital density increases exponentially, organizations can take advantage of the generated big data by anticipating patterns and trends that the data reveal. Therefore, anticipation in this context means the ability of making predictions, that is to say, using existing data to generate new data that organizations do not have. In the same way that automation was widely used by companies as the result of having affordable computation, the inclusion nowadays of anticipation in many of the new value propositions is the consequence of prediction becoming cheap (Agrawal et al. 2018).

We can find an example of a value proposition using anticipation in the aeronautics company Rolls-Royce, which can inform an airline when a plane that is landing needs preventive maintenance in advance of the scheduled date. In this way, the airline can avoid unscheduled stops, leading to substantial savings, given that an unscheduled airplane stop due to technical problems costs approximately $10,000 per hour. Rolls-Royce receives real-time operating data, from more than 25 sensors per plane, for each of the more than 12,000 Rolls-Royce engines operating worldwide. By cross-referencing with the records of problems with other engines and applying a predictive algorithm, the company can predict technical problems in specific engines even before they appear. Rolls-Royce's use of AI implied migrating its business model: instead of selling a product (an engine), it offers its customers—the airlines—a service based on the number of airplane engine hours without unscheduled stops (Zamora 2016).

Another interesting example of anticipation in the health sector is Cardiogram, an American company that offers a mobile app acting as a personal healthcare assistant. Cardiogram leverages the data coming from personal wearable devices like the Apple Watch or Android Wear not only to track sleep and fitness activity but also to detect atrial fibrillation. Atrial fibrillation is a type of heart arrhythmia that causes more life-threatening strokes than any other chronic heart condition, and in many cases is undiagnosed, since continuous heart monitoring is needed. In 2016, Cardiogram collaborated in the "mRhythm" study (Health eHeart 2018) together with the University of California in San Francisco (UCSF), training Cardiogram's deep learning algorithm, "Deep Heart," with 139 million heart measurements coming from 9750 users. The result of the study showed an accuracy of detection of atrial fibrillation higher than FDA-cleared wearable ECG devices. Cardiogram is currently deploying "Deep Heart" outside of the "mRhythm" study to offer it to all the Cardiogram App users.

Notwithstanding, a paradigm of using anticipation in new value propositions is IBM's Watson, which has gained a lot of notoriety in the last years. Watson has AI capabilities to process natural language, generate hypothesis, and learning based on evidence. Initially, IBM created the Watson project in 2006 to find out whether a supercomputer could compete with humans' decision-making capabilities when faced with complex challenges. In 2011, after five years of work and training, Watson was sent to compete on Jeopardy!, a television game show, against two of the best contestants from previous rounds. After several rounds of play, Watson won out.

In the wake of the media reporting, in 2013, IBM set up a partnership with the Memorial Sloan Kettering Cancer Center in New York to use Watson for treatment decisions in cases of lung and breast cancer. When making decisions, Watson processes more than two million pages of research articles from medical journals, in addition to an archive of more than 1.5 million patient medical records. To aid physicians in the treatment of their patients, once a physician has posed a query to the system describing symptoms and other related factors, Watson first parses the input to identify the most important pieces of information; then mines patient data to find facts relevant to the patient's medical and hereditary history; then examines available data sources to form and test hypotheses; and finally provides a list of individualized, confidence-scored recommendations. Based on all of this information from tests performed in previous cases, the percentage of successful treatments prescribed by Watson for lung cancer cases is 90%, much higher than the 50% achieved by doctors (Steadman 2013).

Watson's advantage over human beings is obviously its ability to absorb information. In fact, in a 2017 (Wrzeszczynski et al. 2017) study, IBM Watson took just 10 minutes to analyze a brain-cancer patient's genome and suggest a treatment plan in comparison with the 160 h that human experts needed to make a comparable plan. Compared with traditional software, which is based on predetermined algorithms and always yields the same output if given the same input, Watson uses technology based on machine learning, where the algorithm is adapted as a result of the learning that occurs during the training process. In Watson's case, this consists of looking at a treatment's effectiveness among the patients who have received it.

In the financial sector, AI can be applied to improve the credit scoring of a given client. Traditional algorithms do not predict well the deterioration of the credit score over the years. In a study (Khandani et al. 2010) from 2010, an alternative to the traditional credit score was used as a risk classifier using machine learning. It used a 1 terabyte dataset consisting of everyday transactions (e.g., credit card, ATM, etc.), credit bureau, and account balance for a subset of a commercial bank's customers, which accounted for 1% of the data generated by the bank for the period between January 2005 and April 2009. The study showed that machine learning had a better performance as a risk classifier than traditional credit score algorithms.

Some good clients could previously have been rejected because of a low score using the traditional algorithms and conversely some bad clients could be accepted since they were getting a high score. By using this alternative method, banks can get both a cost reduction by better identifying riskier operations and at the same time generate new business with people that otherwise did not have a chance to become their clients.

In all examples above, the use of AI in the form of an anticipation interaction allows organizations to predict the state of the physical world, which is a critical factor to develop new value propositions. The main business drivers of anticipation are: description, prediction, and prescription. First, we can use AI to describe a complex process that otherwise would not be evident to detect, like having a digital microscope, as it is in the case of Cardiogram's app for detecting atrial fibrillation. Second, we can use AI to predict future patterns based on current conditions, as it is in the case of the Rolls-Royce engines or the risk classification for consumer credits using machine learning. Finally, we can use AI to prescribe or recommend a course of action, for example, IBM Watson recommending a specific oncologic treatment for a given patient.

## 11.3.3 Coordination Using AI

Traditionally, organizations have offered their value propositions operating inside the boundaries of the linear value chain of a given sector (e.g., automotive, banking, etc.). This situation derived from the high cost of transactions (e.g., coordination, production, etc.) that made it unfeasible to do it otherwise. As a result, the products and services were fully made and controlled by the organizations themselves with the participation of the providers present in their value chain. However, as digital density increases, it becomes possible to redefine how customers' needs are met beyond what is provided by the traditional value chain. In other words, new value propositions can now be the result of the coordination of disparate and multiple actors (i.e., organizations, people, and things).

As the number of actors involved in a given value proposition increases, the complexity of the coordination increases substantially since the number of possible interactions and learning opportunities grow in an exponential combinatorial fashion. In these scenarios, the use of distributed AI (DAI) can be very helpful to aid building new value propositions. DAI systems consist of autonomous "intelligent" actors, called agents, that are physically distributed and often on a very large scale. One example could be the application of DAI in calculating the optimal routing of a large fleet of vehicles in a mobility platform (e.g., UBER, Cabify, etc.).

In all of these examples, the use of AI as coordination interactions allows different actors to work together in new value propositions, without the constraint of belonging to the same traditional linear value chains, without the limitations of size (i.e., number of actors) or physical location. Nowadays, the use of AI for coordination interactions is not as prevalent as in the case of the other three types of interactions (i.e., automation, anticipation, and personalization). Nevertheless, as we move to a hyperconnected world of high digital density, organizations, people and things could be coordinated regardless of their number and physical locations. For instance, the Chinese city of Guangzhou with a population of 16 million people, with more than 16,000 km of roads and a daily flow of 3.5 million vehicles, uses a "city brain" based on AutoNavi, Alibaba's traffic management system. This "city brain" (ET City Brain 2018) allows the Guangzhou Traffic Police Smart Center to analyze big data coming from video feeds, social media, and traffic information to optimize traffic signals and reorganize their road network in real time.

Therefore, as digital density continues to increase, it will create a new scenario of collective intelligence where people and computers (i.e, computation associated to connected things and/or organizations) might act collectively more intelligently than any person, group or computer (Malone 2018) enabling another level of value propositions based on AI.

## 11.3.4 Personalization Using AI

Until recently organizations were competing in their markets either using pricing or differentiation strategies (Porter 1979), that is to say, by competing in price on a mass market or by developing products for a specific niche market. When digital density increases companies can create a fully personalized offering for a high volume of different customers (Anderson 2006), based on the data reflecting the habits and preferences of an individual consumer. AI is used in the interaction of personalization to predict the right value proposition for a given customer based on the collected data reflecting her/his habits and preferences.

One example of applying AI in a personalization interaction is the American auto insurance company Progressive, where customers could opt-in to plug a small device called *SnapShot* into the onboard diagnostics (OBD) of the car or by installing the *SnapShot* App in their smartphones, which tracks their driving behavior (e.g., how they turn the wheel, how they brake, etc.) and sends the data back to Progressive. The *SnapShot* program had collected more than 13 billion miles of driving data by 2016, all this data is processed by Progressive's partner H2O.ai using predictive analytics. In this way, the company becomes more efficient in its operations (e.g., managing claims, detecting fraud, improving analytics, etc.) and at the same time personalizes the customer experience. Those customers who voluntarily decide to share the data collected by *SnapShot* for the period of the first insurance policy, which normally is half a year, get a personalized insurance rate based on their actual driving rather than the standard car insurance criteria such as age, car model or area of residence.

Another application of AI as personalization interaction can be found in precision medicine by tailoring a medical treatment to the individual characteristics of each patient. Precision medicine involves analyzing patient's various biological characteristics interacting with multiple pharmaceutical molecules to better match drugs to improve patient's heath. However, precision medicine has not become a reality due to the unaffordable costs associated with the required combinatorial explosion of clinical trials that would be needed. For this reason, pharmaceutical companies traditionally have been offering a standard care for a hypothetical average patient. The American GNS Health company processes millions of data points of all types—electronic medical records, genetic, proteomic, genomic, claims, consumer, laboratory, prescription, mobile health, sociodemographic, etc.— to model patient response to treatment *in silico*, that is to say applying computer simulation instead of clinical trials. GNS Health, using machine learning, reconstructs complex diseases into computer models which allows pharma companies to simulate real-world scenarios increasing the speed of discovery of new drugs from years to months.

In the previous two examples of Progressive and GNS Health, the use of AI in personalization interactions allows organizations to create a specific and affordable value proposition based on customer's needs. In many of those cases, the personalization interaction is also related to the anticipation interaction. For instance, the traffic app Waze uses an anticipation interaction to leverage the big data received from the drivers for prediction purposes, whereas the personalization interaction focuses on the personal data (i.e., location of a given car) as the input to change the behavior (i.e., a driver changing his route following Waze's recommendations). Another example is Amazon's recommendation engine analyzing all the client transactions and clustering them in groups of clients with similar behaviors and tastes (i.e., anticipation) to recommend potential products to a given customer (i.e., personalization). As AI algorithms for anticipation and personalization continue improving, Amazon eventually can switch its business model from buying and then shipping to shipping and the buying, as it was hinted by the 2013 Amazon's patent filing about "anticipatory shipping."

## 11.4 AI Implications on Organizations

In the previous section, we saw that AI represents an important technology to build new value propositions as a combination of automation, anticipation, coordination and personalization interactions. However, the introduction of AI in the company's business model has also a big impact on its organizational model. In this section the AI implications are analyzed at three levels: firstly, by identifying the specific challenges when an organization implements new value propositions based on AI; secondly, focusing on new capabilities that an organization needs to integrate AI technology; and thirdly, stressing the importance of some AI governance principles when data becomes the critical asset for any business.

### 11.4.1 Challenges When Introducing AI

Beyond any doubt, an increase in digital density enables organizations to leverage a lot of benefits by creating new value propositions as described in the previous section. However, this scenario also creates new challenges, specifically in the context of AI, where organizations need to recognize and address certain issues that may arise in relation to:

– *Privacy* related to the amount of required personal data to train the AI algorithms
– *Integration* related to the ownership and use of data of value propositions resulting from the coordination of multiple parties
– *Reliability* related to the quality of the outcomes of the AI models
– *Security* related to the vulnerability of AI models against cyberattacks.

## Privacy

However, better personalization implies collecting and storing more and more individual data from the customer and the challenge of privacy is therefore incremented. A near future scenario may involve a company that is able to predict, through biosensors, the likelihood of a person to develop a serious illness. Hence a health insurance provider could potentially discriminate a customer by denying coverage for those with higher risks. This personalization-privacy tension could even be found in a simple vacuum cleaner robot that creates a map of an apartment to know which parts have been already cleaned. For this reason, consumers are only going to embrace these new value propositions if they trust the organization that provides them and it is transparent in its use of personal data. First steps have been done toward increased levels of personal data privacy by introducing new regulation and compliance requirements, such as EU's General Data Protection Regulation (GDPR), which also limits what kind of data an organization can use to train its AI algorithms.[1]

## Integration

In a high digital density world, value propositions are often the result of the cooperation of multiple organizations within richer ecosystems. For this reason, such partnerships require establishing data clauses regarding the ownership and limitation of data usage by participating companies. In the previous example about predictive maintenance for aircraft engines, Rolls-Royce sees its operational value in the aggregated data from all the engines, while the airline and or the aircraft manufacturer, only have access to a fraction of the raw data collected and do not have access to the bigger picture. Industrial companies may not want to share their data for compliance reasons (e.g., medical machines) or competitive concerns, thus limiting the machine learning capabilities (i.e., reduced data training set of the equipment operated by the organization). In order to reconcile industrial companies concerns about sharing their data because of the concern of sharing

---

[1]General Data Protection Regulation focuses specifically on protecting data and ensuring its privacy. Any organization operating within EU will be obliged to gather data legally and under strict conditions and protect it from misuse by third parties, otherwise it will be fined. Organizations are required to use the highest privacy settings, so that the data does not become public. GDPR empowers individuals to challenge organizations to reveal or delete their personal data.

valuable insights about their products, some organizations have decided to share the data for the sole purpose of using it as a data training set for AI algorithms but keeping the ownership of the data to be protected from compliance and security risks.

## Reliability

Reliability in the context of AI encompasses two aspects. On the one hand, the quality of the data that is used by AI algorithms is important and, on the other hand, the reliability of the software of those algorithms represents challenges. Ensuring data quality relates to data governance, which will be addressed later on in this chapter. Regarding the reliability of the AI algorithms, it is important to take into account not only their possibilities but also their limitations. Addressing data quality and algorithm reliability issues within businesses will help organizations discard investments without any return, as well as not to over-sell the results of projects involving AI in order to avoid disappointment and skepticism of the utility of AI.

The AI algorithm learning techniques (Zamora and Herrera 2018) are based on training a model with data. Without this data, training is not possible and therefore it is not possible to generate any model. Many times, companies request evaluation about how much data is needed to train a model. This depends on the particular case and the complexity of the algorithm. However, the right question to be addressed by business executives should not be about the amount of data needed, but rather what problem can be solved with the data available. If an organization does not have a lot of data, it is advisable to use those algorithms that are "more resistant" to learning with less data, however with lower confidence levels. For example, if a prediction model for product weekly sales in a retail store is needed, it is logical to request several years of sales data for each product per week, as well as the time series with potentially explanatory variables (e.g., holidays, weather, macroeconomic indicators, sales channel, etc.).

An AI system with a high quality of prediction may stop performing as well at any time, or, put it another way: an AI system properly trained with past data, can fail to be correct with the present circumstances, if these circumstances change the reasons why the past cases occurred. For example, a customer who buys seasonal clothing for years in a store, can change their habits with the appearance of a competitor that better meets their needs and at a better price.

Due to this limitation, it is essential in the current situation to create AI systems within inbuilt continuous learning but also with the ability to distinguish "noise" in the data, that is to say, events not relevant for the training, but that can distort the results.

The degree of confidence of the resulting model built with a machine learning algorithm can be measured, comparing the prediction of the model with what has happened in the past. The more cases that prediction coincides with reality, the greater the degree of confidence of the model. But not in any case does the degree of confidence of a model fully guarantees its success in the future practical application, since many models suffer what is called as "over-training," that is, the learning process has been too adapted to the data of training, and despite its high degree of confidence, the emergence of circumstances that generate relationships between data different from the past does not make the model work well in practice.

## Security

One of the consequences of a hyperconnected world is that the surface of attack of the organization increases exponentially. For this reason, protecting the integrity of the data from cyberattacks is especially critical when data powers the artificial intelligence algorithms. Therefore, security in the context of value propositions based on AI goes beyond the type of cyberattacks (Sieber and Zamora 2019) we have experienced until now, something that is called adversarial machine learning. This kind of attacks exploits the limitations of a neural network's design, used in many AI algorithms, which do not operate in the same way as a human brain does. A hacker (i.e., a malicious adversary) can manipulate the input data of an AI algorithm, either in the training or operating phase, to fool systems into seeing or listening to something to compromise the whole security system.

A training time attack may happen at a stage of building a machine-learning model by using malicious data. An inference time attack uses specifically synthesized inputs which affect the model. Some examples of AI being hacked may look innocent, like a neural network confusing a turtle with a rifle on a picture. However, some AI mistakes can cause greater disturbances, like a self-driving car not stopping at a stop sign, because it was partially covered by carefully crafted black and white stickers (Eykholt et al. 2018).

As more and more value propositions depend on using AI technology, it is important to identify potential risks related to adversarial attacks beforehand (i.e., secure-by-design principles) and build in certain defenses to protect them.

## 11.4.2 New Capabilities When Adopting AI

When an organization considers implementing new AI technologies, it is advisable to do it progressively in order to assess its suitability and prepare the organizational structure and capabilities both at the operational and managerial level to integrate AI technology in its business model successfully.

Quite often organizations start with a pilot where AI can be used to create a new value proposition for automation, anticipation, coordination and/or personalization interactions. In these initial phases the emphasis should be put on iterative experimentation, building a viable minimum product (MVP) and tracking metrics, which allow testing initial hypotheses or success criteria. Once the new value proposition has been validated in the pilot project, organizations can start implementing it on a larger scale by replacing or improving existing processes. This will translate into cost reduction and/or generation of new sources of revenue. Moreover, the new data generated by the customer using these new products and services can be used in turn to discover or improve new value propositions, through the use of AI as a driver of innovation, closing a virtuous circle.

As a matter of fact, most AI algorithms are widely available. However, access to quality data is the main entry barrier for achieving a sustainable and competitive business model. For this reason, it is critical to define a strategy of continuous data acquisition (e.g., having a unified data warehouse) not only for AI training purposes, but also as a source for future innovations, which requires the development of new operational capabilities in the organization related to the application and correct usage of AI techniques in the organization.

To that extent, many organizations incorporate new professional profiles like the "data scientist" (Zamora and Herrera 2018). An ideal data scientist should have training in applied mathematics and good knowledge of programming languages and database management. Moreover, a "data scientist" must be oriented toward practical results, but with a great creativity component especially when it comes to defining the data training for the AI algorithm.

However, organizations face some problems filling this position. Among the difficulties that organizations encounter when searching for data scientists are: domain knowledge of the business, communication skills, and understanding and identifying the different and heterogeneous repositories of company data. In order to overcome these limitations, data scientist's role often serves in conjunction with other roles, such as "business translators," who interpret business challenges, points of improvement, opportunities, and translate them into proposals that can be implemented using AI.

In addition, organizations should also incorporate profiles specialized in searching for the necessary training data in a more efficient way. In some instances, availability of a unified data warehouse or any other centralized repository of information simplifies the task, but there is always the subsequent enormous search task among the different business attributes that the data training set is composed. Special mention deserves the knowledge that this profile must have to be in compliance with the regulatory requirements when processing personal data (e.g., GDPR).

As AI technology becomes a core technology in the organizations' business models, new capabilities (Daugherty and Wilson 2018) will be needed related to the AI governance, which will be described in more detail in the next section.

## 11.4.3 Some Governance Principles with AI

As described in the previous sections, the introduction of AI technology as a part of new value propositions will face specific challenges of privacy, integration, reliability, and security, as well as difficulties in acquiring new necessary capabilities to manage them. However, since AI technology is used either to substitute or augment human activity, general managers should be aware of the impact of AI on their own decision-making process on employees, on customers using their products, and on society as a whole. For these reasons, general managers should be aware and act accordingly regarding the externalities of AI, specially the negative ones, beyond its impact on their business models.

First, organizations will face important issues regarding the fairness of implemented algorithms depending on the bias[2] embedded in the training data set. Second, as AI algorithms are going to be integrated in the decision-making process, issues about accountability will have to be faced in the event of undesired outcomes. Third, general managers will trust AI systems only if these systems can be transparent and explainable (e.g., ability to explain how certain outcomes were reached) instead of being a "black box." Fourth, general managers should be conscious of the ethical implications of using systems based on the values (utility function) that the AI algorithms were designed with. Lastly, general managers should follow a practical wisdom, acting on the basis to what is right for all stakeholders.

---

[2]In this context, bias does not refer to its statistical meaning but to the inclination or prejudice for or against one person or group, especially in a way considered to be unfair.

With the current state-of-the-art of AI technology, the current problems that organizations are facing do not relate to the possibility that AI systems achieve a superintelligence (Bostrom 2014) power overriding any human control but, on the contrary, based on the shortcomings of today's AI technology lacking inherent human abilities such as generalization, abstract thinking and the ability to make analogies. In the words of Pedro Domingos, Professor at the University of Washington and a leading AI researcher (Domingos 2015), "people worry that computers will get too smart and take over the world, but the real problem is that they're too stupid and they've already taken over the world." This means that AI algorithms do not have yet the capability of understanding things the way humans do, which may result in dangerous outcomes.

These AI limitations are directly related to the quality of the data used and the design itself of the algorithms. Therefore, organizations should know and trust their data before starting using AI technology. "Data for Good" (Wing 2018) has been advocated for in the scientific and technology field as a guiding principle of data usage through the entire data life cycle. In the management world, a similar principle should be used when adopting AI in the decision-making process and integrating AI in the company's offering. This guiding principle of data usage and design algorithm design is also known by the acronym F.A.T.E. (FAT/ML 2018; FATE 2018). In the specific context of the general management, we propose to add an additional guiding principle based on practical wisdom, to address the issues of:

- *Fairness* related to the bias introduced by the data training set of the AI algorithms
- *Accountability* related to the responsibility of the decisions based on AI models
- *Transparency* related to the explainability of the AI models
- *Ethics* related to the values that the AI systems are built
- *Practical Wisdom* related to the good judgment of the general management whether to use or non-use AI on the basis of what is right for all stakeholders.

## Fairness

As we have seen in this chapter, AI is a powerful technology to serve customers better and to get more enhanced insights into the organization. However, these advantages should be realized avoiding exposing people to any kind of unfairness as a result of potential biases introduced by the adoption of AI. In this context, fairness means that the adopted AI models must produce unbiased classifications or predictions. One trivial example can be found in the image search engine Google Images, which for the query "CEO" overwhelming produces images of men in suits, reflecting how historically women have had difficulties to access to high executive positions in equal conditions than men. In this case, the training data set contains the gender bias of having many more men than women in CEO positions.

Since an AI model is the result of training an algorithm with data, the bias comes from either the data used or from the algorithm itself. However, algorithms reflect the values of the people who designed and coded them, something that we will cover below considering the ethical implications of AI. For this reason, organizations should pay special attention to the bias contained in the data training set used by AI algorithms. Although many AI systems were made with the best intentions, these AI systems increasingly have a direct impact on people's lives (O'Neil 2016). As a result, biased data should be a concern for many organizations, due to important liability consequences in areas like access to housing, law enforcement, and employment.

A recent study (Buolamwini and Gebru 2018) evaluated the bias in three commercial facial recognition software applications (Microsoft, Face++, and IBM). The study showed that the software was 99% of the time right white men in photos. However, the error rate was nearly 35% for images of women with darker skin. The study concluded that the gender and race biases were due to the data set used to train those software programs. As a matter of fact, it was estimated in the data training set used by the facial recognition software, about 75% of the pictures were portraying men and more than 80% of them were white men. These results indicate that there is an urgent need to fix the gender and raced biased data, if companies want to incorporate this type of software in their commercial offerings.

Notwithstanding, the AI model bias can have even more serious consequences causing social stigmatization by stereotype reinforcement. This seems to be the case of the software Correctional Offender Management Profiling for Alternative Sanctions (COMPAS) developed by the American company Northpointe, which is used across the US courts to predict recidivism of criminals. COMPAS has become a tool used by judges to guide them in producing sentences by identifying potential re-offenders in a future crime. According to a recent study published in ProPublica (Anwin 2016), COMPAS predicted the recidivism correctly 61% of the time. However, it showed a strong bias toward black people, who were labeled with high risk of recidivism 44% of the time, but then finally did not re-offend. In contrast with only 23% of the time for white people labeled high risk, but who finally did not re-offend.

For those reasons, the quality of data utilized by algorithms should be addressed by managers in advance of AI development and deployment. Intel in their Public Policy Opportunity white paper (INTEL 2017) suggests mitigating bias by using verified algorithms, data models and well-curated training sets, performing extensive validation of AI systems, and being alert to possible fairness implications from AI-based decisions. To that extent, as companies are using multiple sources of data to feed their AI algorithms, a role of a "data hygienist" (Daugherty and Wilson 2018) will be required. Her/his role will be to free the data of any noise or hidden bias.

## Accountability

Accountability has been always a crucial concept in management. According to Peter Drucker (1973), leaders in any organization are responsible and accountable for the performance of their institutions and also responsible for the community as a whole. Therefore, accountability implies the acknowledgement and assumptions of responsibility for actions, products, and decisions within the scope of the management role. However, in the context of AI, accountability can be more challenging since behind a decision or a product are also data and algorithms. One example is the 2015 study (Datta et al. 2015) of Google ads, using a tool called AdFisher developed by Carnegie Mellon University, which runs experiments using simulated user profiles. The study revealed that ads for high-paying jobs were shown more to men than women on Google. Nevertheless, in this situation it is not clear who is accountable for this discrimination outcome. It could be the advertiser's targeting the ad, or the design of the Google advertising platform, or the fact that men click more on this type of ads translates into increasing the frequency of these ads, or even that there is more competition for advertising space to women reducing the frequency of appearance of these ads.

Previously in this chapter, it was mentioned how IBM Watson helps oncologists in the diagnosis and type of treatment of their patients. However, if Watson provides a treatment recommendation with fatal consequences for the patient, who will be accountable for this undesired outcome: the oncologist, the hospital, or IBM? This scenario could potentially happen as pointed out by the health-oriented news website STAT (Ross and Swetlitz 2018) reporting in July 2018 "multiple examples of unsafe and incorrect treatment recommendations" in cancer treatments produced by Watson.

Reflecting on these issues of accountability, the Future of Life Institute held the Asilomar (Future 2017) Conference on Beneficial AI in 2017, creating a set of 23 guidelines for AI researchers, that can be extended to managers of organizations, as they are the main stakeholders in the moral implications of the use, misuse, and actions related to AI technology. Organizations should commit to responsibility to shape those implications and adopt internal policies consistent with external social criteria. Companies should implement the necessary systems and training programs for managers to use AI tools and hold accountability for the outcomes.

## Transparency

The third guiding principle in the use of AI is transparency. Organizations will only implement AI systems if those systems can be transparent and explain how they reach an outcome instead of acting as a "black box," or a system for which we can only observe inputs and outputs. To that extent, transparency can enable accountability in the use of AI technology. When organizations and managers start to rely heavily on algorithms to make increasingly important decisions, they will be required to have the right explainability mechanisms in place if the results turn out to be unacceptable or difficult to understand. For instance, if IBM Watson recommends a patient treatment, which seems incorrect to the physician, she or he will trust Watson's (IBM 2018) recommendation if the system explains in understandable terms the factors (e.g., MRIs, scientific papers, etc.) contributing to the final outcome.

Moreover, transparency is also required to provide a fair treatment to any person affected by the outcome of AI. This was the case of Sarah Wysocki (O'Neil 2016), a fifth-grade teacher in the MacFarland Middle school in Washington DC. After two years in that school, she was getting excellent reviews from the principal, as well as, the student's parents. However, at the end of the 2010–2011 academic year, Wysocki was fired because of a very bad score on her IMPACT evaluation. IMPACT is an AI tool adopted in 2009 by the chancellor of Washington's schools with the aim to turn around the city's underperforming schools. IMPACT tries to measure the effectiveness of a given educator in teaching math and language skills. Although the initial intention of IMPACT was to minimize human bias like "bad teachers can seem good ones," at the end of the day it is extremely complex to calculate the impact that one person may have on another over a year since there are many other social impacts playing in the equation. Nevertheless, when

Wysocki, as well as other fired teachers demanded details of the evaluation criteria, many school administrators were unable to provide a detailed explanation since they did not know the inner workings of IMPACT.

Transparency is challenging for organizations as it may require revealing intellectual property by forceful publishing of the AI models. Therefore, it is important to clarify situations when explanations should be given and if they need a detailed description of AI's inner workings or rather a justification for the particular outcome (Doshi-Velez and Kortz 2017). Moreover, the new EU GDPR regulation includes the "right to explanation" by providing "meaningful information about the logic involved."

Because of the nature of current AI algorithms, especially those based on deep neural networks, it has been almost impossible to understand how the AI reached their impressive results. Nevertheless, as explainability is becoming more and more important, researchers (Binder et al. 2016) are looking at explainability mechanisms for AI algorithms, such as the Layerwise Relevance Propagation (LRP). These mechanisms can take an AI's outcome and work backwards through the program's neural network to reveal how a decision was made. In addition, organizations will need to hire a new type of AI professional called "AI explainers" (Daugherty and Wilson 2018), whose main role will be to explain the inner workings of complex AI algorithms. In some cases, these professionals could act as algorithm forensic analysts to provide a satisfactory explanation, auditable by a competent authority, of an organization's AI system.

## Ethics

The fourth guiding principle in the use of AI is ethics. As humans delegate more and more certain decisions to AI systems, sooner or later we will face moral dilemmas. An adapted version of the "trolley problem" (Thomson 1976) dilemma could be found in self-driving cars. Imagine that an autonomous vehicle has a mechanical failure and is unable to stop, the AI system (acting as the driver) has two options. Either the car continues running over and killing a family crossing the street, or the car swerves crashing into a wall and hitting a bystander. Which is the moral ethical option? Killing two (the passenger and the bystander) or five people (the family)? In the case of a human driver, this dilemma would be solved by the judgment of the driver. However, in the case of a self-driving car using AI, ethical decisions, some of them without a right or wrong answer, should be programmed beforehand. In these situations, regulation would be needed to reflect how society (Edmond 2017) as a whole wants to deal with these ethical dilemmas.

To that extent and inspired by the well-known Asimov's Three Laws of Robotics (Asimov 1950), Oren Etzione, Professor of Washington University and Chief Executive of the Allen Institute for Artificial Intelligence, proposes three AI "laws" (Etzione 2017) related to the ethical issues that this technology is creating. The first one is "An A.I. system must be subject to the full gamut of laws that apply to its human operator." The second one is "An A.I. system must clearly disclose that it is not human." And the third one is "An A.I. system cannot retain or disclose confidential information without explicit approval from the source of that information."

## Practical Wisdom

The previous four principles of Fairness, Accountability, Transparency, and Ethics have the main focus on the externalities of AI on employees, customers, and society at large. However, from the perspective of general management, we propose to introduce an additional principle: Practical Wisdom. A concept from the virtue ethics (Hursthouse and Pettigrove 2018), that is understood as the knowledge or understanding that enables its possessor to "do the right thing" in any given situation.

To that extent, ethical issues are also present when deciding spheres where organizations can apply AI technology (e.g., development of lethal weapons guided by AI). In November 2018, The World Economic Forum in their Annual Meeting of the Global Future Councils stated (Sutcliffe and Allgrove 2018): "There is a need for clearer articulation of ethical frameworks, normative standards and values-based governance models to help guide organizations in the development and use of these powerful tools in society, and to enable a human-centric approach to development that goes beyond geographic and political boundaries," that is to say, being conscious that the focus should be the impact of AI on people, extending the concept of human rights to the digital sphere. Something that is also reflected on the 11th AI ASILOMAR principle (Future 2017): "AI systems should be designed and operated so as to be compatible with ideals of human dignity, rights, freedoms, and cultural diversity."

Therefore, organizations using AI technology in their value propositions, as well as, the decision-making process, will need the new role of "AI sustainers" (Daugherty and Wilson 2018) to ensure that each of the AI systems satisfies its purpose of serving humans. Their overarching activities might include setting limits for AI to comply legally and ethically, managing the performance of AI and checking output quality. Future sustainers roles, like ethics compliance manager and automation ethicist, will also include roles related to enforcing AI algorithms to operate within human ethical and moral rules. Humans deciding which AI systems should be demoted or, in contrary, promoted based on their performance will perform a role similar to HR management, however in this case applied to AI.

In the context of management, beyond controlling the outcomes of using AI in the organization, the use or non-use of AI must be also guided by the good judgment of the general manager, who must act on the basis of what is right for all stakeholders. This translates to manage a complex, interconnected system: the institutional configuration, the internal context, the external environment, and the business, which constitutes the four genuine responsibilities of general management (Andreu and Ricart 2014). This judgment must be informed by the mission of the organization or the ultimate raison d'être of the company.

Therefore, we propose to extend the guiding principles of data usage and design algorithm with the inclusion of the Practical Wisdom principle related to those genuine responsibilities of the general management.

## 11.5 Some Conclusions

We have seen in this chapter that organizations should not consider AI as a technology in isolation. AI is becoming a reality as a consequence of living in a world with an exponential increase in digital density, where more and more data is available from the activity of companies, people and things. The increase of digital density is the underlying driving force for the process of digital transformation that business units, organizations, sectors and the society as a whole are currently undergoing. This transformation touches different dimensions in the organization: Technology Platform, Business Model, and Organization Model. Once the organization has the required IT infrastructure in place to manage AI technology (i.e., algorithms and data), companies can leverage the benefits of AI by using it in new value propositions as part of their business models, as a combination of automation, anticipation, coordination and personalization interactions. To that extent, not only AI is a powerful technology for automation purposes in many industries; but also, AI can be implemented as an anticipation interaction to predict outcomes or recommend actions in a multitude of scenarios. Moreover, as value propositions are more often than not the result of the participation of many actors (companies, people, things), AI can play an important role as a coordination interaction of complex and heterogeneous ecosystems. Finally, AI technology as a personalization interaction can be used to offer affordable highly personalized products and services.

Nevertheless, in order to integrate AI technology in a business model successfully, managers should be aware of AI implications in their organization at three levels: challenges, capabilities, and governance. In turn, these challenges are categorized into four categories: privacy, integration, reliability, and security. Firstly, operating a business model with new value propositions based on AI requires addressing issues regarding the privacy of data derived from the human activity. Secondly, organizations need to establish the ownership of the data used to train the AI models specially when the value proposition requires the participation and integration of many actors. Thirdly, organizations need to ensure the reliability of the outcomes of an AI model both when it is used in new value propositions as well as in the decision-making process of the organization. Lastly, organizations must address the specific security concerns that AI poses beyond the traditional cyberattacks.

Furthermore, as data becomes a critical asset to create and capture value, organizations must acquire the required capabilities both at the operational and managerial level to integrate AI in their business model successfully. Last but not least, managers should be conscious of the potential externalities of AI on their employees, customers, and society at large. To that extent, AI governance should follow the five principles of fairness, accountability, transparency, ethics and practical wisdom. Only by fully understanding the potential benefits, as well as, the implications on the organization, AI technology will fulfill its promise to become a positive transformation technology of companies, sectors, and society.

Figure 11.4 summarizes the impact of AI on the Business Model and Organizational Model dimensions that general management should take into account when managing AI in a holistic way within the digital density framework.

In the same way that AI currently has more potential as an augmentation rather than a substitution of human activity, general managers should be aware that there is nothing artificial about AI since machine values are derived from the human values that designed them, as well as, any bias in the input of AI systems will translate into a bias in the output. To that extent, general managers should not consider AI technology only as a tool to gain efficiency in the organization, they need to understand the consequences beyond the business model such as the external and internal context and the institutional configuration. These implications call for general managers to develop a digital mindset to enable them to manage AI in a holistic

| Value Propositions based on AI | Automation | Doing more with less resources by reducing manual steps of routine tasks. |
|---|---|---|
| | Anticipation | Knowing the state of the physical world in real time by describing, predicting and/or prescribing actions to be included as part of the business model. |
| | Coordination | Making disparate actors work together in new value propositions without the limitations of size or physical location. |
| | Personalization | Meeting better customer needs by using data to reflect the habits and preferences of a given customer |
| AI Challenges | Privacy | Establishing transparent policies about the use of personal data to preserve a relationship of trust with customers. Fulfilling compliance requirements about data privacy. |
| | Integration | Establishing data clauses regarding ownership and right of use of data when the value proposition derives from the participation of multiple actors. |
| | Reliability | Understanding the impact of the quantity and quality of the data used to train the AI algorithms, as well as, the limitations and applicability of those algorithms. |
| | Security | Including potential risks related to adversarial attacks in the cybersecurity policies (prevention, detection and reaction) of the organization. |
| AI Governance Principles | Fairness | Identifying and eliminating beforehand noise or hidden bias in the data sources (internal and external) feeding AI algorithms. |
| | Accountability | Training programs for managers to asume the responsibility of the use, misuse and actions related to AI technology. |
| | Transparency | Excluding the use of AI systems if the results are either unacceptable or difficult to understand. |
| | Ethics | Enforcing that all AI systems are designed and operated to be compatible with ideas of human dignity, rights, freedoms, and cultural diversity. |
| | Practical Wisdom | AI must be also guided by the good judgment of the general management, who must act on the basis of what is right to all stakeholders. |

**Fig. 11.4** Impact of AI on the business model and organizational model dimensions

way, preparing the IT infrastructure and acquiring and developing the required new capabilities, creating and capturing value through new value propositions based on AI, addressing the specific new challenges that AI poses to the organization, and implementing a good AI governance based on fairness, accountability, transparency, ethics and practical wisdom principles.

# References

Agrawal, A., J. Gans, and A. Goldfarb. 2018. *Prediction Machines: The Simple Economics of Artificial Intelligence*. Boston: Harvard Business Review Press.

Anderson, C. 2006. *The Long Tail. Why the Future of Business Is Selling Less of More.* London: Hyperion Books.

Andreu, R., and Ricart, J.E. 2014. The Genuine Responsibilities of the CEO. *IESE Insight* 23 (Fourth Quarter): 15–21.

Anwin, J., et al. 2016. Machine Bias. *ProPublica*, May. https://www.propublica.org/article/machine-bias-risk-assessments-in-criminal-sentencing. Accessed January 31, 2019.

Asimov, I. 1950. *I, Robot*. New York: Gnome Press.

Binder, A., et al. 2016. Layer-Wise Relevance Propagation for Deep Neural Network Architectures. In *Proceeding of Information Science and Applications (ICISA)*, 913–922.

Bostrom, N. 2014. *Superintelligence: Paths, Dangers, Strategies*. Oxford: Oxford University Press.

Buolamwini, J., and Gebru, T. 2018. Gender Shades: Intersectional Accuracy Disparities in Commercial Gender Classification. In *Proceedings of Machine Research, Conference on Fairness, Accountability, and Transparency*, 77–91.

Casadesus-Masanell, R., and Ricart, J.E. 2011. How to Design a Winning Business Model. *Harvard Business Review* 89 (1/2): 100–107.

Datta, A., M.C. Tschantz, and A. Datta. 2015. Automated Experiments on Ad Privacy Setting. In *Proceedings on Privacy Enhancing Technologies*, 92–112.

Daugherty, P.P., and H.J. Wilson. 2018. *Human + Machine: Reimagining Work in the Age of AI*. Boston: Harvard Business Review Press.

Domingos, P. 2015. *The Master Algorithm*. London: Allen Lane.

Doshi-Velez, F., and M. Kortz. 2017. Accountability of AI Under the Law: The Role of Explanation. Working Paper, Berkman Klein Center Working Group on Explanation and the Law, Berkman Klein Center for Internet & Society.

Drucker, P. 1973. *Management: Tasks, Responsibilities, Practices*. New York: Harper & Row.

Edmond, A. 2017. Moral Machine: Perception of Moral Judgement Made by Machines. Masther's Thesis, MIT, May.

ET City Brain. 2018. Alibaba Cloud. https://www.alibabacloud.com/et/city. Accessed December 27, 2018.

Etzione, O. 2017. How to Regulate Artificial Intelligence. *The New York Times*, September. https://www.nytimes.com/2017/09/01/opinion/artificial-intelligence-regulations-rules.html. Accessed December 27, 2018.

Eykholt, K., et al. 2018. Robust Physical-World Attacks on Deep Learning Visual Classification. In *Proceeding of the Conference of Computer Vision and Pattern Recognition*, 1625–1634, April.

FATE: Fairness, Accountability, Transparency, and Ethics in AI. 2018. https://www.microsoft.com/en-us/research/group/fate/. Accessed December 27, 2018.

FAT/ML: Fairness, Accountability, and Transparency in Machine Learning. 2018. https://www.fatml.org/. Accessed December 27, 2018.

Future of Life Institute. 2017. Asilomar AI Principles. https://futureoflife.org/ai-principles/. Accessed December 27, 2018.

Health eHeart. 2018. https://www.health-eheartstudy.org/study. Accessed December 27, 2018.

Hursthouse, R., and G. Pettigrove. 2018. Virtue Ethics. In *The Stanford Encyclopedia of Philosophy*, ed. Edward N. Zalta, Winter 2018 ed. https://plato.stanford.edu/archives/win2018/entries/ethics-virtue/. Accessed January 20, 2019.

IBM Watson. 2018. Trust and Transparency in AI. https://www.ibm.com/watson/trust-transparency/. Accessed December 27, 2018.

INTEL. 2017. Artificial Intelligence: The Public Opportunity. https://blogs.intel.com/policy/files/2017/10/Intel-Artificial-Intelligence-Public-Policy-White-Paper-2017.pdf.

Káganer, E., J. Zamora, and S. Sieber. 2013. The Digital Mindset: 5 Skills Every Leader Needs to Succeed in the Digital World. *IESE Insight Review* (18, Third Quarter): 15–22.

Khandani, A., A.J. Kimz, and A.W. Lo. 2010. Consumer Credit Risk Models via Machine-Learning Algorithms. *Journal of Banking & Finance* 34 (11): 2767–2787.

Malone, T. 2018. *Superminds*. New York: Little, Brown.

O'Neil, C. 2016. *Weapons of Math Destruction*. New York: Broadway Books.

Osterwalder, A., and Y. Pigneur. 2010. *Business Model Generation. A Handbook for Visionaries, Game Changers*. New York: Willey.

Porter, M.E. 1979. How Competitive Forces Shape Strategy. *Harvard Business Review* 57 (2): 137–145.

Ricart, J.E. 2012. Strategy in the 21st Century: Business Models in Action. IESE Technical Note, SMN-685-E.

Ross, C., and I. Swetlitz. 2018. IBM's Watson Supercomputer Recommended 'Unsafe and Incorrect' Cancer Treatments, Internal Documents Show. STAT, July. https://www.statnews.com/2018/07/25/ibm-watson-recommended-unsafe-incorrect-treatments/. Accessed December 27, 2018.

Sieber, S., and J. Zamora. 2019. The Cybersecurity Challenge in a High Digital Density World. *The European Business Review,* January–February: 75–84.

Steadman, I. 2013. IBM's Watson Is Better at Diagnosing Cancer Than Human Doctors. *Wired*, February. https://www.wired.co.uk/article/ibm-watson-medical-doctor. Accessed December 27, 2018.

Sutcliffe, H., and A. Allgrove. 2018. How Do We Build an Ethical Framework for the Fourth Industrial Revolution? *World Economic Forum*, November. https://www.weforum.org/agenda/2018/11/ethical-framework-fourth-industrial-revolution/. Accessed December 1, 2018.

Thomson, J. 1976. Killing, Letting Die, and the Trolley Problem. *Monist: An International Quarterly Journal of General Philosophical Inquiry* 59: 204–217.

Wing, J.M. 2018. Data for Good: FATES, Elaborated. Data Science Institute, Columbia University, January. https://datascience.columbia.edu/FATES-Elaborated. Accessed December 27, 2018.

Wrzeszczynski, K., et al. 2017. Comparing Sequencing Assays and Human-Machine Analyses in Actionable Genomics for Glioblastoma. *Neurology Genetics* 3 (4): e164.

Zamora, J. 2016. Making Better Decisions Using Big Data. *Harvard Deusto Business Review*, May: 6–14.

Zamora, J. 2017. Programming Business Models Through Digital Density. *IESE Insight* (Second Quarter): 23–30.

Zamora, J., and P. Herrera. 2018. How Prepared Is Your Business to Make the Most of AI? *IESE Business School Insight* (151, Winter): 64–73.

Zamora, J., K. Tatarinov, and S. Sieber. 2018. The Centrifugal and Centripetal Forces Affecting the Digital Transformation of Industries. *Harvard Deusto Business Review* (279): 18–31.

# Index

**A**

Abertis 49
Accountability 207, 226
Activist investors 59
Advertising clutter 155
Advertising effects 155
Advertising spending 153
Agrawal, A. 23, 39
AI governance principles 207
AI Universities 16
AI winters 6
Algorithmic decision-making 3
Algorithmic management 103
Algorithms 10
AlphaGo 31
Amazon 16
Amit, R. 55
Analytical insights 142
Anand, B. 46
Andrew Ng 208
Artificial general intelligence (AGI) 8
Automated assistant 170
Automation 24, 39, 141

**B**

Barnard, C.I. 53
Bayesian networks 41
Best performers 104
Biased data 44
Biased indicator 98
Birkinshaw, J. 46
Birthrates 74
BlackRock 38
Blockchain 32
Board of directors 54
Brand choices 151
Brand equity 158
Brand strength 160
Broader social impact 60
Brynjolfsson 23
Budget deficits 74
Business model (BM) 25, 55, 185, 210
Business model renewal 188
Business operations 11

C

Canals, J. 47, 54
Capabilities 31
Capitalism 59
Cappelli, Peter 57
Carbon emissions 59
Carter, C. 54
Casadesus-Masanell, R. 55
Castells 24
Causal discovery 109
Causality 131
Cellnex 49
Chatbots 3
Classification functions 209
Cloud computing 205
Cognition 40
Cognitive process 13
Collective action 69
Collective intelligence 166
Computer power 44
Computer vision 7
Computing power 133
Conditional prediction markets 177
Connected data 205, 206
Conscious capitalism 82
Consumer experiential metrics 160
Contextual understanding 27
Coordinating activities 28
Corporate social responsibility 47, 60
Corporate strategy 175
Correlation 45
Cost of group decision making 193
Creative destruction 135
Credit scoring 214
CRM 212
Crowdsourcing 192
Customer equity 158, 161
Customers 62
Customer satisfaction 159, 162
Cut emissions 59
Cyberattacks 221
Cyber-human strategy machine 181
Cyber-human systems 168

D

Data clustering 41
Data labeled 14
Data literacy 118
Data science 93
Data storage 126
Decarbonize the economy 59
Decision making for mergers and
    acquisitions 12
Deepfakes 41
Deep learning 4
Deep learning networks 7
Deep-learning powered customer
    chatbot 9
Deep Thought 6
Demand transportation systems 194
Demographic diversity 107
Developing talent 57
Develop people 56
Digital advertising media 151
Digital data 7
Digital density 205
Digital density architecture 210
Digital marketing 151
Digital transformation 205
Dignity of every person 61
Diminishing returns to marketing 153
Discrimination 45
Dispersed shareholders 59
Disruptive production 127
Distinctive qualities 33
Distributed AI (DAI) 216
Division of labor 121
Drucker, P. 53, 190

E

Economic anxiety 125
Economic concentration 68
Ecosystem 193
Employee data 101
Employees 62
Employee well-being 69

Employment decisions 107
Engagement 46
Engagement of employees 56
Enterprise value 160
Entrepreneurial mindset 46
Environment 59
Environmental sustainability 84
ERP 212
Established predictors 104
Ethical values 61
Ethics 207, 228
Expert systems 6
Explainability 10, 227
Exploitation 31
Exploration 31
External environment 186

F

Fairness 16, 107, 207
Fake news 41
Ferraro, F. 82
Firms 59
Focus 175
Four Ps 151
Francisco Reynés 50
FW Taylor's Scientific Management 30

G

Game playing 5
Gans, J. 23, 39
General AI 4, 8
General Data Protection Regulation
    (GDPR) 219
General intelligence 166
General purpose technology 38
Generative Adversarial Networks
    (GANs) 12
Generative tasks 12
Generic AI DevOps 11
Geo-political factors 59
Ghemawat, P. 55

Ghoshal, Sumantra 30, 81
Golden years of AI 5
Goldfarb, A. 23, 39
Good job 72
Governance model 53
Governing 188
Graphical processing units (GPUs) 7
Group decision making, benefits of 193

H

Hamel 26
Hanssens 55
Health care costs 77
Healthy workplaces 86
Hebb, D. 5
Hebbian learning 5
Hedge funds 59
Hierarchies 165
Hiring algorithms 108
Hiring practices 94
Home assistants 7
HR outcomes 95
Human assistant 170
Human engagement 13
Humanistic literacy 118
Human life 85
Human-machine system 130
Human resources 43
Human values 57
Human work 39
Humility 46
Hyperconnected digitized world 208
Hyper-intelligent machines 23

I

IBM 5
IBM's Watson 12
Image labelling 3
Income maintenance 74
Incumbent firms 185
Inditex 37

4th Industrial Revolution 24, 117
Industrial Revolution 120
Information Technology (IT) 3
Institutional configuration 186
Intelligence 166
Internet of Things (IOT) 151
Investment decisions 42


J

Jensen, Michael C. 30
Job creation 57
Job destruction 39
Job losses 57
Job performance 79, 109
Judgment 46


K

Knowledge 119
Kogut, Bruce 30, 32


L

Labeled data 14
Labor market 70
Labor organizations 81
Labour compensation 67
Lafley, A.G. 172
Large shareholders 59
Layoffs 78
Learning algorithms 16
Life-long learning 132
Life-long self-learners 130
Lorsch, J.W. 54
Low wages 80


M

MacGregor 30
Machine learning (ML) 4, 38
Machine learning algorithms 209
Making decisions 29
Malone, T. 46

Management 46
Managerial functions 39, 63
March 32
Marketing 11, 12
Marketing elasticity 153
Marketing impact assessment 152
Marketing mix 153
Market leadership 159
Market share 159
Martin, R.L. 172
Massa, L. 55
Masstige strategy 174
McAffee 23
McCarthy, John 5
McKinsey 72
Meaning 69
Meckling, William H. 30
Medical diagnostics 7
Metric of marketing effectiveness 154
*Mine* these data 151
Minsky, M. 168
Mintzberg, H. 52
Mobility 195
Moral dilemmas 228
Moran, Peter 30
Mortality 77
Moss Kanter, R. 53
Motivating employees 30
Motivation 32
Multi-agent system 12


N

Narrow AI 8
Neural nets 10
Neural networks 4, 5
New economy 67
Nohria, N. 46, 52


O

Objective setting 29
Online retailing 151
Operational effectiveness 26

O'Reilly III, Charles A. 31
Organizational change 143
Organizational model 210
Organizations 67
Ownership structures 59

P

P&G 175
Pearl, J. 41
People 62
People's health 70
Percent change as a focal metric 152
Personalization 217
Personal selling 156
Pfeffer, J. 57, 70, 82
Platform 193
Platform businesses 26
Platform business model 193
Polman, Paul 47
Porter, M.E. 52, 55, 175
Positioning of the firm 55
Practical wisdom 207, 229
Prahalad 26
Prediction markets 177
Predictions 39
Price elasticity 154
Price management 154
Principle literacy 118
Principle of linear alignment 29
Privacy 45
Private equity 59
Process automation 40
Product innovation 157
Productivity 79
Product quality 156
Product reviews 157
Project Debater 31
Promotion 98
Proprietary systems 181
Prudence 46
Public–Private Collaboration 196
Purpose 32, 52

Q

Quantitative marketing knowledge 152
Quantum advancement in computing 126

R

Relational databases 14
Reliability 10
Renaissance 120
Response elasticities 156
Responsible citizens 60
Ricart, J.E. 55, 191
Risk 141
Risk scoring 3
Rivkin, J.W. 172
Robo advisors 27
Robotic process automation (RPA) 15
Robots 3
Role of the CEO 185
Routine jobs 126

S

Safety 10
Sales-to-distribution relationship 157
Samuel, Arthur 5
Schumpeter, Joseph A. 135
Self-driving cars 3
Selznick, P. 53
Semi-automated tools 178
Semi-autonomous machines 37
Senior managers 39
Sensors 126
Shared purpose 56
Shareholder capitalism 81
Shareholder interests 80
Shareholders returns 52
Siggelkow, N. 172
Simon 32
Skills assessment 98
Smart city 133
Smith, Adam 121

Social goals 48
Social identity 30
Social institutions 63
Society 62
Society of mind 168
Specialized intelligence 166
Speech recognition 7
Stakeholder capitalism 80
Stakeholders 60
Strategic decisions 55
Strategic planning 11
Strategizing 188
*Strategy and M&A* 43
Strategy recombinator 176
Strong AI 8
Superminds 166
Susskind, Daniel 23
Susskind, Richard E. 23
Sustainability 49, 59
Sustainable performance 58
Sutton, R.I. 82

T

Technological innovations 58
Technology automating work 24
Technology complementing human
    effort 24
Technology dysfunctions 67
Technology supporting 24
Temporary price cuts 154
The moral dimension of the CEO's job
    61
Theory X 30
Thinking machine 5
Threat to labor 69
Tobias Martinez 50
Training 74
Training data 9, 140
Training programs 76
Trambe, Prasanna 57
Transformation process 48
Transparency 45, 207, 227
Trust 16, 62

Trust of AI 10
Turing, Alan 5
Turing test 5
Tushman, Michael L. 31

U

Uncertainty 141
Unemployment 57
Unilever Sustainable Living Plan
    (USLP) 47
Uniqueness 55
Unit of activity 205
Universities 118

V

Value chain 187
Value of business education 124
Value of university education 127
Value proposition 55
Virtue ethics 229

W

Wasserman, N. 46
weak AI 8
Williamson, Oliver 30
winner-takes-all 127
Wisdom 55
work 24
workers' satisfaction 111
workplace practices 70
World Economic Forum 72

Y

Yakubovich, Valery 57

Z

Zander, Udo 30, 32
Zott, C. 55

Printed by Printforce, the Netherlands